MARKET AND HEALTH

Also by David Reisman

ADAM SMITH'S SOCIOLOGICAL ECONOMICS

ALFRED MARSHALL: Progress and Politics

ALFRED MARSHALL'S MISSION

THE ECONOMICS OF ALFRED MARSHALL

GALBRAITH AND MARKET CAPITALISM

THE POLITICAL ECONOMY OF HEALTH CARE

THE POLITICAL ECONOMY OF JAMES BUCHANAN

RICHARD TITMUSS: Welfare and Society

STATE AND WELFARE: Tawney, Galbraith and Adam Smith

THEORIES OF COLLECTIVE ACTION: Downs, Olson and Hirsch

Market and Health

David Reisman

150th YEAR
M
St. Martin's Press

First published in Great Britain 1993 by
THE MACMILLAN PRESS LTD
Houndmills, Basingstoke, Hampshire RG21 2XS
and London
Companies and representatives
throughout the world

A catalogue record for this book is available
from the British Library.

ISBN 0–333–59480–0

Printed in Great Britain by
Antony Rowe Ltd
Chippenham, Wiltshire

First published in the United States of America 1993 by
Scholarly and Reference Division,
ST. MARTIN'S PRESS, INC.,
175 Fifth Avenue,
New York, N.Y. 10010

ISBN 0–312–09981–9

Library of Congress Cataloging-in-Publication Data
Reisman, David A.
Market and health / David Reisman.
p. cm.
Includes bibliographical references and index.
ISBN 0–312–09981–9
1. Medical economics. 2. Supply and demand. 3. Health care rationing—Moral and ethical aspects. I. Title.
RA410.5.R449 1993
338.4'33621—dc20 93–17299
CIP

Contents

1 Introduction

Market means demand and supply. The subject of this book is demand and supply. The specific area of demand and supply is health.

The first part of the book examines the demand for care that is derived from the demand for health. It shows that the quantity demanded is determined by the complex interaction of three key constituencies: the patient, the practitioner and the public. Health is quintessentially individual – only the patient can quantify the pain, or compare a wait with a price, or say when his health status lives up to his personal expectations. Health is also quintessentially social – defensive of its morals and its resources, resistant to externalities like epidemics, the public puts in its oar even when the health-holder and the treatment-centre wish most sincerely to contract in private. In between the atom and the collective stands the clinician – responsive to professional conventions, uncertain about entrepreneurial alertness, the servant of the insurer with the money as well as of the patient with the symptoms, the practitioner too has an effect upon demand, but still his freedom of choice must remain within determined bounds.

Part II is concerned with the supply of finance. So much of the payment for care being refracted by the risk-averse through the intermediation of the third party, a discussion of health insurance is required in order to establish what happens when it is the consumer who presents the demand but the agency that covers the bill. Just as the private sector can provide insurance in the form of the occupational plan and the individual plan, the prepaid maintenance organisation and the autonomous sickness fund, so, Part II shows, the public sector can fulfil many of the same functions through self-funding and residualism, citizens' universalism and the National Health. The inclusion of socialised agencies alongside commercial carriers must serve as a reminder that the State's involvement in the managed market can extend far beyond the compulsion, the regulation and the subsidisation that are the familiar responses to private sector deficiencies in the mixed health economy.

Part III turns to the provision of care. Arguing that care, like air, is all around, it considers the contribution to health that can potentially be made by the individual, the community, the doctor and the hospital. Bringing in the family and the pharmacy, the social services and the voluntary bodies, the schools and the newspapers, the control of pollution and the infrastructure of sewers, the conclusion is reached that good health can be delivered by a multiplicity of suppliers. Good bolts are properly manufactured by good bolt-makers but good health is too important to be left to the experts alone.

Part IV closes the book with the value of life. Part IV ends the book where it began, with the patient, the practitioner and the public who form the constituencies that shape the demands. Most members of the community will have a view on the trade-off between medical care and industrial investment, the prohibition of high tar cigarettes and the preservation of individual freedom. Not, however, the same view: thence the need to compare arguments and contrast explanations such as constitutes the primary objective of the present book.

One man's meat is another man's poison; and that is why this book does not specify the optimal point on the continuous spectrum that runs from free market to managed market to no market at all. One man's *explicandum* is another man's *conundrum*; and that is why this book makes no recommendation as to the ideal relationship between market and State in the modern health economy. No specification and no recommendation – save this: where people disagree, welfare-maximisation can only mean the just process of discussion and negotiation, debate and argumentation, without which we would surely fight.

Part I

Demand

2 Principal and Agent

The demand is for health and not for care. Isolated and lonely people no doubt value doctoring because it is contact and sympathy. Obsessives and addicts are known to seek out treatment and sometimes even surgery because they regard the intervention as satisfying in itself. The tastes of such unrepresentative consumers must be given the respect that even a minority has the right to command. Still, however, those preferences must be recognised to be the exceptions and the means–ends orientation to be the rule. The normal pattern is for health care to be demanded because of the positive contribution to health status that that care is expected to make.

Many things make a positive contribution to health status, including nutritious food and regular exercise, a sound genetic endowment and a supportive partner, an unpolluted environment and a reasonable education, moderate speed limits and clean drinking-water, housing that is warm, dry and safe and a level of income that is sufficient to facilitate the purchase of these and other health-promoting goods and services. Formal care, it is widely accepted, ought to figure prominently on any such list. The demand for healthy life is closely identified in the popular mind with the demand for trained attention. To some people the terms are all but interchangeable. The over-stressed executive sitting down to a large plateful of fat complains that there are too few doctors and not enough hospitals. His good lady wife, faithful to nothing so much as the principle that every good smoke deserves a gin, deplores the costliness of the drugs and the bossiness of the nurses. It is always a temptation for the rational to point up the inconsistency that is revealed by such preferences. Justifiable as the inference might well be in the frictionless vacuum of the ideal textbook, nonetheless it does nothing to alter the fact that some people somehow do not see their myopia. For them at least the demand for health status is, rightly or wrongly, all but identical with the demand for health care.

This chapter, and the next, is concerned with the demand for health, and most of all with the demand for health through care. The theme of the two chapters is the three constituencies. Taking the view that the demand in question has in truth a treble source, the chapters examine in turn the independent contribution to the articulation of wants and needs that is made respectively by the patient, the practitioner and the public.

In few areas of social life is the public interest more frequently invoked than it is in the case of health. The influence of the whole upon the care of the parts is the subject of Chapter 3. The present chapter is devoted to a consideration of the principal and the agent, the individual client and the individual professional. The demand for the standard economic tradeable originates with the single decision-making unit that is the final consumer. The demand for health, as this chapter and the next will seek to show, is rather different: where three instead of one are invited to register an opinion, there the commodity must be treated as an unusual one and analysed in a manner that reflects its special characteristics.

2.1 THE PATIENT

Typically it is the patient who initiates the sequence. Sometimes it is not, as where the consumer arrives an unconscious casualty after an accident, or is oblivious to a mental illness, or is called in by a proactive doctor who takes the repeat prescription as an indication that something is wrong, or is required by a health-conscious employer to undergo an annual check-up, or is guaranteed a six-monthly home visit by a prudent insurer bent on prevention, or falls into an at-risk category that is offered routine immunisation or a cervical smear as a simple matter of course. Most frequently it is. Most frequently it is the patient who, ignorant and uncertain though he undoubtedly will be, still takes the first step in the direction of diagnosis and cure by visiting the practitioner to complain that he 'doesn't feel well'.

Yet the perception that one 'doesn't feel well' is a world away from an accurate understanding of *why* one 'doesn't feel well'. The patient, even if enviably articulate in the description of the symptoms, will always be at the layman's disadvantage with respect to the likely causes of the problem. In that sense the patient cannot even be confident that the visit to the doctor is itself fully warranted: stomach pain can indeed be the first sign of life-threatening cancer but it can also be as transitory and unimportant as the passing consequence of poor hygiene in the kitchen. The patient, lacking an expert's knowledge, might demand formal care when he is not ill (obtaining, of course, the far-from-valueless reassurance that he continues to be well) or might fail to demand formal care when he has a real need (unaware, perhaps, of an asymptomatic malfunction or of the implications of not securing early intervention once a problem has been detected). The patient, lacking an expert's knowledge, can hardly be said to be exercising consumer sovereignty in the economist's sense where he, the patient, knows enough to know how little he himself knows about illness and about treatment.

Some individuals admittedly will make it their business to educate themselves in the fundamentals of body maintenance. Building on medically-relevant background knowledge gleaned from classroom biology, driven by a curiosity to learn more about pathology and a desire to remain in a state of felt well-being, such individuals watch television documentaries on arthritis and read newspaper features on septicaemia. Most individuals, however, will probably elect not to make themselves particularly well-informed: lacking background or curiosity, they will probably regard information-gathering as unacceptably expensive in the light of the competing demands on their time and money.

Economically speaking, there is a certain rationality in the decision of maximisers to hold back on investment. Some future needs can be anticipated: witness the life-cycle predictabilities, the age-related normalcies, such as chickenpox and mumps, contraception and childbirth, menopause and prostate. The bulk of medical requirements cannot be. The pay-off to investment in information is hardly likely to be high where no data more individualised than the statistical probability is to be had. The gain will be discounted still further by virtue of the fact that the marginal benefit is distant as well as putative whereas the marginal cost is definite and here-and-now. Economically speaking, in short, the likelihood is great that rational individuals will hold back on the collection of precautionary intelligence concerning each and every hypothetical contingency with which they might one day have to cope.

Present illness is, of course, a different matter. The contingency translated from a potential *might-be* into a current *is*, the return to specific and targeted information will then almost certainly be perceived by the individual afflicted as exceeding the means – ends contribution of general education behind the veil of unknowledge. Even so, however, still the rational might continue to abstain from investment. The anxious sufferer, perhaps seriously ill, might believe himself to be too emotional and distressed properly to sift what he reads. The ailing consumer, convinced that she will not uncover a cure, might see no logic in the purchase of facts that are unlikely to produce an outcome. The existence of the insurer who pays reduces the financial incentive to the consumer to become well-informed. The existence of the practitioner who advises frees the symptom-holder from the need to do anything more taxing than to report that he 'doesn't feel well'. The risk-bearing hived off to the insurer, the decision-making delegated to the practitioner, the economic patient, deliberately passive and intentionally under-informed, is likely to derive considerable satisfaction from his access to the division of labour.

The opportunity to consult a specialised adviser must inevitably count as an important cause of rational ignorance: if the doctor knows best, the logical economiser will conclude, then the patient has no real need to know at all. Information in such a context is a marketable commodity like any other. With, however, certain differences, as Kenneth Arrow has explained:

> The value of information is frequently not known in any meaningful sense to the buyer; if, indeed, he knew enough to measure the value of information, he would know the information itself. But information, in the form of skilled care, is precisely what is being bought from most physicians, and, indeed, from most professionals. The elusive character of information as a commodity suggests that it departs considerably from the usual marketability assumptions about commodities.[1]

The consumer who purchases an apple is able both to imagine the tastiness in advance of the eating and to evaluate the realisation of the expectation once the event has occurred. The consumer who purchases advice and analysis is in a somewhat less attractive position. Seldom able to state in advance the precise nature of the diagnosis which he requires, seldom able to assess afterwards if the recommendation supplied was optimal or even accurate, the consumer of information will in a very real sense be as lacking in confidence after he has purchased the commodity as he was before he entered the marketplace with the desire to trade.

The patient seldom knows *ex ante* precisely what it is that he needs nor *ex post* if the explanation was correct and the treatment of good quality. In the infrequent cases of conspicuous and flagrant negligence such as may be typified by the removal of the spleen instead of the splint, the patient is in a strong position to sue for redress on grounds of malpractice. In the far more frequent cases where the patient is given inappropriate attention or where the workmanship is shoddy the injured party is far less likely to seek compensation through damages. The reason is simple: his information being deficient, the consumer is far less likely to become aware of the abuse. Some patients undergo the same medical intervention more than once. Learning by doing, such individuals will gradually acquire a measure of facility in the assessment of the procedures: this will be the experience, say, of a woman reporting for a succession of pregnancies, or a long-term sufferer from a chronic complaint, or a dental patient observing that sometimes an offending tooth is laboriously filled and sometimes it is quickly extracted. Where the medical intervention is once-for-all, however, the patient will be less well-placed to pass an enlightened opinion. The patient will not previously have consumed an appendectomy and will not therefore be able to apply any personal standard of comparison. So long as nothing goes radically wrong, the patient is unlikely, realistically speaking, ever to discover if the service delivered was first-class or, alternatively, barely competent.

Human nature being what it is when autonomous *homo sapiens* is first anaesthetised and then cut up, the consumer will want *ex ante* most sincerely to trust the producer, *ex post* to wake up to the best-possible outcome. Fearing the worst at least as much as he hopes for the best, the consumer will have a not unnatural propensity to filter the whole of the medical encounter through the rose-tinted wishful thinking of the anxious health-holder determined to affirm the complete recovery while blotting out the chance of mistakes and failures. Such fears, such hopes, complicate still further the task of evaluation. Biased in favour of optimism as well as ignorant of medical technique, the outsider can never be the equal of the expert upon whom he relies when he 'doesn't feel well'. Power in that sense will always be asymmetrically distributed as between the patient and the practitioner. Logically so, since it is that very inequality of knowledge and skill that provides the *raison d'être* for the contract which they conclude.

Information is asymmetrical. The inequality in the endowments, the 'information impactedness'[2] in the sense of Oliver Williamson, is undeniably a problem for the patient who is at a disadvantage with respect to medical technique. It would be wrong to neglect the vulnerability and the susceptibility of the consumer of service in so unbalanced a situation. What should not be overlooked, however, is the sense in which the supplier of service is himself exposed to an 'information impactedness' all his own. The doctor is trained to supply the objective input: he is taught to recognise the warning signs of an incipient coronary, to assign a statistical probability to a lump in the breast, to prescribe an ointment that can clear up an infection, to stop a bleed by means of a tourniquet. What the doctor cannot do is to supply the subjective input that is the *sine qua non* for a medical system that is genuinely committed to the felt welfare of the unique individuals who absorb the care. Just as there is more that the practitioner will know about medicine, so, it is clear, will there be more that the patient will know about himself. Impactedness is a two-way street.

Only the consumer of the pair of fashion shoes can say if the beauty and the emulation are genuinely worth the pinching and the expense. The same principle holds true in the health care field. Only the patient can weigh the pain of the treatment against the pain of the condition if left untreated; or compare the unpleasant side-effects of chemotherapy with the perceived risk of complications from surgery under anaesthetic; or contrast the relief of symptoms with the total cure in the borderline case where the cure involves a cost (loss of earnings while off work, significant fees that cannot be shifted to insurers, increased burden on family carers of a recovery period spent at home, inconvenient journeys to and from treatment centres) and also carries a small but non-negligible probability that the operation if successful will nonetheless leave the patient permanently confined to a wheelchair (an eventuality which some patients will no doubt regard as even less desirable than the initial complaint). Only the patient can know where it hurts and with what intensity; or what felt quality of life he himself regards as his personal best; or precisely what she understands by 'full' in phrases like 'enjoy life to the full' and 'possess full command of faculties'; or whether a private room in hospital would make him 'feel better'; or whether she prefers the drug to take the form of the tablet, the linctus, the patch, the suppository or the injection; or what standard of good but not perfect health he would accept as tolerable; or what level of disability or disfigurement she would regard as worse than death. Only the patient can know these things – and the practitioner is not the patient.

The locksmith can repair a lock without asking it to state the perceived discrepancy between *what is* and *what ought to be*. The veterinary specialist can set the fracture of an injured sheep without inquiring too closely into the felt impairment of function experienced by that notoriously non-verbal bleater. The medical practitioner faces a more difficult challenge. Aware as he is that his subjects are neither inanimate nor unreflective, he is conscious at the same time that his knowledge of the unique and sentient individualities with which he deals must always be incomplete and partial. Ideally the sensitive practitioner will want to read the mind and plumb the subconscious of the patient. That option not being on offer, what the sensitive practitioner will probably do instead is to consult the patient on tastes and preferences even as the client consults him on diagnosis and cure. Each party in that way becomes the other party's adviser. Each party, recognising the symbiosis, lightens the other party's darkness. The outcome is a quantity demanded that is in a real sense a joint product. Decisions made by wise shepherds for a passive flock can never be as finely-tuned nor as individually-differentiated.

Consultation, clearly, can be a valuable part of a medical relationship that is orientated towards total persons and not simply towards disembodied symptoms viewed in clinical isolation. An institutional acknowledgement that there is ignorance not on one side alone of the contract but rather on both, the substitution of *in collaboration with* for *on behalf of* may be expected to moderate (even where it does not eliminate) the potential dominance of the supplier over the purchaser of care than can at its most malign represent a full-blown conversion of consumer's into producer's sovereignty. It is well-known that the patient normally retains a right to reject the advice that is given: because of the cost, perhaps, or because of a religion that prohibits a blood transfusion, or because of the spoiled self-image that is associated with a scar, or because of a fear of death in the operating theatre, the fact is that the patient normally can and sometimes does refuse the informed consent that is needed for a recommendation to become a treatment. What the advocates of consultation and collaboration would propose is that the traditional freedom to reject and refuse should become the model for an amplified freedom to shape and specify. In that way, it is argued, the patient who initiates the sequence and chooses the doctor would not subsequently fall victim to a constraining system in which it is the agent who seizes the initiative and makes the decisions.

Yet consultation is expensive and resources are scarce. Time spent listening and learning is time *not* spent treating and healing. Advocates of the democratic benefit would do wrong to neglect the opportunity cost that is the slower throughput. On the one hand there is the expectant mother, told in detail about discomfort and sedation, home delivery and hospital delivery, the role of the midwife and the likelihood of complications. Her freedom of choice would be much reduced were the referring doctor and the antenatal staff too busy to explain the options. On the other hand there is the battered housewife, bruised psychologically as well as physically but rushed through with only a bandage because the system is unable to pay for therapy – therapy that could be afforded if doctors spent less time sharing intelligence and matching perceptions with unique patients and discrete individualities.

Further cost is incurred where different people want different things. Consultation without consequences is as insubstantial as a grin without a cat. Consultation followed by differentiation, however, can mean that the same money comes to command less care. Non-standard services can be an expensive luxury in the currency of scale economies foregone: cod liver capsules flavoured with a choice of raspberry or mint can cost more to produce than a longer run of equivalent capsules flavoured with the taste of cod. Besides that, the non-standard can be an efficient administrator's nightmare and a significant cause of disruption to professional routines and institutional practices. The economic burden might be consensually acceptable if the differentiation were believed to have a therapeutic pay-off. Where the benefit is believed to be comfort instead of healthiness, however, the community as a whole may be somewhat less sympathetic to the expense imposed by the idiosyncratic.

Then there is the private cost that is borne by the patient himself when, having consulted a doctor, he finds the doctor determined to consult him. The rational and the intellectual when in good health and spirits will probably find the idea of the bilateral relationship a profoundly attractive one. They must not expect that their valuation of involvement will necessarily be shared by the typical and the median when presenting themselves in the doctor's offices to complain that they 'don't feel well'. Where time and money are at stake, the representative patient might feel, there it is only logical for the consumer to select bounded rationality in preference to extended search, deliberately entrusting the care of his health (as if sealed in a blind account) to a valued agent employed expressly to provide sensible leadership. No one buys a car and then walks to work, the representative patient might conclude. Most of all might the real-world client want to rank benevolent despotism above democratic involvement where it is the psychic and not the paid-out costs on which the consumer is most anxious to economise. These psychic costs are the fear-of-freedom costs of which McGuire, Henderson and Mooney have written that, present the problem and absent the knowledge, 'it is not surprising that the consumer becomes reliant upon the supplier. In fact if the anxiety costs become too high the consumer may be unwilling to participate in the choice process and default on making decisions, in which case the doctor/supplier takes over this decision-making role.'[3] The consumer asked in such circumstances for an opinion might have not a single preference to reveal save for the perception that consultation involves a cost and is therefore a burden.

Consultation can prove superfluous (as where the patient, consulted, merely duplicates the recommendation that the practitioner unassisted would in any case have provided). It can prove functionless (as where the patient, consulted, demands gold fillings for which the insurer will not pay or requests a drug which the State has banned as unacceptably toxic). And it can prove second-best when compared with the decentralised spontaneity of the economic price. The argument for consumer consultation through demand and supply is a familiar one, that market-determined user-charges may be relied upon sensitively to quantify the patient's aversion to a given symptom, the patient's attraction to a given therapy. Because of consumer's ignorance and third-party payment, professional cartels and barriers to entry, the assertion that the economic is also the epistemological will perhaps carry less conviction in the market for doctors and hospitals than it will, say, in the market for apples and oranges. Further complications are caused by technical indivisibilities, inevitably a real impediment to anything approaching textbook pricing. In the words of Peter Smith: 'It must always be borne in mind that many of the services in the NHS have high fixed and low marginal costs, and that the neat attribution of all costs to specific patients, so beloved of accountants, is therefore a highly questionable procedure.'[4] As with the National Health, so with all other capital-intensive delivery systems. Perhaps it is not the supply-and-demand price but rather the face-to-face interview that will in the last analysis provide the better insight into the unrevealed preferences of the invisible mind.

Consultation remains problematic, however, and a final difficulty will be the quintessential heterogeneity of individuals' expectations. Tweedledum can eat no fat: acculturated by his privileged schooling to the leadership role, accustomed in his managerial position to commanding and demanding, Dum will want explanations and be resistant to other-directedness. Tweedledee can eat no lean: educated to do as he is told, too ill and too afraid to contemplate a stressful confrontation with a doctor who knows best, Dee will be prepared for the paternalist to make the choices and will not be insulted when given to understand that the business which he ought to mind does not extend to the body which he is permitted to lease. The expectations of Dum are evidently not the expectations of Dee. Patient-centred medicine would seem in the circumstances to dictate that unlike should not be forced into the participation that is designed with like in view. Instead, it would appear, respect for persons must ensure that each party be offered the specific mix of consultation and abdication that he finds best suited to his own circumstances.

There is a powerful logic which says that the patient's wishes ought to be taken into account not just in respect of the demand for care but also with respect to the demand for consultation that influences the demand for care. The logic admitted, so, however, must be the complexities. Morally speaking, a tolerant society might be entirely happy for Dum to read his notes to tatters, Dee to delegate all his decision-making to the skilled mechanics – but still have reservations about allowing the articulate bully to monopolise the doctor's time while the shy and the self-effacing hold back lest they be a nuisance. Besides that, and speaking practically, the doctor will not always be certain just how much consultation a specific patient actually expects when he presents himself for treatment. Life would be much simpler for the practitioner if the patient agreed to wear a badge labelling him clearly as a Dum or a Dee on the day. Badges being improbable, the truth must be faced that a real mismatch will often exist between patients' perceptions and practitioners' perceptions of those perceptions.

Such a mismatch was identified in the study conducted in the United States by Strull, Lo and Charles. The authors concentrated on one complaint (hypertension) and three treatment settings (the community hospital, the health maintenance organisation and the Veterans Administration clinic). Questionnaires were returned by 60 clinicians (41 doctors, the remainder nurse-practitioners or clinical pharmacists) and 210 patients (half male, half white, less than half with the same clinician for more than two years, one-third with education beyond high school, two-thirds hypertensive for more than five years). The survey revealed that 41 per cent of patients wanted to be given more information but that clinicians, apparently not perfect judges of clients' preferences, under-estimated the desire for discussion in no less than 29 per cent of cases. Only in 11 per cent of cases was it over-estimated. Decision-making was quite different, however. Turning from explanations to choices, what Strull, Lo and Charles established was that 53 per cent of patients wanted to share in the selection of treatment whereas clinicians mistakenly believed that 78 per cent wished to do so.[5] Thence the conclusion, that the patient wants more disclosure of information but less involvement in decision-making than he or she is believed by the practitioner to desire.

Studies such as that of Strull, Lo and Charles (allowance made for the limited pool and the problem of cross-national generalisation) will no doubt do much to reduce the mismatch in attitudes and expectations as between the consumer and the counsellor. The mismatch may be reduced but it is unlikely ever to be eliminated. Faced with a unique individuality, the sensible doctor will never ignore the possibility of the dispersion in order to concentrate exclusively upon the probability and the median. Tentatively the doctor will test the nexus by inviting the patient to ask questions in order to regulate the flow. The doctor will do his best. Still, however, some patients are bound to end up under-consulted in their own estimation while others will regret that they were over-consulted at a time when they were ill. Fundamental heterogeneities serve at any rate to reinforce the observation that, just as the patient is likely to be less than perfectly informed about medicine, so the practitioner is unlikely to be perfectly informed about the patient. Impactedness is a two-way street. It is often also a hurried thoroughfare where noise speaks loudly and communication is debased.

What matters most, of course, is the arrival at the destination. The demand being for health status and not for health care, the patient who loses the symptoms and gains the recovery might feel that the journey was entirely worthwhile even if the companions' conversation left much to be desired. The bone set, the bleeding stopped, the ringworm arrested, the tooth capped, the patient might feel entirely satisfied with the outcomes brought about even if the techniques employed were never made the focus for discussion and debate. All well and good – where alternatives are limited and the optimal is acceptably the habitual. Frequently, however, there will be no professional convergence on a single standard of bestness. Where medical practice is subject to variation, there, clearly, the patient who has in mind a given endstate will often be obliged to make a discriminating choice of the practitioner as well.

Thus it will frequently be the case that the doctors disagree on the specification of a need – a need being, as Cooper indicates, 'a medical opinion, not a medical fact':

> It is one of many possible points along a continuum. What levels, for example, of blood sugar or emotional stress are abnormal are not matters which readily attract medical unanimity. It is likely to be only those conditions at the extreme end of the continuum, where life is immediately threatened by inaction, that will be universally considered as need.[6]

The patient contributes the want by articulating a disparity between the actual and the ideal. The doctor validates the want, thereby elevating it to the status of a need. The doctor confirms that a technique exists for producing the desired improvement: a want for a hernia repair is therefore more likely to be ticketed a need than is a want of equivalent intensity for a lifespan of two hundred years. The doctor in addition affirms that the want in question properly merits the trained professional's scarce attention: the hypochondriac's want for ever more proof that a negative is not a false one will presumably be less often dignified as a need than will the want of the cardiac case for the emergency drill. Doctors confronted with the impossible at the one extreme, the urgent at the other, will probably gravitate to the same knee-jerk reaction in respect of the validation of a want as a need. Doctors working in the discretionary range, however, will be led by their personal predilections significantly to differ in their attitudes. Doctor A will tell the patient complaining of sadness that he should not be wasting the professional's time with self-pity and self-indulgence; doctor B will take the view that the depressed state is a medical condition fully deserving of the resources that are devoted to the drugs, the counselling, the ECT; and thus it is that the patient who aspires to the endstate of intervention would be well-advised to select the instrumentality of B while leaving A for the patient who will go home satisfied if told to drink fruit juice and take up a hobby.

Medical opinion is frequently divided in the identification of a need. It is frequently divided as well in the choice of the appropriate therapy. Where care is a range that admits of alternatives, it can hardly be expected that doctors will adopt a single cookery book procedure, a unique and agreed-upon routine. Doctors will differ in their attitudes to pain and risk; in the reward systems which they face and the practice-culture of their local peers; in their access to manpower and plant and their sensitivity to patients' preferences; in the vintage of their training and the cost-consciousness of their administrators. Doctors will differ; and so in consequence will the treatments that they endorse. Immediate surgery or delayed action, care in hospital or care in the community, the seventeen-day in-patient convalescence or the day-case turn-around, the optional hysterectomy rationed by wait and the elective tonsillectomy put on the priority list – it is differences such as these that lead Andersen and Mooney to call into question the technological determinism of those thinkers who expect single-valued correctness somehow to emerge: 'Substantial variations in utilisation of modern medical care seem to be more of an overwhelming rule than an exceptional phenomenon. Practice variation has revealed to a greater extent than ever before, and in a way which denies the essentialism of modern medicine, that medical practice floats on a sea of uncertainty.'[7] There is a strong temptation to assume that each and every detached counsellor will tend to home in on the same solution. A more realistic view would, however, be to accept that different doctors will tend to treat different patients in different ways. To choose the doctor is in that sense also to choose the treatment that one is likely to receive.

Where there is dissensus among the doctors as to the wants that ought to be labelled needs, as to the effectiveness of care inputs in the attainment of status objectives, there, clearly, it is of some importance that the patient be in a position to make an informed choice. Where doctors disagree, the patient will want not unnaturally to know the nature of the differences. Doctor A always treats abortion as a valid need but never refers for cosmetic surgery. Doctor B advises on diet and exercise in a Sunday morning clinic but pleads lack of experience when asked to perform minor surgery in the office. The differentiation of A from B is a promise of pluralism that is very much in keeping with the differentiated wants of a heterogeneous community. Yet it is a promise that is likely to remain a hollow one so long as the consumer is unaware of the services that are available.

One possibility would be for insuring agencies to sponsor second opinions and to buy in a diversity of views: they would then be able to diffuse collated information on quantity and quality and to advise their clients on the range of options. Another possibility would be for the State to insist that track records and utilisation reviews be made easily accessible in public libraries and citizens' advice bureaux: comparative data on doctors and hospitals would at the very least give the ignorant consumer a set of benchmarks against which to measure the performance of individual contractors. Nor should the potential contribution of commercial advertising necessarily be rejected merely because the crying of the wares is always and everywhere an invitation to the manipulative and the unscrupulous to prey on the ill-informed and the desperate. Monitors and law courts will understandably have to make it their business to protect the purity of information against the exaggerated claims of the fraudulent. What is often forgotten is the extent to which market freedom may itself be expected to provide a defence against misrepresentation and concealment. As Sorkin puts it:

> In some industries, where consumer ignorance is important, an individual obtains some measure of protection through the competitive behavior of producers, as in the automotive repair industry. If the producers engage in vigorous competition with one another, some of them will make an effort to inform the consumer about the merits of their product or service as well as those of their competitors. In the case of physicians' services the reverse is true.[8]

In the case of physicians' services, the profession's resistance to commercial advertising in effect raises up an artificial barrier to the dissemination of information on the differentiation of product. The impediment is by no means the only instance where the profession acts not to relieve the consumer's ignorance but rather manufactures a new ignorance that is entirely of its own contriving. Suspicious of price competition, susceptible to medical jargon, secretive in their evaluation of one another's work, reluctant to testify against one another in negligence proceedings, unwilling to criticise standard procedures in public, determined to keep notes and records so confidential that they remain inaccessible even to the patient to whom they refer, doctors in corporate bodies are themselves contributing causes of consumers' ignorance to an extent that would only be justifiable if there were genuinely no choices for the individual to make. In the consensual complacency of medical confidence, the consumer might indeed be prepared to accept with Lord Horder, physician to five crowned heads, that 'only the doctor knows what good doctoring is.'[9] In the real-world conditions of disagreeing doctors and scientific uncertainties, on the other hand, the consumer might harbour real reservations about endorsement without involvement.

Superintendence by consent (the 'heteronomous management of life') will be still further called into question by the warnings of radical individualists like Ivan Illich that 'any kind of dependence soon turns into an obstacle to autonomous mutual care, coping, adapting, and healing, and, what is worse, into a device by which people are stopped from transforming the conditions at work and at home that make them sick':[10] 'Beyond a certain level, the heteronomous management of life will inevitably first restrict, then cripple, and finally paralyse the organism's non-trivial responses, as what was meant to constitute health care will turn instead into a specific form of health denial.'[11] Medical and social iatrogenesis joins the observed non-uniformities in undermining the consumer's confidence in monoliths and monopolies. The consumer might or might not have *adequate* information if the clinicians were to relax their grip. What is certain is that the consumer would have *more* information – and that the age of involvement cannot but welcome the open door.

The consumer is ignorant about health. Yet he or she is not ignorant *only* about health. Culinary illustrations over-simplify cases. Perhaps the consumer does know enough to squeeze a melon for ripeness or to recognise a lemon so rotten that it merits a refund. Quite different, however, is the position when the consumer inspects a roof for structural soundness, or buys a second-hand motor that appears to run, or tries to pick out a computer from a plethora of properties and characteristics. In cases such as these the typical consumer lacks the technical background to make a rational choice. Confronted with the mechanic who insists that his dishwasher must be gutted, the consumer is not likely to be able to conclude a significantly more intelligent transaction than he is when confronted with a surgeon who says that his intestines require immediate restringing. In the one case as in the other the consumer may want to bring in an outside opinion, or to read a specialist survey such as a *Which?* report, or to rely on word-of-mouth recommendation to identify a reliable supplier. In neither case nonetheless is the consumer likely to be perfectly informed at the moment of choice: the intestines are the same as the dishwashers in that particular at least.

The implications of the ignorance, admittedly, may not be the same. A defective television can be refused and returned but a botched appendectomy can mean instant death. A rotten lemon can be discarded with the rubbish but a careless operation can mean an irreversible handicap. Thence the argument that health care is distinguished from other purchases by the greater gravity of the risks that sanction the failure to make the 'correct' decision at the 'right' time. Yet the distinction is not in truth an entirely convincing one. Not all formal care is life-and-death: consider the doctor's sympathetic counselling of an overworked executive deserted by his wife. Mortality, morbidity and indigence can be the unexpected by-products of ordinary consumables: witness the car with faulty brakes, the electrical appliance with exposed wiring, the lounge-suite that is not flame-resistant, the toy that chokes or blinds. Some kinds of medical care will probably involve more risk than the use of a microwave oven but others, one reflects, are likely to involve significantly less. Here once again, one concludes, health and care would seem to have much in common with other goods and services in the household's choice-set.

As with the spot, moreover, so with the forward, where once again the difference is unambiguously hedged about with blur. Uncertainty reinforces ignorance in the case of health: no one would dispute that the patient and the practitioner will be in a state of unknowledge with respect to the future that must at least be the equivalent of the darkness in which they seek to negotiate the present. Few individuals can say today from what serious illnesses, if any, they will one day be suffering; or whether the doctor-to-come will be successful in steering a middle course between the Scylla of the false positive and the Charybdis of the mistaken oversight; or what the optimal treatment will in 20 years be for a sickly child unlikely to be born for another 10; or when, if ever, the need for an in-patient bed will arise; or whether the organ for transplant will be available when it is required; or whether the organ transplanted will prove unsuitable and be rejected by the body; or whether too much or too little of the anaesthetic will be administered; or whether the scalpel will slip, the operee be dropped, the blood transfusion bear the free gift of serum hepatitis if not something infinitely worse. One tries to remain healthy; but still the unexpected might happen, happen again, and thereafter keep on happening.

The unforeseen and the unforeseeable compound the problems associated with a hidden present. They remind the reader just how approximate is the market for health. What is true of the *species* is no less true of the *genus*, however; and the market for health is in truth not unique in its vulnerability to surprises, shocks, discontinuities and errors. A hospital not built in the here-and-now may mean the subsequent death of the speculating tax-payer who opposed the investment. Yet a factory converted from guns to butter may mean unexpected gluts and inconvenient shortages where uncoordinated rivals secretly employ identical strategies. A theatre without a surgeon cannot operate. Nor, however, can a production line without intermediate inputs produce warm winter coats. Health care, in short, may be subject to uncertainty, but so too is the whole of human life and enterprise. Recognising that intended sequels can be frustrated by what Shackle calls 'the plurality of rival possibles'[12], accepting that imagined outcomes can be reduced to a skein of fantasies by what Shackle stresses can be 'the upshot of any one of several paths of history-to-come'[13], the best that can be expected is that the patient will do no worse than the rest of us when he seeks to exercise his rational choice and to articulate his demand for care.

2.2 THE PRACTITIONER

The doctor plays an important role in the shaping of the demand for care. Given the asymmetry of information that underlies the patient–practitioner relationship, given the extent to which the principal is dependent on the agent for advice and instruction, it must be true by definition that the doctor will exert an autonomous pressure on the resources that are earmarked for health.

Ideally the doctor in the liberal democracy will do so on the principle that the individual is the best judge of personal interest. The individual being deficient in medical knowledge, what this would mean in practice is a double constraint. First, the agent would strive to decide precisely as the principal would have done if only the principal had enjoyed the agent's command of technical expertise. Second, the practitioner would endeavour to acquire a sound stock of subjective intelligence concerning the one-off patient's non-generalisable perceptions. The conditions will self-evidently not be easy to satisfy. To be perfectly informed about Alter it would be necessary for Ego not simply to interview Alter but actually to *become* Alter. So intimate a degree of participant observation being inconceivable and impossible, the real-world position is then likely to be that the agent has no option but to exert an autonomous pressure precisely because completeness of information is not to be expected in a second-best environment.

At least the practitioner in such an environment will be prepared to accept that autonomous pressure builds second-bestness into the model. Not so the paternalist who is convinced that the doctor knows best – and still less the commercialist who supplies with a view to gain. The doctor in the liberal democracy will regard autonomous pressure as a deviation from the patient-centred ideal. The paternalist and the commercialist will not. The former because he regards the patient as a monopolist of sensory data from whom no reasonable shopper will want to buy, the latter because he faces a conflict of loyalties which he resolves Hobbes-like by maximising his own return, neither the doctor who sees the patient as a ward nor the doctor who sees the patient as a target will regard autonomous pressure as anything other than the norm and the rule.

The orientations are different. The revised sequence is the same. In the market for lemons it is demand that traditionally induces supply. In the market for health, as Evans explains, the order and the lead are frequently reversed:

> The physician can exert direct influence on the demand function of the consumer by altering the patient's perceptions of his needs and of the capacity of medical technology to satisfy them. Thus, the medical service market cannot be simply dichotomized into demand side and supply side, with price serving as the only nexus between the two; rather we must allow for shifts in the demand curve itself in response to supplier behaviour. Market clearing may take place directly through the information which suppliers pass to consumers as well as by adjustments in price.[14]

Supply frequently shapes demand in the market for health, where autonomous pressure in league with manipulation by consent undeniably complicates the interpretation of the signals. A high price in the market for lemons arguably conveys useful information concerning the intrinsic wants of independent consumers. A high price in the market for operations must always be that much more difficult to decipher.

Supply-side guidance need not in itself be a bad thing: where a patient in unaware, say, of a life-threatening condition on the point of turning malign, no one would suggest that an exogenous shift in the consumer's demand function brought about by that consumer's doctor will be anything other than in the client's own best interests. Such a shift, manufactured by a liberal democrat or engineered by a committed paternalist, clearly interferes with the freedom of the uninformed unassisted to make their own mistakes. If, however, the ignorant genuinely feel that outside advice, acted upon, would leave them better off in their own estimation than would no counsel and no influence, then it would have to be accepted that a small infringement of freedom in order to secure the elimination of the threat to life might well prove the friend and not the enemy of welfare.

Non-ego guidance need not be incompatible with patient's welfare. Yet doctors are human too. Sometimes tired and bored, sometimes worried about an unpaid mortgage or anxious about a drop-out child, sometimes desperate to help or determined to experiment, doctors are identical to their patients in this particular at least, that each has his or her own goals and objectives. Those goals and objectives will shape and colour the guidance that is provided. The shaping and the colouring will not on all occasions be directed solely and exclusively towards the welfare of the patient whom the practitioner notionally sets out to serve.

Thus it might happen that the patient expresses a want which the doctor is not prepared to call a need. Where the demand is for sympathy and care, where the request is for cosmetic surgery to straighten the nose, there the doctor might well refuse to get involved. Time and energy limit the extent to which even the attentive physician can play the father-figure. The service budget imposes a fundholder's ceiling on the luxuries that can be afforded. And there is the pressure of superiors where the doctor is paid not by a fee for a service but by a salary from an organisation. In the words of Maynard, Marinker and Gray:

> No form of contract would be less sensitive to the consumer than a contract based on salary. Although it could be said the salaried doctor would have his performance measured in relation to professionally negotiated health care goals, in effect the general practitioner in such a bureaucratic structure would be answerable to his professional superiors. It is possible that his performance would therefore be geared to pleasing them rather than to fulfilling the health care needs of patients.[15]

This is not to say that patients will deliberately be maltreated, only that a system based upon salary and standards is less likely to bend with the client's wishes than is one in which the patient pays for what he or she demands.

Where extra care attracts no extra reward, there the practitioner will face an undoubted temptation to consult his own ease by declining the optional and ignoring the dispensable. Such supplier-reduced demand will often be entirely in keeping with the letter of the contract (which omits any guarantee of love). Still, however, it can prove somewhat restrictive and unimaginative in the broader human context that refuses to treat the doctor – patient relationship as the goal-directed equivalent to the straightening of the panels on a dented car. As Alan Williams has written:

> A treatment, known to be ineffective in relation to the patient's physiological condition, may still be given as a demonstration (to him or his loved ones) that someone cares, and this may give satisfaction to them and indeed to other members of the community unknown to the patient who sympathise with the plight of the sick generally, so that the treatment may be quite 'effective' in this broader sense.[16]

In the broader sense, Alan Williams is saying, a range of basic human needs (for reassurance, friendship, even death with dignity) can be met through medical care which would simply go unnoticed by a rational gatekeeper who evaluated success and failure from too narrow and technical a perspective. In such a situation, it is clear, a reliance upon supply to determine demand would lead to an under-provision of the service and of the benefits it might have generated.

The influence of supply upon demand can be malign in the downward direction – the case where *too little* is supplied by a medical profession determined to do the minimum. Equally, the influence of supply upon demand can be malign to the extent of *too much* – as where a venal gatekeeper anxious to maximise revenues (or, at the very least, to secure a target income in combination with a rent that is paid in leisure) yields to the entrepreneurial incentive and opens wide the doors to an under-employed capacity. The patient is ignorant, the practitioner has discretion – and the potential for bias is clear enough.

It may well be that it was just this mix of conflicting interests and unequal power that Fuchs was observing when, comparing different areas within the United States, he isolated an upward-sloping demand relationship for surgery: 'Where surgeons are more numerous, the demand for operations increases. Other things being equal, a 10 per cent higher surgeon/population ratio results in about a 3 per cent increase in the number of operations and an *increase* in price. Thus, the average surgeon's work load decreases by 7 per cent, but income per surgeon decreases by much less.'[17] Greater availability, in Fuchs's study, is evidently correlated both with a rise in quantity *and* with a rise in price. The perverse sign would appear to call into question the extent to which user-charges may be relied upon to deter consumption at times when suppliers are, for financial reasons, actively involved in the business of boosting demand. Fuchs's study relates exclusively to in-patient care. The author is, however, if anything even more convinced of the reality of supplier-induced demand in the world outside the ward: 'The ability of surgeons to shift the demand for outpatient services is probably greater than for operations. Thus the total impact of supply on demand may be larger.'[18] Fuchs is not alone in drawing attention to the rapid expansion in doctor-initiated intervention. Nor is he alone in speculating on the possibility that *too much* might have been the unwelcome outcome of a distorting incentive structure.

Yet a possibility is not a fact; *too much* is seldom an incontrovertible observation; and the fee-seeker's opportunism is in the circumstances always far easier to suspect than ever it can be to measure. Of course tissue committees occasionally find that healthy organs have unnecessarily been removed. Of course second opinions sometimes discover that the patient sentenced to perpetual psychoanalysis hosts no mania. Error and variation are no proof, however, that the doctor has in practice been self-serving in defiance of the duty of care. Patients expect something to be done: marginal tests cannot properly be taken as evidence of a practitioner's greed where it is the consumer and not the producer who demands the reassurance. Medical omission can damage even as medical commission can cost: critics who regard 'when in doubt, take it out' as the profession's own admission of wasteful over-treatment should remember that excessive postponement is money-saving only in the obvious sense that the patient might then die for want of care. Doctors and their families receive at least as much treatment as do other consumers: if any inference can be drawn from Bunker and Brown's discovery that, in California, 'the appendectomy rate for physicians remains nearly twice as great as the national rate from age 25 to 40'[19], it can only be that no rational agent would knowingly expose himself and his loved ones to risky superfluities if he were simultaneously involved deliberately in exaggerating the medical needs of his ill-informed clients. Considerations such as these must put the reader on his or her guard against the obvious temptation to see *too much* treatment – and *too much* selfishness – in the marginal demands which the interested supplier seeks assiduously to induce.

Mental states being inaccessible to the outside observer, there is no way of testing the hypothesis that doctors have consciously supplied treatments of zero marginal productivity exclusively because, recognising impactedness, they wanted to exploit the inequality for gain. The evidence simply cannot be collected which would show unambiguously whether the representative practitioner genuinely abuses the representative patient for money or whether, alternatively, the trust that is the essence of the relationship is likely to remain well-founded despite the discretionary power that so complicates the contract. Two approaches to testing the hypothesis have been employed by investigators. Neither permits of convincing generalisations concerning the practitioners' motivation in the consultations that validate the supplier-induced demand.

One option is to rely on the time-series to track the co-variance between increased availability on the one hand, increased take-up and increased price on the other. The method would have a certain logic were nothing else to change but the number of merchants. The method is that much more problematic, however, where so much else is in rapid and continuous flux. Technology changes: to make the patient aware of state-of-the-art novelty is not necessarily the same as to advertise innovation purely in order to sell. Tastes change: to satisfy a demand for longer consultations is not necessarily the same as to supply an unnecessary service because of an irresponsible attitude. Incomes change: to sell what consumers at last can afford is not necessarily the same as to trigger off an artificial exogeneity purely and simply to reap a pecuniary reward. Insurance changes: an increase in coverage and a decrease in patients' co-payments introduce additional ambiguities into the interpretation of the time-series. As Phelps observes:

> Decreases in the coinsurance rate facing individuals will rotate the demand curve (around its quantity intercept), causing the equilibrium price, quantity, and importantly, the equilibrium of number of doctors, all to increase – all without inducement. Since physician supply will then naturally correlate with price and quantity, the appearance of inducement can emerge due to omission of the relevant coinsurance variable.[20]

Very sensitive corrections would clearly have to be made if the comparison through time truly were to be trusted to measure the availability effect and no other change.

The alternative to the comparison through time is the comparison through space. Rejecting the time-series in favour of the cross-section, it is the convenient property of this second approach that it is able to abstract from temporal mutation through a date-stamped concentration on spatial variation. Change in that way is netted out. Not netted out, however, are the multiplied independent influences other than practitioners' availability that can have so significant an effect on the quantity and the price of care. Communities differ in levels of income, education, health-consciousness and general culture: the fact that doctors like to live in middle-class areas and that their affluent neigbours like to consume medical attention cannot evidently be taken as proof that the professionals are cynically manipulating the suburbs until such a time as the *post hoc/propter hoc* has adequately been amplified by the *ceteris paribus*. Communities differ in payment-practices and thus, as Calnan points out, in that socialised guilt which makes the patient ashamed to utilise the availability: 'It is a product of a particular type of system where providers will define need. It is doubtful whether such a finding would be identified in studies of use of privately financed medical care, where both supply and doctor's income is claimed to respond to patient demands.'[21] Allowance having been made for patients' restraint, further allowance must be made for patients' travel. In isolated areas the consumers might find a higher charge for a local service an economical alternative to the time wasted and the fares paid that might, indeed, actually have compelled clients to cut back on care that was itself cheap. The increased availability in isolated areas will tend not so much to induce new demand as to release pent-up pressures previously dammed by cost. Travel is less of a burden in more accessible areas: there patients' costs are less likely to fall even as doctors' fees are seen to rise and the impact of increased availability is less likely to be the simple satisfaction of a pre-existent frustration. All of which is to say that the comparison through space will never be entirely convincing so long as the communities being compared remain so heterogeneous as to impede meaningful generalisation.

Hypotheses relating to supplier-induced demand may be tested using evidence through time or evidence through space. Whichever the approach that is adopted, still the chicken-and-egg problem of the line of causality is unlikely ever to be satisfactorily resolved. The reason for the on-going ambiguity is the exceptional difficulty of distinguishing supply-led demand from demand-led supply in a real-world context in which separate identification may be all but impossible. In the words of Auster and Oaxaca: 'Generally, we observe only one quantity at any given moment – the quantity transacted.'[22] The evidence, always mean with the *what*, is little short of miserly with the *why*. Perhaps *too much* treatment is even now the flawed consequence of *too much* selfishness – and perhaps it is not. There is no way to say for certain.

There is no way to say for certain if the autonomous pressure of the practitioner with the vested interest constitutes a serious challenge to the effective functioning of the market for health. What is more certain is the bounded nature of the producers' power: 'If suppliers can influence demand, there must exist limits on their ability to do so.'[23] The doubts expressed by Auster and Oaxaca concerning the ability of the medical professionals Galbraith-like to shift the demand function into any position of the suppliers' own choosing are valid and logical. They invite a search for the countervailing forces that constrain the conflict of interest. The following inhibitors of abuse are potentially the most powerful.

First, return visits and personal recommendations. Like the lawyer and the educationalist, the doctor enjoys considerable standing in the community (much of it reflected prestige derived from the high status of a life-saving calling); and, again like his fellow professionals, he is seldom regarded by his community as a tradesman, a salesman or a merchant. The unique nature of the unusual relationship the practitioner enjoys with the patients is captured by the language used to describe the contract. The plumber is 'hired' or 'employed'. The doctor is 'consulted'.

Only so long, however, as he commands the patient's confidence. Just as the carpenter's workmanship forms the basis for his repeat business, just as the hairdresser's skill is the commercial asset upon which he pyramids his reputation for service, so the doctor must be trusted and believed to be deserving of trust if he is successfully to attract and to retain patients. The perceived breach of trust is the ultimate threat to the doctor–patient relationship. Aware of the risks, there will be definite limits beyond which no future-orientated practitioner will allow himself to go. One inference might be that inducement will be more of a threat in the short-term context of one-off surgery than it will be in the continuing context of general practice.

Product differentiation admittedly confers upon each practitioner a degree of monopoly power with respect to his own image and catalogue of talents. The search costs of seeking and sampling reinforce the bias in favour of the known that is the consequence of monopolistic competition: thus Pauly and Satterthwaite have argued that, information costs rising with physician density, a given doctor may actually enjoy a stronger monopoly in an urban than in a rural area.[24] Such tendencies undeniably extend the limits of tolerance. They expand the realm of discretion but they do not eliminate the ceiling. Just as a particular butcher will cease to be a conditioned reflex once his prices are believed not merely to exceed but to double his rivals' avarage, so a particular doctor will lose the edge of inertia once the consumer loses faith in the standard of the service.

Second, medical referrals. Sometimes a return visit (for a second appendectomy, say, in contrast to a second pregnancy) is as unlikely as a personal recommendation (for suspected gonorrhea, say, or chronic delusion). Even then, however, it can be the prospect of future patients that keeps the medical specialist on his toes. The reason is the need to please the referring generalist whose task it is to shop around on behalf of a steady flow of varying clients, most of them unlikely more than once to experience the same intervention.

Bunker's results are of especial interest. Bunker, finding the ratio of operations to population twice as high in the United States as it was in England and Wales, concluded that the British practice was more nearly the medical optimum: 'Until new evidence is available, it is reasonable to assume that there is a disproportionate number of surgeons in the United States, at least in relation to the total medical manpower pool.'[25] The British, Bunker said, had the advantage over the Americans with respect to the suppression of unnecessary surgery. A significant reason, he inferred, was the British approach to the division of labour:

> The British surgeon is a true consultant. He sees patients only as they are referred to him by the general practitioner or internist, and he is entirely hospital based. The American surgeon, by contrast, may

> function as consultant exactly as his British counterpart, he may accept patients without referral, or he may be the primary physician-general practitioner, referring the patient to himself for surgery and thus creating his own demand.[26]

Bunker may perhaps have underestimated the problem of general practitioners who happen to be weak, lazy or simply over-sympathetic, of referrals that occur too early and recur too frequently. His overall inference is nonetheless quite an important one: through initial screening prior to referral, through evaluation of service after the event, the referring doctor acts as an inhibitor of abuse.

Third, mode of payment. The fee for service is an obvious incentive to multiply the services supplied. Remuneration by capitation or salary opens the door to under-performance at the margin. The difference in the financial arrangements has an undoubted impact on the treatments provided which Vayda's Canadian study is by no means unique in being able to identify: 'Surgical rates were compared for two sets of Sault Ste. Marie residents having similar age and sex characteristics. The rates for all surgical procedures studied were lower for the people served by a prepaid group-practice program and their tonsillectomy rate was less than half the rate of the physicians in fee-for-service practice.'[27] The conversion from the indemnity *ex post* to the prepaid maintenance organisation would evidently do much to cut the work and trim the cost. Whether the weakness of will in the opposite direction would adversely affect the health of the patients is less well documented.

Fourth, insurance arrangements. Suppliers are more likely to provide elective and borderline services where they are confident that their bill will be paid. Much of the reimbursement is, however, third-party – and insuring agencies have a financial interest of their own actively to discourage the over-provision to which moral hazard so frequently exposes the self-employed practitioner.

Insurers have an incentive to contain the needs for which they can be asked to assume the liability. They also have an incentive to involve themselves in quality control and medical audit, peer review and practice standardisation, in order to minimise the extent to which they will be obliged to pay for waste. Their endeavours, as Bunker records, will sometimes meet with remarkable success: 'When a requirement was added that all operations be endorsed by preoperative specialist consultation, the number of operations fell by as much as 75 per cent for hysterectomies, 60 per cent for appendectomies and 35 per cent for hemorroidectomies.'[28] Monitoring picks up the excessive, guidance keeps it down, and suppliers are faced with limits beyond which further demand may not be induced.

Fifth, internalised self-policing and normative self-constraint. No sensitive practitioner will want, guilty of conduct which he himself knows to be unscrupulous and improper, to become that pathetic creature that Adam Smith recognised to be 'the object of his own hatred and abhorrence.'[29] Every sensitive practitioner will therefore strive, desiring 'not only praise, but praise-worthiness', to be and to know himself to be 'that thing which, though it should be praised by nobody, is, however, the natural and proper object of praise.'[30] Not every practitioner, admittedly, will be all that sensitive; while even among those who are sincerely disposed to conform to standards and conventions there are bound to be some sturdy souls and independent egos who will be prepared to support the psychological burden of spoiled self-image provided that they are offered a substantial sum of money in return. Exceptions there will always be, but still it remains the conviction of the optimistic moralist that the typical doctor is a man or woman of integrity and honour. It is just as well that this is so. Conscience is ubiquitous, the constable is not, and 'only *I* can see everywhere I litter.'[31]

The internalised ethic is more easily enforceable than are the laws and regulations propounded by the State. It economises on decision-making costs at the treatment stage by pointing to professional practice and nothing else. It reassures the anxious patient that clinical freedom will be exercised responsibly and not harnessed to the plough of profit. It plugs the gap to avert the market failure by compelling the practitioner to be honest and impartial in the face of the obvious temptations to which the unequal relationship must inevitably give rise. The absolute moral code that transcends opportunism and stigmatises selfishness is quite clearly a thing apart from the market mechanism. Not a component of the marginalism and the maximising, its functionality in the case of health may indicate nonetheless that it is an infrastructural complement without which supply and demand are more likely to end up less satisfactorily matched.

Sixth, peer pressures and professional organisations. Spoiled identity is a self-imposed sanction. Its deterrent effect is amplified by the external sanctions that are mobilised by professional collectivities committed to standards. Those sanctions include ostracism, loss of contacts, denial of malpractice insurance (where commercial alternatives are prohibitively expensive), withdrawal of hospital privileges, expulsion from a professional body such as the British or the American Medical Association, revocation in the limit of the license to practice. Such measures serve to discourage the medically unnecessary procedure such as the deliberate removal of a healthy appendix purely for financial gain. In that sense they are the corporatised counterpart to the more formal sanctions of the courts and the police in respect of the illegal intervention such as the purchased organ transplanted from the living donor.

Yet no remedy is ever entirely free from side-effects; and the professional standard, successfully employed though it may be as a check on the unwelcome pathologies of supplier-induced demand, is no exception to the rule. The contra-indication in question is the blinkered narrowness of a convention that is the property of a single group alone. The truth is the whole. The profession, however, is not.

Thus it is possible, *looking backward* to the *first section* of this chapter, that doctor-led medicine might mean the pursuit of objectives that are somewhat different from the goals that would have been selected by the patients. The consultant might fight shy of the routine procedure that she finds marginal, boring, lacking in challenge, devoid of prestige – but the client might take the view that the treatment would make a non-trivial difference to his felt quality of life. The gynaecologist might refuse ultrasound scanning for a foetus which he believes to be free from abnormality – but the mother-to-be might insist that no one can make a rational decision on abortion without first being told the gender of the child. Examples such as these remind the observer that the patient and the practitioner might not after all be in total agreement as to which of their number it is that actually knows best.

There is, one senses, much truth in Enthoven's warning that there is more to efficiency than technique alone:

> There is a broader and more important concept of efficiency: what are the needs and wants of patients and how can they be served most effectively with the resources available? It seems to be taken for granted in the NHS that patients' needs are without limit, so the NHS doesn't need to spend any effort finding out what they are. The NHS does no market research. Such research might turn up valuable insights into patients' priorities and might help the NHS to allocate resources more effectively.[32]

Enthoven's specific focus is Britain's National Health Service. His plea to interpret respect for persons as incorporating respect for patients would appear nonetheless to have a relevance that transcends the national frontiers.

As with the patient who is the first constituency, so with the public that is the third. Thus it is equally possible, *looking forward* to the broad thrust of the *next chapter*, that the standards of the corporatised clincians might to some extent be at variance with the norms entertained by the wider community. Resources being constrained and choosing therefore inevitable, many will conclude that no society can afford the luxury of allowing its doctors the last word and the right to decide. Not least among the critics of clinical freedom is the cardiologist Hampton who, stressing that 'one man's provision is another man's deprivation'[33], has gone so far as to praise the suppression of medical independence in no uncertain terms:

> Clinical freedom died accidently, crushed between the rising cost of new forms of investigation and treatment and the financial limits inevitable in an economy that cannot expand indefinitely. Clinical freedom should, however, have been strangled long ago, for at best it was a cloak for ignorance and at worst an excuse for quackery. Clinical freedom was a myth that prevented true advance. We must welcome its demise.[34]

Not everyone, of course, would be prepared to accept the diagnosis of the demise or, still less, to welcome the collectivisation of the practitioner's duty. Democratic accountability conspicuously conflicts with patient's welfare where the doctor is prohibited by law from reattaching the amputated limb of a convicted thief, or where the doctor is required to perform tranquillising lobotomies on recidivist thugs. In a case where society denies a woman the sterilisation she needs to secure employment or to win promotion, in a case where consensus refuses a rapist the chemical castration that he himself prefers to a prison-sentence, there, it is clear, the patient will press for the practitioner to put aside the *I–We* in favour of an *I–Thou* that is preceived the better to advance the felt welfare of the unique individuality. Where resources are scarce and values are shared, however, the popular choice might strongly resent the decomposition of social obligation into consumer sovereignty on the one hand, clinical freedom on the other. The demand for health being treble and not double, the popular choice might be for the public interest to be properly represented in the consulting-room when the client removes his clothes.

3 The Public Interest

The first decision-making unit to be considered in the preceding chapter on the demand for health was the patient, the second the practitioner. The discussion in the circumstances has been strongly imbued with normative individualism and the atomistic ethos: consumer sovereignty and client consultation, clinical freedom and disinterested service, all have figured prominently, to the virtual exclusion of societal dispositions and collective preferences. The butcher, the brewer and the baker pay sincere tribute to Kenneth Boulding's defence of revealed preference: 'Only the slave has needs; the free man has demands.'[1] The good neighbour and the Good Samaritan are quick to endorse the absolute commitment to a unique sufferer's genuine best interests that is captured by the doctor's Hippocratic Oath in the following words: 'I will use my power to help the sick to the best of my ability and judgement.'[2] The economic man and the medical deontologist have, in short, this in common, that they believe the whole to be no more than the sum of the parts: the patient ignorant and uncertain, the practitioner torn between ethically-orientated conduct and supplier-induced demand, still it remains the reductionist's *credo* that the interaction can only be dyadic and that the wider society is not present in the consulting room when the client removes his clothes.

The third decision-making unit is, however, the public; and it is at this point that the latent tension between individualism and atomism on the one hand, social pressures and political interference on the other, must finally be acknowledged as an important causal influence in its own right on a nation's demand for health care. Just as patient's want must not be confused with medical need, so, it would appear, must medical need not be confused with social need. Thus Durkheim warned that factoring down is artificial, inappropriate and inconsistent precisely because the life in groups inevitably gives rise to the constraining force of a 'collective being which is, itself, of a *sui generis* nature': 'It results from special development which individual minds undergo in their association with each other, an association from which a new form of existence is evolved.'[3] Where all constrain each, it is clear, the freedom of the patient or of the practitioner can never be absolute and must always be bounded. There is much to be said in the circumstances for the proposition that the biological organism should be kept discreetly wrapped until such a time as the surrounding social organism has assembled for debate.

It is easier to explain the demand for care that emanates from the patient and the practitioner than it is to explain the influence of the wider society. The patient harbours the abnormality and the practitioner searches out the cure: that joint effort of the principal and the agent is far easier to comprehend than is the determination of an intervening community to coerce its members and to guide its parts. Easy or difficult, what cannot be denied is the fact: the public interest is widely believed to have an independent existence and the public itself generally regarded to be the third of the three decision-making constituencies. The nature of the collective mind is usefully examined in terms of three interdependent arguments: values, externalities and institutions.

3.1 VALUES

Durkheim conceived of ethical *ought-to-bes* as social facts: 'Society', he wrote, 'is not a simple aggregate of individuals who, when they enter it, bring their own intrinsic morality with them; rather, man is a moral being only because he lives in society, since morality consists in being solidary with a group and varies with this solidarity. Let all social life disappear, and moral life would disappear with it, since it would no longer have any objective.'[4] Even the law of contract, Durkheim maintained, was supra-individual and supra-utilitarian in its essence. Property rights and their alienation through market exchange, Durkheim said, can only be rooted in the value consensus of a specific collectivity. Where there is no consensus there can be no legitimacy: to that extent, in his view, even *laissez-faire* is ultimately *sui generis*.

As it would be in the market for health where the public, consulted, came down fully in favour of patient-led care. Thus, with respect to the exchange mechanism, the public might be of the opinion that effective demand is the best standard in terms of which to rank alternative treatments. Individuals themselves assign values to desiredness; doctors and hospitals are compelled by competition to be efficient; and these advantages might widely be regarded as so decisive as to make it the majority view that the decentralised system will on balance produce outcomes superior to those associated with the politicised option. The citizen who sees himself first and foremost as a consumer will wish in the circumstances to take issue with Brian Abel-Smith when that distinguished interventionist asks, however rhetorically, the following question of the monetarists and the libertarians: 'Why is the consumer always right and the citizen usually wrong?'[5] The dichotomy is a false one, the reply will be, wherever the consumer and the citizen are in truth but one and the same person. No less suspect is the implicit call for State: where it is as a consumer that the citizen happens first and foremost to see himself, there it might be the thrust of consensus that the public interest is always best served where public policy most strongly favours not the public sector but the private. Besides which, of course, it might also be the thrust of consensus that good procedures are at least as important as good outcomes – and that the free market is a good procedure quite explicitly because of the autonomy and the dignity that are automatically enhanced whenever the discrete health-holder is entrusted with the chance to choose.

Laissez-faire is legitimated by *sui generis* where the public, consulted, comes down in favour of patient-led care. It is legitimated in an analogous manner in the case of clinical freedom where the public, consulted, takes the view that the doctor knows best. Ignorance and expertise being so unequally distributed, the public might reason, the community cannot do better than to rely on its trained professionals with their service ethic to act the gatekeeper with respect to the *what*, the *when* and, most difficult of all, the *for whom*. Such a confidence in the wisdom of the practitioner was expressed by the White Paper of 1944 even as it proposed the introduction of the National Health Service: 'The practice of medicine is an individual and personal art, impatient of regimentation. Whatever the organisation, the doctors taking part must remain free to direct their clinical knowledge and personal skill for the benefit of their patients in the way which they feel to be best.'[6] Clinical freedom is humane and it is sympathetic: putting people first, it is an absolute commitment 'to help the sick' irrespective of the patient's financial circumstances and the economist's careful valuations of costs and benefits. The absolute commitment of one to one is bound to be a source of comfort and reassurance to the ailing health-holder, uncertain and afraid. It will in the circumstances come as no surprise to find clinical freedom so frequently supported by popular pressures and public opinion.

Where the society is entirely satisfied with the processes and the outcomes that are associated with patient-led care and with clinical freedom, there the nation will see no need to posit a public interest that transcends the bargain struck between patient's payment and practitioner's commitment. Where the society is not, however, so satisfied – where it remains convinced that there is more to the *summum bonum* than is captured by patient's willingness and practitioner's service – there the public will look elsewhere than to the markets and the clinicians for the defence of the shared objectives.

If the availability of health care inputs were not rigorously resource-constrained, it is possible that the public interest would be less often invoked in emotionally-charged discussions of ranking schemes and allocative criteria set against a backdrop of frustration and resentment, disability and death. Yet the fact is that care is scarce; that perceived wants are open-ended; and that no society, however wealthy, can afford to offer all individuals equal access to best-possible treatment for every possible complaint. The age-old problem of choices rendered mutually exclusive by an inescapable limitation of supply is well encapsulated by Newhouse in the following words:

> Individual A is a child with asthma; and individual B is a child that needs orthodontia. Who should receive treatment if treatment is equally costly and resources suffice to treat only one of these individuals? Individual C is a teenager with acne; individual D is a teenager with hay fever. Who is to be treated? Individual E is an adult who needs psychotherapy; individual F is an adult who requires physical therapy to recover from a stroke. Who is to be attended?[7]

Supply is limited; not every demand can be met; choices must be made; and Newhouse's crucial question of 'who?' is continuously being answered, day and night, somewhere in the system. There is no reason to think that the society will necessarily be satisfied with the answer that automaticity will provide. Where the *sui generis* comes to entertain a notion of the public interest that is strongly at variance with the bias of *laissez-faire*, there it will be to the elected representatives and the civil servants, not the patients and the practitioners, that the public will look for the defence of the *summum bonum*.

Thus a society with an overarching commitment to economic prosperity might decide to substitute collective need for individual want in the case of the dysfunctional purchase of medical care. A growth-orientated society will normally hold the allocative and dynamic efficiency of spontaneous coordination in high esteem. Should the commodity be not apples and pears but doctors and nurses, however, it will often want to make an exception to its rule. Thus a growth-orientated society, reasoning that there is no material benefit to be derived by the wider community from a scarce transplant being purchased by a wealthy pensioner, might insist that gains from trade or indisputable physical disorder may be a necessary but cannot be a sufficient condition for care. Public opinion might then decree that the interaction of effective demand with medical need ought altogether to be suppressed in the case of the elderly non-productive in order that limited resources (both preventive and curative) be concentrated on the producing members of the current labour force. Fewer working days would be lost through avoidable illness; premature death would less frequently waste scarce skills, and economic growth would in that way accelerate in consequence of the improved performance that better health makes possible. It cannot be said in such a case that there will necessarily be a rise in the felt welfare of the community as a whole: there being no interpersonal measure of utility, it cannot conclusively be proven that the felt diswelfare of the aged dysfunctional condemned to death is not in effect so great as completely to cancel out the marginal satisfaction of his fellow-citizens from the possession of the marginal electric toothbrush. What can be said in such a case is simply this, that social values and common beliefs (strongly held and broadly consensual) would appear to dictate a hierarchy of social needs that is simply not congruent with the pattern that would have emerged in the absence of intervention.

Not that the public interest will inevitably be linked in so materialistic a manner to the rate of economic growth. Just as a society might wish, in the face of finite health budgets, to divert resources from the long-stay mental ward to regular check-ups for middle-aged high-flyers, so, clearly, can it articulate a need for geriatric beds and drug abuse clinics. Public opinion is quintessentially itself; and if it in the event backs the claims of the prematurely tattooed even at the expense of the highly-qualified in need of brain scans, then that preference must be taken as an indication of what the public itself happens to see as its interest. More materialistic or less materialistic, what matters most for the specification of the social need in a political democracy is not the content of the consensus so much as the fact that the members of the community are allowed bottom-up to give voice to their choices and their rankings.

The social input is likely to be perceived as being of particular importance where medical intervention intrudes into emotively-charged areas such as those surrounding the inception and the termination of life. Embryo research, genetic engineering and religious circumcision at public expense all raise ethical issues with respect to which a concerned community might wish to be consulted. So does the artificial insemination of a virgin or a lesbian; the preselection of a child's gender; the easy availability of chemical contraceptives to teenage women lacking parental consent; the deliberate abortion of a malformed foetus; or the month-after abortion as the consumer's alternative to charts and caution. Popular attitudes can undeniably produce unintended outcomes in cases such as these. Thus a policy of abortion on demand as a woman's right to choose might be the cause of a dramatic shortage of labour; while a prohibition of contraception on moral grounds might breed unwanted pregnancies and equally-unwanted venereal diseases. Such outcomes, unintended and dysfunctional, are a great nuisance. Democracy has its contradictions as well as its attractions.

As with the beginning, so with the end; where popular attitudes governing the marketability and allocation of organs can easily influence who lives, popular attitudes with respect to euthanasia easily influence who dies. Death by consent is always a problem for a practitioner whose Hippocratic Oath is known to include the following undertaking: 'I will not give a fatal draught to anyone if I am asked, nor will I suggest any such thing.'[8] Medical realists will, of course, point out that doctors have long paid lip-service only to authority's dogma when deciding when to switch off the life-support system of the terminally ill. Reflecting that the Oath is easier to cite than it is to operationalise (the medical profession is believed to have particular difficulty with the clause 'I will be chaste and religious in my life and in my practice'), such realists will presumably go as far as to propose a compromise wording: 'Thou shalt not kill, but needst not strive, officiously to keep alive.' Even that, however, is unlikely to satisfy the dying consumer, conscious and in pain, who expresses a wish for a lethal injection only to be told that it is prohibited by medical ethics – and by social ethics as well, should popular attitudes reinforce the view of the medical paternalists that there are some choices which even rational adults should not be allowed to make. The sovereign consumer will no doubt contend that there is something priggishly self-righteous about an Oath, something intolerantly totalitarian about a consensus, which enjoins the supplier to reject the customer's considered demand for a convenient death. The sovereign consumer will no doubt contend that Mill on State intervention can usefully be regarded as of lasting relevance to medical intervention as well: 'The only purpose for which power can be rightfully exercised over any member of a civilized community, against his will, is to prevent harm to others. His own good, either physical or moral, is not a sufficient warrant.... Over himself, over his own body and mind, the individual is sovereign.'[9]

Mill will be tabled. Not, however, necessarily taken up. Social *ought-to-bes* are curious constructs. Sometimes they will stand as one with Mill in defence of the priorities and preferences of the physiological capitalist towards whom the procedures are directed. Sometimes they will insist that the drip be secured with a padlock and the hydrocyanic acids stored where the suicidal cannot reach them. Popular attitudes, whatever they are, must at any rate be conceptualised as the basis for the public interest that informed voters communicate upwards to sensitive politicians and obedient bureaucrats. It is those values that make health policy *social* policy in the strictest and most literal sense – shared and common policy, in other words, and thus a phenomenon *sui generis* which has an identity of its own that remains behind even after the patient's demand for medical care and the practitioner's ethic of best-possible service have somehow been factored out.

3.2 EXTERNALITIES

When elephants fight it is the grass which suffers. When fans attend a football match it is the neighbours who are disturbed by the noise. When smokers seal contracts with tobacconists it is the passive who share the exposure to the carcinogens. Spillovers such as these argue eloquently for an approach to the public interest that goes beyond the dyadic. Where the costs and the benefits are fully internalised by the partners in the trade, there the bystanders may perhaps invoke values but they cannot reasonably appeal to externalities. The position is different when Alter dealing with Ego stores his fist in the space that is the consensual reservation for the nose of Id. Such an externality will give rise to a demand for consultation that even a broadly contractarian community will be quick to acknowledge as legitimate.

Externalities are common in the area of health; and one of the most distressing of these is the awareness of some fellow human creature under threat from sickness and death. Whether the sentiments involved are altruistic or egotistic is a line of inquiry that is best pursued with a good dictionary. It is one which for all the effort is unlikely to repay the research with unambiguous results. Given that A's utility-function will often incorporate B's health status as a discrete argument, given that Alter will often derive pleasure from Ego's pleasure while Ego will often experience pain in consequence of Id's pain, it is no easy task to prove that a citizenry identifying as a social need the succour of the ailing and the assistance of the afflicted will be burdening itself with the transfer because it is exclusively concerned with the plight of the distressed. It might, at the more mundane level of self-interest, be doing so because it is exclusively concerned to square with its own conscience the knowledge that fellow creatures who could be helped are continuing to suffer from leprosy, glaucoma, scabies and leukaemia. Some thinkers will emphasise the self-denying humanitarianism of the sympathetic sentiments while others will point to feel-good selfishness and the repulsion of an irritating pollutant as the proper explanation of the stranger-gift. Whatever the reasons for the interdependence of utilities, few observers will want, however, to deny either the existence of the externalities or the extent to which they are common in the area of health.

Thus Gavin Mooney, writing of the other-orientated element in social man's attitude to his fellow's health, concludes that the caring spillover

> does seem to be an important form of externality which, while not unique to health (we can be concerned for the poor, for example), is more pervasive (we care about the rich being ill as well as the poor) and stronger (we are probably more likely to give, at the margin, to charities concerned with alleviating ill-health than those aimed at alleviating poverty). It is interesting to note that even with a national health service, as in the UK, there are still many people who donate funds and give up their time to buy dialysis machines, scanners, TV sets for hospitals, and so on. Indeed, this 'humanitarian spillover' has been suggested as one of the reasons for the UK National Health Service being established.[10]

Mooney clearly believes that A obtains happiness from the extra health that is consumed by B – and that the awareness of ill-health is a negative externality so widely perceived as intolerable that it motivates social man actively to *do* his share as well as merely to *get* his share. In this way do other-regarding psychological predispositions engender other-regarding social attitudes and other-regarding public policies precisely because, as Anthony Culyer says, 'the state of health of others is itself an object of interest to all': 'One individual is not affected merely by the possibility of another passing some disease on to him.... but also, and much more importantly, by the state of health of the other in itself. Individuals are affected by others' health status for the simple reason that *most of them care*.'[11]

Care in the sense of Culyer is one reason for the attitude that is described by Mooney – for the recognition, in other words, that A's health status is not only a private good to A but a public good to A's community as well. The humanitarian spillover is one explanation that can be found for group intervention intended to prevent or to cure a negative externality. The threat to all from the infection of each provides a second explanation of active involvement. The latter explanation will for most people be the more immediate of the two. The guilty conscience whispers. The epidemic plague screams.

It is the spillover diswelfare that, in the case of the communicable disease, constitutes the most immediate reason for not permitting A's health care choices to lie where they fall. Where the disease can spread, it is clear, A puts not only his own health at risk but that of other members of her community as well when a decision is taken to forego preventive measures (in the form, say, of immunisation against smallpox or polio) or to abstain from curative treatments (for syphilis, for tuberculosis, for typhoid). Those other individuals in the community might have a valuation of good health that is superior to A's own. If so, those risk-averting conservatives are likely to react with justifiable adversity to the lawyer's recommendation that they sue the gambler *ex post* for full and proper compensation. The tort-feasor might be impossible to identify where more than one contact carries the disease. The guilty party might not have the funds to pay the damages. The person infected, most important of all, might not regard any sum of money as adequate redress for the grievance imposed. Gifted with a complaint that is incurable and terminal, one would have thought, the litigant will obtain limited satisfaction from an action against the estate of a defunct surgeon whose needle-stick bled into an incision or of a discarded lover who thought that a sheath was a dress. In such circumstances the recourse to law will not solve the problem and the health-conscious community will want therefore to adopt a more interventionist stance. Where A's sickness can be transformed without consent into B's ill-health, there a responsible society will want almost certainly to circumscribe the personal freedom of the patient and the practitioner in the broader interests of the collectivity that surrounds the individual.

Consensus condemns contagion: thence the legitimation for a wide range of measures intended to defend public interest against private volition. One option will be the public health campaign such as strives to educate (to warn, say, against the hazards of unprotected coughing), to examine (the case of the chest X-ray to spot a tubercular lung) and to treat (not least through mass vaccinations performed in school halls). Another possibility will be the statutory prohibition: obvious candidates for regulation will include drunken driving, noxious emissions, cigarette smoking in non-designated areas and the immoderate display of affection while suffering from a notifiable disease. The statutory prohibition can usefully be complemented by the statutory screen: in such a case the State would require compulsory check-ups of all workers in externality-intensive industries (in, say, the catering trades), it would institute mandatory blood-testing for all at-risk minorities (including addicts believed to be involved in sharing needles), and it would check and test freely at all ports of entry (tourists and immigrants being easy targets for coercion in view of their obvious lack of citizenship rights). Then there is the specific incentive: this selective inducement, aimed at the modification of behaviour patterns, can take the form either of a pecuniary bonus (such as the payment made to parents who present their children for prophylactic immunisation against measles or whooping cough) or of some other concession (such as the priority given in the choice of school for his existing children to a father who volunteers for a free vasectomy in an over-populated country). Yet another option will be the subsidy to medical research: public funding will be especially of value where the private sector sees no profit in diffuse developments (however generous the patient protection) and where consensus nonetheless supports advance in order that negative externalities might effectively be minimised.

A consensus which condemns contagion will, however pro-market in net, almost certainly endorse public investment in good sewers and clean drinking-water, the drainage of swamps and the construction of roads. The consensus may even demand public housing schemes and adequate income-supplementation, if only because the poor who under-consume in areas such as accommodation and food are particularly vulnerable to germs and viruses which they then pass on. And there is medical care. The doctors and the hospitals have a social role to play which is fundamentally distinct from the specific service they provide to the unique patient. In limiting the unwanted spillovers while encouraging a healthy resistance, the doctors and the hospitals are conferring a genuine benefit on potential sufferers which is quite separate from the current benefit that they deliver to the present-day victim of cholera or flu. The doctors and the hospitals would seem in such circumstances to be the agents not of one but of two principals, and indeed they are. Social as well as individual benefits are clearly involved; and medicine has therefore no alternative but to take social as well as individual preferences in some measure into account. To that extent it would have to be conceded that every health care system, however private its property rights may be, is *willy nilly* a national health service as well.

At least some of the benefits being external, a rational community will therefore take the precaution of itself shouldering at least some of the costs. As Mark Pauly explains:

> If an individual's consumption of medical care does provide benefit to others, this must mean, that at some level of consumption by that individual, other persons would be willing to pay for him to consume an additional unit of medical care. That is, at some level of consumption by the particular individual, other persons have a positive, marginal evaluation of medical care.[12]

The public's willingness to pay may be motivated by empathetic compassion with a human being in distress: where A's illness causes unhappiness to

A's community, there, it is clear, the felt welfare of A's fellow citizens will be increased when market demand is abandoned in favour of collective action such as negates the negation. Alternatively, the public's commitment to care may be explicable in terms of a self-centred desire to dam a problem before it spreads: where A's illness at best means days off work, at worst the infection of his neighbours, it will be hard-headed interest and not warm-hearted altruism that causes the community to pay the practitioner 'to help the sick'. Whatever the motives, the implications are as unambiguous as the sentiments are varied: should externalities arise, should good health be generally regarded as a public good like good defence and good lighthouses, a concerned public will frequently turn to the public sector for the solution that uncoordinated individualism is believed to be incapable of supplying.

3.3 INSTITUTIONS

The institutional framework in the functioning democracy reflects the social consensus and the national culture. The institutional framework is in that sense a practical embodiment of the public interest as defined by popular attitudes. Just as different communities will assign different rankings to different consumables, so too will different collectivities entertain different preferences with respect to the finance and the provision of care.

Some collectivities will find the market model the more in keeping with their perspectives. Such societies will probably be suspicious of pooling schemes and cross-subsidisation, favourable to individual autonomy and family responsibility. In sympathy with the value of voluntary exchange and the primacy of freedom to choose, such societies will almost certainly find much to admire in Milton Friedman's libertarian *critique* of State-coerced uniformity:

> The characteristic feature of action through political channels is that it tends to require or enforce substantial conformity. The great advantage of the market, on the other hand, is that it permits wide diversity. It is, in political terms, a system of proportional representation. Each man can vote, as it were, for the color of tie he wants and get it; he does not have to see what color the majority wants and then, if he is in the minority, submit.[13]

Continuous consultation through decentralised negotiation will undoubtedly have a considerable appeal to a society imbued with the awareness that the human condition is infinitely varied.

Other collectivities will be unconvinced. Fearful lest the self-seeking independence of the heroic individualist make him as uncaring as a tank, as unfeeling as a wolf, such societies will warn that life can be desperately empty and totally unfulfilling where the free man chooses to cut himself off from the organic solidarity of a cohesive community. Such societies will therefore take the view that rationing by price should be eschewed in a wide range of integration-orientated areas in order to ensure that the members of the team retain an adequate sense of belonging and attachment. Fred Hirsch on the museum charge will usefully be cited in support of the proposition that exclusion by economics harms the *ins* even as it rations away the *outs*: 'This charge removed not only 10 pence from the pocket but also the pleasure derived by some visitors from the existence of a part of the cultural heritage as common property available freely to all.'[14] Such a diminution of pleasure the moderate interventionist clearly regarded as indicative of an institutional framework deplorably repressive of the deep-seated human need for perceived involvement. Just as the State can undeniably restrict the individual's freedom, so, Hirsch cautioned, can the excessive reliance on the market choice. In view of the wide range of socialised institutions that complemented the free market in Hirsch's own Britain, it is to be inferred that the median citizen in that cordial collectivity shared the perspective that I-aloneism may reasonably be selective but must never be allowed to become general.

Thus it was that Richard Titmuss, strongly opposed to the greediness and the divisiveness that he associated with unbridled *enrichissez-vous*, consistently argued that it had been popular attitudes first and foremost that had pressed for liberation *from* enterprise through the adoption of shared welfare institutions. Titmuss's commitment to democracy led him to the conclusion that social policies are legitimate policies purely and simply because they are endorsed by consensus: 'All collectively provided services are deliberately designed to meet certain socially recognized "needs"; they are manifestations, first, of society's will to survive as an organic whole and, second, of the expressed wish of all the people to assist the survival of some people.'[15] It was Titmuss's considered opinion that it had been 'society's will' and the 'expressed wish of all the people' that more than any other factor had been responsible for the introduction of the National Health Service in 1948. The revolution in the institutional framework, he concluded with pride, had more than justified the social democrat's instinctual confidence in the judgement of the common man:

> The most unsordid act of British social policy in the twentieth century has allowed and encouraged sentiments of altruism, reciprocity and

> social duty to express themselves; to be made explicit and identifiable in measurable patterns of behaviour by all social groups and classes. In part this is attributable to the fact that, structurally and functionally, the Health Service is not socially divisive; the universal and free access has contributed much, we believe, to the social liberties of the subject in allowing people the choice to give or not to give blood for unseen strangers.[16]

Richard Titmuss, using the supply of blood as a sensitive social indicator, reached the conclusion that a valuable contribution indeed had been made to the moral health of the British people by the symbolic interaction of the National Blood Transfusion Service with the National Health Service. The former makes no payment to the donor. The latter makes no charge to the patient. There is evidently more to individual freedom than the freedom to choose the market price.

Titmuss assigned particular value to compassion, commitment, fellowship, empathy, sympathy, citizenship and generosity in the context of health care and health systems. His emphasis had been anticipated by no less practical a politician than Aneurin Bevan when that great architect of the Welfare State wrote as follows of the other-orientated humanitarianism that the British socialists of the 1940s had regarded as the cause and effect of classless, coordinated, responsible and universalistic health care institutions: 'Society becomes more wholesome, more serene, and spiritually healthier, if it knows that its citizens have at the back of their consciousness the knowledge that not only themselves, but all their fellows, have access, when ill, to the best that medical skill can provide.'[17] Bevan, like Titmuss, believed that the health of the individual and the health of the community were closely connected, the vital link being the common culture of common institutions. Other thinkers will no doubt be somewhat less confident that equity and efficiency, the relief of deprivation and the promotion of dignity, are best brought about by a collectivism that emanates from community and subsequently reinforces consensus. The precise characteristics of the ideal framework are likely long to remain a matter for debate. There will be less disagreement, however, in respect of the proposition that institutions as well as treatments are properly a focus for social choice.

In the case of the market-orientated scenario, the contribution of the consensus is at its minimum. The members of the national club are duly asked to assent to the contractual nexus that binds the patient to the practitioner. Having confirmed the legitimacy of the paired relationship, the members of the national club are then encouraged to go about their business. Of course their values will be an input and externalities will remain a consideration. The minimal scenario is not the invisible scenario; but still the probability is low that the wider society will want continuously to make observations when, in the consulting room, the client removes his clothes.

The national health model is more problematic; since it is there the case that the consensus must not merely validate the framework but must also provide ongoing guidance on shared rankings and democratic priorities. The undertaking to involve would not present any insuperable difficulties if an unambiguous Social Welfare Function could rapidly be contacted on the telephone or if the General Will were known to be at home to visitors at alternate tea times. The reality is that social life is not so simple. The Function having gone *ex directory*, the Will refusing to come to the door, the Eden of full information has undeniably been superseded by the East of Eden in which the only thing that is not obscured by a veil is the client when he removes his clothes.

Consensus is problematic; but that does not mean that the invisible mind must remain forever hidden. Questionnaires and surveys reveal preferences *ex ante*. So do parliamentarians' postbags and constituency feedback. Popular practices are an *ex post* indicator of social attitudes (as where it is inferred that a nation addicted to tobacco would also like to see a liberalised access to prescription drugs). So are popular pressures in response to media revelations (as where the discovery that a hole-in-the-heart baby has been lost for want of staff provokes a scandal that augments the budget). At the clinical level a health district will often institute a user's council: the members will be local worthies rather than patients in beds, the forum is susceptible to capture by the nominees of the producer interest, the delegates are commonly appointed and seldom elected, but at least the council is an institutional acknowledgement that consumers have opinions. Damage done, the health ombudsperson hears the complaints and the legal profession dines out on the malpractices. Sadly, neither the commissioner nor the solicitor has any real interest in recording successes or passing on congratulations: to that extent the viewpoints registered will necessarily tell only a part of the story. Even so, they can clearly make some contribution of their own to the uphill struggle of reconstructing the national consensus in the light of the shadows thrown on the wall.

The task is not unlike the challenge faced by the archaeologist who wishes to reassemble the shards in such a way as to reconstitute the urn. Yet there is a difference, and it is an important one. The pieces of a shattered urn add up to a harmonious whole – whereas the preferences of an individualised citizenry need not add up at all. Different persons might value different things; there might not be one consensus so much as a multiplicity of clusters; and in such circumstances the problematic task of reconstructing the consensus must give way to the even more problematic task of reconciling disparities and negotiating packages. Titmuss and Bevan were able to neglect the threat that there might be significantly more than a single representative citizen because of their conviction that a society almost by definition must enjoy a high degree of consensus in its attitudes, a high degree of unanimity in its rankings. Their confidence in the shared and the common bears witness to the optimism with which they approached not just the altruism but also the integration of the nation. Where the nation is simply a place on the map, however, where its people are a *Gesellschaft* that resolutely refuses to identify the *Gemeinschaft* with the many millions who make up the whole, there, it is clear, the national health model will be that much more difficult to operationalise without some viewpoints being neglected and some groupings getting hurt.

Public opinion in the heterogeneous society will not speak with a single voice. The sheer plurality of the competing alternatives inevitably makes the community a locus of conflict and disagreement as rival factions vie with one another for relative shares in the compromise that, satisfying no section ideally, is nonetheless defined to be the public interest. The ultimate responsibility lying with the political leadership, the final result will almost certainly reflect the distortions and imbalances that are associated with inequality of access. The policy that emerges from constrained consultation will by its very nature be *partially* social rather than *completely* social. Biased as it normally will be towards the vocal and the powerful (the doctors and their professional bodies, for example), biased as it so frequently is against the silent and the weak (the lobbies speaking, say, for the mentally handicapped or the victims of sickle-cell anaemia), the politicised mix is bound to prove as disappointing to excluded groupings as is always the loser's-eye view of the zero-sum game. Where there exists a strong consensus, the pathologies of the majority's tyranny can at least console themselves with the thought that coerced conformity is the outcome of unambiguous values. Where there exists no consensus but merely sharp elbows, the neglected will probably feel that much more resentful and frustrated.

The adoption of a politicised system presupposes a considerable measure of confidence in the politicians and the bureaucrats to whom the decision-making role is delegated. The motivation of the leadership introduces a further complication and perhaps a further bias as well.

Thus bureaucrats, obedient servants though they are generally believed to be, might in truth have occupational targets and personal objectives which they bring with them when they filter information and make proposals. William Niskanen, for example, has argued that there is an inherent tendency towards empire-building and organisational megalomania in the very logic of the structured administration itself:

> Among the several variables that may enter the bureaucrat's utility-function are the following: salary, perquisites of the office, public reputation, power, patronage, output of the bureau, ease of making changes, and ease of managing the bureau. All of these variables except the last two, I contend, are a positive monotonic function of the total *budget* of the bureau during the bureaucrat's tenure in office.[18]

Anthony Downs, more cautiously, has pointed out that while some bureaucrats are no doubt entrepreneurial expansionists, others are inertial conservatives with a deep-seated attachment to the *status quo*: 'Both their underlying values and their expectations contribute to their net belief that negative change would be very bad, but positive change would not be very good.'[19] Whatever may be the precise direction of the bias, the point that both Niskanen and Downs are keen to make is that self-interest remains the compass even when men and women desert the supermarket for the civil service. If Niskanen and Downs are correct in their interpretation of the bureaucrat's motivation, then the implications for the definition of the public interest can be grave indeed. The zealot in paediatrics will say that today's babies are tomorrow's affluence when he puts in a claim for above-average funding. The conserver in geriatrics will discount reports of forgotten prostate when she defends her ministry against the change of unsupported dentures. Neither is likely to make frequent use of the deliberate untruth. Neither will see any need to do so where consistent selectivity can so easily produce the identical result.

Politicians too might be fully aware of a private interest that is corporatised, professionalised, and independent of the preferences of the public. Self-selected at the initial stage when he sets his sights on a career in leadership, the politician will probably hold an above-average stock of ideological capital which he will wish to see transformed by active policy into the national purpose. Thus it is, as Buchanan explains, that the public interest even in a democracy will often come to be promulgated top-down and not bottom-up:

> Within what he treats as his feasible set, the politician will choose that alternative or option which maximizes his own, not his constituents',

> utility. This opportunity offers one of the primary motivations to politicians. In a meaningful sense, this is 'political income', and it must be reckoned as a part of the total rewards of office.[20]

Such a constraint of conviction will have important implications for the health care sector. An advocate of privatisation who is also an opponent of deficits will call for cuts in national health spending in response to macroeconomic exigency. A proponent of integration who is also a spokesperson for the hard-to-reach will demand female doctors for housebound Asian housewives. Advocates and proponents will call and demand, but they need not be doing so in passive response to some clearly-defined and strongly-supported consensus. Rather it will often be the case that it will be the politicians who seize the initiative. Their fiduciary power admittedly legitimated *ex ante* by democratic process, still it would have to be conceded that the public interest they proclaim will frequently originate nowhere else than in their personal and private perceptions of the nation's needs.

Election and re-election naturally impose limits to the leadership's autonomy: in that sense the politician's vote motive is also the ultimate defence of the citizen's expressed wish. The politician, an entrepreneur in competition with rival suppliers for the prize of power, simply cannot allow himself to propose policies or implement programmes that are at variance with public opinion or are likely to cost popular support. In this way do the people retain control, as if guided by the invisible hand of opportunism in the manner described as follows by Gordon Tullock: 'The market operates by providing a structure in which individuals who simply want to make money end up by producing motor cars that people want. Similarly, democracy operates so that politicians who simply want to hold public office end up by doing things the people want.... There is no reason why we should be disturbed by this phenomenon.'[21] No one would want to be too critical of a social process that so sensitively converts private vices into public virtues. Yet no one by the same token would want to deny the possibility of distortion and neglect even in a political market where it is the sincere intention of the passive democrat not to lead his citizenry but exclusively to follow it. Scarce resources will be skewed towards the glamorous and the newsworthy (laser surgery to improve blood flow, say, inside a toddler's heart) but not towards the sordid and the uncomfortable (the early detection of liver disease, for example, among elderly down-and-outs sleeping rough). The squeaking wheel gets the oil (as where popular pressures to cut waiting times lead to an accelerated throughput of elective surgery) while the invisible consumer gets the dross (as where budgets are restructured from capital to current, inputs shunted from preventive to curative, in support of the proposition that the least expressed of all needs will be those of future generations). Above all, action will be taken. The median voter, confused though he may well be about his wants, is in no doubt about one thing at least, that there is little point in paying political dividends to a democratic leadership that is not seen to be keeping busy.

Nothing will come of nothing, in political as in family life. It is this compulsion to do *something* that is, arguably, an important reason why support and regulation so often win more votes than does the abolition of price guidelines, why hospital admissions without delay are eulogised but prudent elimination of excess capacity is castigated, why an expansion in insured entitlements is popular but cash-limiting designed to boost internal efficiency is not, why the socialisation of provision is welcomed (on the grounds that it speeds the patient's recovery by reassuring him that his community cares) whereas privatisation with the cash-nexus is criticised (on the grounds that it encourages unnecessary treatments and makes doctors untrustworthy). If the public were clear in its own mind that what it wanted to demand was health status and not simply health care, it would not be quite so quick to acclaim intervention and enactment irrespective of the proven successes and failures of the activity so conspicuously put in evidence. Sadly, the public is all-too-prone to identify health care inputs with health status outcomes and to take it on trust that more of the eggs will mean more of the omelette. Thus does the incentive-structure of the elected politician reinforce the expansionary bias of the patient and the practitioner. Whatever care is, whatever care does, this at least is subject to little ignorance and less uncertainty: wants and needs in the politicised system will inevitably point to more and more.

Optimists tend to argue that the politicised framework is a viable option specifically because of the ability of wise democrats sensitively to identify the collective priorities that transcend the discrete wants of the single symptom-holder, the clinical freedom of the isolated practitioner. Thus David Owen, rare among commentators in having been both a medical doctor and a Minister of State for Health, has written as follows in support of the accountability to the wider society that can be superimposed on the dyadic contract by a responsible leadership that recognises the 'general good': 'The doctor is primarily involved with the individual, the politician inevitably predominantly with groups of individuals.... The politician is concerned to ensure that scarce skills are allocated for the general good; the doctor, confronted by an ill patient, sees the good of that patient as the dominant issue.'[22] Pessimists will not, however, share Dr. Owen's confidence in the capacity of elected collectivists accurately to take the national pulse: uncertain about a 'general good' that is independent of the doctor–patient relationship, doubtful that the politician will have the omniscience and the beneficence that are required for the arbiter's role, such sceptics will argue instead for a market-orientated institutional framework that leaves it to consumers and producers to prescribe the optimal dosage and the component services of the national health commitment. Optimists will welcome politicised direction, pessimists will call for individualisation and exchange, but still there is likely to be general agreement that the choice of the framework is itself a collective choice and a shared undertaking. Institutions, like values and externalities, are always and everywhere a reflection of the public interest. Even when the number of seats is strictly limited to two, yet, it would have to be conceded, the wider society will nonetheless be present in the consulting-room when the client removes his clothes.

Part II

Finance

4 Health and Insurance

Some people cannot afford to pay for care. Bereft of entitlements and claims, they fall back upon the safety-net residualism of private charities, factory nurses, altruistic practitioners and public clinics. The concomitant of free treatment is often stigma and lack of courtesy, the care itself is often rushed and second-rate, but at least the indigent are granted access to trained personnel and specialised facilities. Denied such access, they attempt to treat themselves with a poultice or an aspirin, or they rely on the body to heal itself of its own accord. In the limit, they die.

Some people are so poor that they are unable to pay at all for care. Other people are so rich that they can fund their consultations exclusively from current earnings: their ability to do this will be especially marked where incomes are high and costs are moderate. Some people are in possession of accumulated wealth: they can finance care by means of depleting their savings or remortgaging their homes. Other people have prearranged lines of credit such as the medical credit card or the State-guaranteed loan: they are in a position to pay for what they need through unsecured borrowing at an agreed interest rate. And there is insurance.

Insurance permits of the pooling of risks and the sharing of uncertainties. In few areas of social life is the anxious individual more exposed to the potential buffeting of a cruel fate than where it is unpredictable health in an unknown future that is at stake. Statistics teach that there will be losers as well as winners but no one can know in advance if she will end up the victor or he the victim. Thus it is that the pooling and sharing of the insurance policy, conspicuous by their absence from the markets for apples and pears, tend to have so great an appeal in the market for health, where so much can go wrong that can prove desperately expensive to put right.

Insurance is the subject of this chapter, which is divided into three sections. The first section is headed Uncertainty and Risk, the second Choice and Compulsion, the third Redistribution and Reappraisal. Uniting all three sections is a sense of paradox. The patient and the practitioner decide on the treatment but it is the membership of the insuring pool that will ultimately settle the bill. Market capitalism is a system of achieved rewards but the market for insurance pays out for need alone. Individual responsibility leads to the purchase of insurance but insurance then absolves the individual of any further responsibility. Opponents of socialism have long recognised the penetration of the enemy in the service ethic of clinical freedom and the emotive solidarism of team sports. The sense of paradox which runs through this chapter suggests that those opponents ought also to be directing their challenge towards the insuring agencies, State-owned or commercial. The market may be red in tooth and claw but the market for insurance would seem marely to be red. As red as blood or as blue as Bournemouth, the exchange of care for money is undeniably an extraordinary transaction where it is a third party who takes out his wallet the moment that the client takes off his clothes.

4.1 UNCERTAINTY AND RISK

Insurance arises out of uncertainty as to the need for and the cost of care-to-come. If individuals had perfect knowledge of the amount and timing of the future burdens that a drunken driver not yet born or a serious disease now familiar only to apes would one day call upon them to shoulder, there would be earmarked savings schemes and interest-bearing deposit plans but no health insurance at all. If perfect knowledge were the norm, there would be no demand for a partner willing to share the risks of a factual future that is fully foreseen. A rational individual might be willing to pay an agreed fee to an insuring agency that takes over from him the possible costs of an unanticipated calamity. Not so where the contingency is a certainty: no rational individual will call it value for money to put down a known stake in exchange for a known reimbursement that is (after the deduction of profits and overheads) a smaller sum than that which had been paid in. Insurance arises out of uncertainty and in the absence of uncertainty there will be no demand for the contract.

Nor, in the absence of uncertainty, will the contract be supplied. Just as no rational bookmaker can afford to accept bets from well-informed insiders with unrestricted access to the facts which are the gamble to the uninitiated, so no insurance fund that wishes to remain solvent can permit itself to quote odds to consumers who know precisely what they will require. The insuring agency cannot afford to promise the omniscient a benefit that is in excess of the premium. It will perhaps agree to guard and invest the private capital of the chronically ill or the infirm elderly but it will nonetheless be reluctant to insure guaranteed loss-makers against a risk which is a certainty.

Thence the significance of the veil of unknowledge. The insuring agency cannot pay out to all subscribes a sum in excess of the contribution that each has paid in. Its very *raison d'être* is, however, to make such payments to some. Its protection is today's ignorance of tomorrow's randomness, its requirement that all members should agree in time of health to assist some members in time of need. The insuring agency in this way sells peace of mind even as a High Street publican sells gin and tonic. The healthy who lose out in the game will not in the circumstances be motivated too strongly to complain. Few people are so pleased never to see their money again as are the consumers of health insurance, none of whom is heard to complain that he took out an option on major surgery and then fell well instead. Illness is an unpleasant thing; imagination is worse; and the widow who bought at auction the plaque 'John Smith, Dentist'[1], on the grounds that 'You never know what might happen' was in truth confessing to a degree of uncertainty which less courageous souls are too frightened to contemplate. Except, of course, when they buy insurance.

Insurance arises out of uncertainty, but still the insuring agency is not quite in the desperate state of radical ignorance that characterises the gambler whose stake is the random number. The reason is that the agency is able to extrapolate probabilities from past experience and to rely on the law of large numbers for the purpose of estimating risks. If the statistics suggest that one person in a thousand will fall victim in a given year to a wasting disease, the one person might be taken unawares by the bolt from the blue whereas the insuring agency might long have been incorporating the cost in its calculations. Probabilities are easier to estimate for known groups than for named individuals: it is precisely this property of pooled data that, modulating uncertainty into risk, confers upon the agency its power to insure. Aware that no prediction is ever perfect, it will nonetheless be the conviction of the insurer that the predictions will be accurate enough for premiums to be set that bear an adequate resemblance to the underlying parameters of the probability distribution.

From the point of view of the contributor the ideal premium will be that value which equals the actuarial mean of the pool's probabilities. So low a price, however, the insurer will simply not be in a position to set. Encumbered as it is by the deadweight burdens of marketing and administration, concerned if a commercial organisation with earning profits as well as covering transaction costs, the agency will have no choice but to quote a premium that lies above the actuarial mean which is the consumer's ideal. To that extent all insurance contains a built-in deterrent in the form of the loading which must not be confused with the conceptually-separate deterrent of the premium *per se*. Every premium has a tendency to discourage consumption on the part of the risk-indifferent and the absolutely deprived. The loading has an independent tendency to price out even the risk-averse at the margin. It will not price out the prudent across-the-board: resentful of paying over the odds but sensitive nonetheless to the accidents and diseases that love to entrap the unwary, the risk-averse will not abandon insurance altogether because of a surcharge that they regard as unfair. What they are likely to do, however, is to economise at the margin by contracting only selectively and by retreating into the cheaper option of self-insurance through saving.

The disincentive gap that separates the actual from the actuarial will be especially conducive to self-insurance where the financial loss that might arise is potentially very small. No one needs insurance to pay for a packet of aspirins; and the same may also be said in many countries of the cost of an occasional filling or a new pair of glasses. A similar reluctance to pay above the pure premium will be observed where the probability of use is extremely low. Thus an elderly monk will rationally economise at the margin by foregoing comprehensive cover in favour of an exclusion clause that expressly denies him protection against the vicissitudes of venereal disease. Coincidentally, the reluctance to insure that is observed where the probability of use is extremely low will be matched by the reluctance to insure that is recorded where the probability of use is especially high. The premium being high as well, it will clearly be to the bank account and not to the insurance policy that the calculative will turn when they estimate how best to finance the six-monthly visit to the dentist, the annual check-up by the doctor, the repeat prescription required at regular intervals. Conversely, the willingness to insure will be most marked where the potential costs are exceptionally burdensome and the estimated risks neither so low as to be negligible nor so high as to be certainties. This would be the case, for example, with insurance to pay for hospitalisation in the event of a medical catastrophe such as would exhaust savings and could not be financed out of income. Where the possible losses are believed to be great and the measured risks are known to lie in the intermediate range, there, it is likely, the rational risk-averter will be most willing to trade uncertainty for protection and to purchase insurance.

4.2 CHOICE AND COMPULSION

A hypochondriac rushes to the doctor for a brain scan at the first sign of a headache. A gambler chases excitement even at the price of calamitous accident. A stoic neither rushes nor chases but impassively waits to see. An optimist maintains resolutely that 'it can't happen to me'. Differentiation of tastes and preferences is the essence of the pluralistic society, tolerant acceptance of that differentiation the essence of the free one. Thence the case for choice in insurance: in a community in which a wide variety of characters and types rub shoulders on a daily basis, it would clearly be more than unlikely that a uniform, a homogeneous, a standardised product could be designed which would somehow maximise the discrete satisfactions of the distinctive individualities that aggregate upwards to become the whole.

Risk-lovers will choose not to join a pooling scheme and the risk-neutral will studiously choose to remain indifferent. Their attitudes and anxieties will self-evidently set them apart from the risk-averse who eagerly insure. Yet it must not be thought that the risk-averse are identical merely because of their aversion to risk. For from it: risk-averters differ significantly not only from risk-lovers and the risk-neutral but also from one another in the focus and intensity of their concerns.

Thus the head of a family will want to ensure that all dependants are covered by the shared policy whereas the single person will have no occasion to contemplate the possibility of lower quality at greater expense that might so easily be the residual entitlement of the excluded spouse or child. Similarly, the individual who neither drinks nor smokes will raise no objection to a special-risks surcharge whereas the candidate with a hazardous lifestyle will prefer a less-judgemental policy that quotes a constant premium without embarrassing distinctions. Some risk-averters will be so alarmed at the prospect of sudden, unexpected and concentrated burdens that they will select the most comprehensive bundle they can find: they will demand a full range of medical, dental, ophthalmic and psychiatric benefits, perhaps with cover for loss of earned income as well. Other risk-averters, concerned with cure but also with comfort, will want to know that their policy guarantees them a certain standard of luxury: they will insist, for example, on a generous entitlement to good hotel facilities in the event of hospitalisation (including, frequently, a private room and an appetising choice of food). Some customers will opt for a low level of cost-sharing at a time when they expect to be at their most vulnerable: they will be especially attracted by the promise of 'first-dollar coverage' without any user-charges whatsoever. Other consumers, less fearful and less obsessive, will be attracted instead by the lure of low premiums: they will opt in the circumstances for a policy that is low-priced but which relies on high deductibles and hefty co-payments. All of which is to say that, while all risk-averters are averse to risk, still they are able to differ significantly from one another in the focus and intensity of their concerns.

Nor should it be forgotten that one and the same risk-averter might have different requirements in different situations. The fact that one and the same individual might demand low cover at low cost in one period but high cover at high cost in the next period should not for that reason be taken as evidence of intransitivity and contradiction. Seeing that health status is not a constant but a variable for the vast majority of human beings, such mutable flexibilities might be nothing less than the sensible choices of rational calculators who recognise when it is appropriate even for the decisive to re-think and to re-contract. Particularly evocative is Enthoven's example of a situation in which prudent economisers able to control the timing of elective treatments made the circumstances serve their interests by means of planning ahead and shopping around:

> How people can use this control to their advantage was illustrated by one California family that had an annual choice between a 'low-option' insurance plan with high deductibles and low benefits and membership in a health maintenance organization (HMO), with comprehensive benefits paid in full. The family chose the 'low-option' plan in order to pay low premiums, until the discovery that all four children needed open-heart surgery. At the next annual enrollment, the family switched and had the heart surgery at the expense of the HMO. At the subsequent enrollment period, the family switched back to get the low premiums again. Less spectacular examples are commonplace.[2]

Commonplace, however, only where individuals remain free to choose. Where a single option is made compulsory, by definition they no longer have that freedom. The consequence can be that diminution in perceived welfare that has been made the object of warnings issued by consumer-orientated economists such as Fuchs and Pauly.

Thus Fuchs has written as follows in praise of the decentralised subjectivity:

> One of the problems that should be squarely faced in framing a social policy for health services is that people differ in the relative value that they place on health, just as they differ in the relative value that they place on other goods and services. Any system which attempts to force all people to buy the same amount of health services is likely to result in a significant misallocation of resources.[3]

And Pauly, similarly concerned about the felt utility of the cat that was forced to eat the dog food (and to pay for it), has observed that heterogeneity of preferences may well render compulsion antithetical to welfare:

> If individual demands for medical care differ, it is possible that the loss due to 'excess' use under insurance may exceed the welfare gain from insurance for one individual but fall short of it for another individual. It

> follows that it may not be optimal policy to provide compulsory insurance against particular events for all individuals.[4]

The fact that tastes *might* differ does not, of course, mean that they *will* differ. Nor is it obvious that anything less than a *significant* non-optimality will necessarily stimulate the harried and the rushed to value the search for insurance above the search for attractive consumables or lucrative investments to which the same resources could equally well have been devoted. Where the consensus approaches unanimity, where personalisation adds only marginally to happiness, there, it is to be inferred, the negative impact of compulsory cover upon perceived welfare will be considerably less than it would be in the alternative case where individuals were as heterogeneous as chalk and cheese and the meat-eater's beef were true poison in the vegetarian's lunch. Even where minorities are not significantly inconvenienced by compulsory standardisation, however, still it is likely to be true that the command *in itself* will impose a welfare cost upon rational individuals acculturated to think of themselves as free agents. To such individuals a law making obligatory the opening of the umbrella in the event of rain will not enjoy as high a ranking as the autonomous decision to perform precisely the same action. Procedures matter as well as endstates; and the libertarian are understandably refractory to compulsion.

Refractory, no doubt; but still even the autonomous democrat is seen frequently to vote for coercion by consent. Even where the rational individual is normally opposed to the monopoly of force, in other words, nonetheless there are seen to be instances in which the sensible pragmatist demonstrably rejects the decentralised market in favour of a politicised lead that is strongly tipped to be the more effective option. Two such instances of market inferiority are of especial importance in the specific context of insurance for health.

The *first* reason why coerced conformity might become the democratic choice is the possibility of a popular preference for coordinated interaction. The problem is the tyranny of small decisions; the prediction is 'what each of us can achieve, all cannot'[5]; and the paradigm is the paradox of individual extravagance in a society consensually committed to the public good of price stability. Thus Mancur Olson, stressing that each of us is never personally so alone as when a part of a massive crowd, has warned that the self-interested economiser in the large group is always and everywhere at war even with a public interest that he himself supports: 'The rational individual in the economic system does not curtail his spending to prevent inflation ... because he knows, first, that his own efforts would not have a noticeable effect, and second, that he would get the benefits of any price stability that others achieved in any case.'[6] The rational individual, it is clear, 'has no incentive to sacrifice any more than he is forced to sacrifice'[7]. Nor, however, has he the incentive to sacrifice any less: thence the argument that compulsion legitimated by consensus, where the social need is for a coordinated response, might become the democratic choice.

Extended from inflation to insurance, what this result indicates is that there are likely to co-exist in the sector at once a threat and a solution. The threat is that atomistic decision-makers in a society committed to a welfare minimum will rationally choose to evade altogether the cost of private insurance because of their guaranteed access to a public service intended specifically for residuals: the safety-net then becomes as crowded as Oxford Circus in the evening rush hour as each seeks simultaneously to squeeze into a congested commons planned to support the part and unable to support the whole. The solution is that wise coordinators, aware that rational volunteers are all-too-frequently thin on the ground, will legislate to make the purchase of insurance a mandatory commitment: *each* is in this way prevented from attempting to travel free on the altruism of a generous *all*, *all* are in this way protected from the rational depredations of a calculating *each*, and thus is coercion not the antithesis of liberty but rather the precondition for it. The model is the rules of the road, where creative spontaneity is generally acknowledged to be a threat to health – but coerced conformity consensually regarded as the solution that, prescribing the direction of traffic, ought to be ranked above anarchy by everyone committed to the saving of lives.

A *second* reason for the popular espousal of compulsion in insurance might be the shared desire for an integrated community, a cohesive citizenry unified not least by overlapping experiences while in the state of illness and dependency. A distinguished proponent of this perspective was Richard Henry Tawney, who formulated his theories of welfare with his eyes fixed firmly on the ideal of the common language that would permit Eliza Doolittle at last to communicate with Henry Higgins: 'What a community requires, as the word itself suggests, is a common culture, because, without it, it is not a community at all.'[8] Richard Titmuss, similarly, recommended a National Health that was truly in the service of the *national* health. The advice on health and development which he and his colleagues gave to the government of Tanganyika is a case in point: 'We want to see a health service developing which will not be separate and aloof from the life of the nation but an expression and reinforcement of national unity.'[9]

Social democrats like Tawney and Titmuss have consistently warned against the loneliness and the isolation that is the free enterpriser's purgatory. Voters sympathetic to their organicist insights might in the circumstances demand compulsion given consensus expressly in order to strengthen the ties of the tribe. The compulsion could be the compulsion to join in (as where no taxpayer is spared the contribution to the national health service) or it could be the compulsion not to opt out (as where no individual is allowed to purchase a differentiated plan from a private source). Joining in or opting out, the principle is clear, that compulsion in insurance might result from a public interest in perceived fraternity such as is generally judged to transcend the shopkeeper's *quid pro quo*.

Two reasons have now been adduced to explain why an alert citizenry might rank the mandatory above the free. A useful illustration of coordination and of citizenship combined is provided by the relief of distress. It involves the case where the market demonstrably fails the deprived because the poor cannot pay.

There are elements of interest in the concern to assist, if only because the future is uncertain and no one can guarantee that he will not himself stand one day most powerfully to benefit from Rawls's principle that 'social and economic inequalities are to be arranged so that they are ... to the greatest benefit of the least advantaged.'[10] No doubt there are elements as well of compassion and sympathy, human dignity and moral obligation, the Good Samaritan's Christian Charity and Richard Titmuss's 'social and ... biological need to help'[11]. Yet private giving is vulnerable to the coordination problems of Olson's free riders while separate facilities are a threat to the equal respect that Tawney associated with common institutions. If the deprived are indeed to be given entitlements, then the theorists of interest and of altruism alike would appear to be in some agreement that the payment for access must not lie where it falls but must instead be governed by a rule of coerced conformity. The employer may be mandated to sponsor insurance or the taxpayer may be required to credit-in the neglected; but still it will be to compulsion and not to discretion that the community will look when it sets itself the objective of the relief of distress.

4.3 REDISTRIBUTION AND REAPPRAISAL

Insurance is sometimes voluntary and sometimes compulsory. Always, however, it is redistributive, and this is true by definition: if all subscribers pay in but only the unfortunate few take out, then it is inevitable that there will be a transfer of resources from those lucky enough to remain healthy to those unlucky enough to fall ill. The redistributive bias is an inescapable characteristic of any risk-pooling scheme. It is, after all, the very reason why the anxious are able to buy mental tranquillity even as they pay their premiums. The insured are seldom happy to sacrifice a certainty for a probability. Paying their money, they nonetheless find consolation in the knowledge that the insurer has in exchange taken over from them the financial liability for the future burden that the named contingency might happen unexpectedly to engender.

The carrier, not wishing to be encumbered with drains in excess of gains, will himself be seeking protection. To that end he will set a premium (unless he is heavily cushioned by a dependable grant from outside the agency) that is actuarially related to the statistical needs for which he has made himself responsible. An insuring agency with a high proportion of high-drain policy-holders will *ceteris paribus* set a high premium whereas a competitor with a low proportion will *ceteris paribus* set a low one. Assuming that the consumer is free to choose his carrier (and is able to back up his legal rights with the spendable resources needed to convert the *de jure* into the *de facto*), assuming further that the carrier is free to choose his consumer (in the sense that he is not prevented by law from turning down bad risks and discriminating in favour of good), then the likely outcome is the multiple-pool society. Even if the supplier were enthusiastically to welcome both the good risks and the bad, after all, the very fact that the premium is based on the *average* burden expected from the mixed population has an automatic tendency to serve as the filtering device that, known as adverse selection to students of commercial insurance, is immediately recognisable as natural selection by the denizens of a competitive jungle that is both praised and feared for its ruthless effectiveness. Thus the low-risk sub-group, deterred by the high premium associated with the mixed population, will be tempted to enrol in a more selective club or even to self-insure through saving. The withdrawal of the healthy from the open-door organisation will no doubt be accelerated by the rise in premiums that will inevitably result as the proportion of the membership that is high-risk rises inexorably in the direction of the whole. The outcome will be the multiple-pool society in which the iron laws of actuarial logic cause even the welcoming supplier to end up risk-stratified by default.

Automaticity promotes segregation. So too does rationality. Commercial competition produces the multiple-pool society by default but conscious action produces it, more deliberately, by design. It is, more specifically, the determination of the rational carrier that it should ferret out the golden goose while not itself becoming saddled with the lame ducks that ought properly to be driven to the wall. On its ability to pick winners depend its profits and its prestige. Alertness and opportunism are clearly not luxuries but necessities to the rational gain-seeker who is determined to stay on top.

One technique that is employed by the economic ferret is the personal medical examination. The transaction costs are high (including the administrative costs of actually processing the information collected) and civil rights present a problem (as where the employee rejected for a company plan is no longer able to conceal an out-of-hours addiction that would otherwise have remained a secret); but at least the insuring agency is given the opportunity to inspect what it is getting. Examination, ranging from the traditional blood test to state-of-the-art genetic screening, has the advantage to the insurer that it makes it possible to assign likelihoods to various contingencies without having to rely on the truthfulness of a consumer in whose financial interest it so clearly is to hide the pre-existence of a condition that, if discovered, would disqualify the applicant from full cover at the standard premium – or at all.

Less accurate but less complicated is the alternative procedure whereby what are risk-rated are not named individuals but rather broad categories of characteristics. Thus applicants can be classified in terms of key correlates such as age, sex, marital status and lifestyle; a differential premium can be demanded from those statistically likely to impose a disproportionate burden (the old, the female, the single, the smoker); and a refusal, complete or partial, can be extended to those whom experience identifies as probable loss-makers (applicants, say, who register high-risk hobbies such as lion taming or who, more controversially, record a preference for high-risk relationships). Occupational group can serve as a useful basis for prediction (the logic behind the denial of all-inclusive cover to lawmen, security guards and mercenary soldiers). So can the branch of industry (a proxy which picks up the hazards of lead, asbestos and falls from heights) and the workplace claims-record (an incentive to firms to improve their safety standards, if also to cut back on the employment of workers likely to impose higher premiums upon the pool). Place of residence can be harnessed in the attempt to track down the high-risk (as where the residents of an area where AIDS is prevalent are all assumed HIV-positive until proven otherwise). So can a history of medical treatments (as where the diabetic, the schizophrenic, the haemophiliac, the cancer patient, are mechanistically branded burdensome and pushed out of the club). Classification in terms of key correlates is less sensitive to individual variation than is disaggregated discrimination. Clearly, however, it does permit of some tailoring of quoted premiums by expected benefits. In that way it provides, however imperfectly, a rational foundation for a multi-pool society.

The insurance contract might itself be designed in such a way as to contribute actively to the filtering process. Thus the offer of a generous no-claims bonus or of a discounted premium for long-standing membership will tend *ceteris paribus* to attract subscribers who know themselves to be healthy; whereas the insistence on sizeable deductibles and a high co-insurance rate is likely to have a deterrent effect on an applicant all-too-aware that undisclosed complaints will probably require costly treatments such as surgery. The lower premium payable by the non-smoker and the non-drinker is an especially interesting technique: not only does it assist the economic ferret to separate the golden goose from the lame ducks that cause the above-average expense, it also provides an incentive to the unhealthy to reform their behaviour patterns and to reduce their consumption of self-inflicted sickness. Such sickness being a burden on the pool, it cannot reasonably be regarded as intolerant of revealed preferences for the representative to require the abnormal either to increase their advance payments or to reduce their expected demands. Nor can it be regarded as illogical for the visible hand of conscious action to be mobilised in reinforcement of the invisible hand of adverse selection: whether through personal medical examinations, risk-rating by categories or insurance contracts with hidden agendas, it must always be the objective of competing agencies to filter in the healthy and filter out the costly. The undertaking is a rational one – and the multiple-pool society is the likely result.

Insurance is always redistributive, if only in the obvious sense that illness is a bad which not all citizens are compelled in equal quantities to consume. Henry Aaron's statistics for the United States well illustrate the extent of the bunching and therewith the potential for the transfer: 'Each year a small proportion of the population accounts for the majority of health care outlays. ... Five percent of the population accounts for more than half of all health care outlays in any given year. One percent of the population spends more than one-fourth of all health care outlays.'[12] Always insurance is redistributive. In the multiple-pool society, however, the redistribution is operative not simply *within* each pool: it is operative *between* the disparate pools as well. Such a bias will not, of course, be perceived as any great hardship by consumers fortunate enough to be classified as good risks. The position of the statistically sickly is less attractive. Turned down by low-premium pools, forced into clubs in which the members share nothing but their coughs and sneezes, the rejects from the agencies that specialise in the healthy will wish most sincerely that the pools and clubs were formed on the basis of some health-neutral characteristic such as love of the countryside or interest in the Bible. Actuarially speaking, their instinct is sound.

Once accepted into the pool or club, once protected by a guarantee that redistributes risks, an otherwise careful party is clearly exposed to definite temptations to let down his guard. This change in the incentive structure is the moral hazard that is faced by the individual when he takes out insurance. It is only one instance of a broad class of cases in which a reappraisal of conduct is the unintended outcome of the purchase of protection. Active as well as permissive, insurance has the important property that it can make things happen and very often does so.

The individual protected by a guarantee is clearly exposed to a temptation to relax his vigilance. Thus the umbrella of a preannounced entitlement will have an undeniable tendency to make the insured more accident-prone, less willing to substitute prevention for cure. Given that tendency, it will have then to be conceded that moral hazard can lead directly to a worsening in health status and to a wasteful over-consumption of care as a consequence. Yet the existence of an attraction can hardly be called the forecast of a dereliction, nor a tendency rightfully be treated as equivalent to a prediction. No doubt there will be some among the insured who are motivated by the contractual guarantee to take fewer precautions than they would have done had the financial responsibility remained sole and not been shared. How significant the change will be cannot, however, be anticipated *a priori*. Some individuals will presumably be stimulated to drive faster and smoke more but others will continue to avoid the crashes and the cancers despite the fact that the treatments are prepaid. The change being indeterminate in advance of empirical investigation, it cannot automatically be assumed that the effect at the margin will necessarily be a substantial one. Nor can it be supposed that the welfare implications are entirely without ambiguity. An insured alcoholic who drinks himself into a liver disorder will lose on the sickness but gain on the drunkenness. An insured sprinter who plays Russian roulette with anabolic steroids will be trading one probability against another in a ratio that accords with his own personal preferences. Generalisation is evidently impossible in the presence of such pluses and minuses: there is simply no way of estimating the net impact upon overall satisfaction that is the joint product of initial insurance, induced indulgence. Were that impact to be positive, the inference would have to be that moral hazard had the effect of raising the general level of happiness. Positive or negative, what is not to be denied is the conclusion that insurance can make things happen and very often does so.

The practitioner like the patient is prone to a reappraisal of conduct as a rational response to the knowledge that the client has acquired the protection of insurance. Where the patient is known to be insured, the sensitive doctor has the soft options of prescription and referral even when the marginal efficacy of formal intervention is almost certain to be negligible; while the maximising doctor has the pecuniary incentive to impose extra costs purely and simply in order to garner extra fees. Often, too, the precise terms of the insurance contract will influence the nature of the treatment that is recommended. Thus the policy will sometimes pay out for expensive care but leave the cost of the cheaper option (the ambulatory as opposed to the in-patient, say) entirely for the consumer to settle. The doctor will clearly be tempted to protect the patient's pocket by selecting the reimbursable alternative, but an unintended outcome will be an unwelcome rise in the total price that is paid for care.

The inflationary tendency is reinforced by the endogenised bias of the research and development industries in favour of the technology-intensive procedures for which the professionals are empowered by the insurers to articulate so effective a demand. Recognising the upward spiral, the consumers, as Weisbrod writes, are increasingly under pressure to take out policies: 'Costly new surgical techniques such as organ transplants and artificial replacement parts spur the demand for insurance; low-cost vaccines diminish it.'[13] More entitlements mean more treatments; new techniques mean more entitlements; and thus it is that insurance will have an active influence on the practice that the practitioner will adopt.

Rising costliness is not, of course, the whole story. Insurance allows the nervous practitioner the freedom of choice to deliver an irreversible service to a patient with whose credit-worthiness he is not familiar. The existence of the outside guarantee means that the doctor has no need to introduce an insurance component of his own by turning away the probable defaulters or by raising his average charges in a bid to compensate himself for unremunerated business. Insurance offers the compassionate practitioner the medical opportunity to treat more suffering and to prolong more life: an additional advantage to the committed Hippocratic will be the green light to supply preventive services on which the patient might have had to economise if required to pay the market price. Undeniably, the influence of insurance is likely to be an active one. Seen from the perspective of the practitioner, the prediction must be that insurance can make things happen and very often does so.

Insurance having the capacity both to shape the done and to stimulate the undone, the insuring agency is clearly in a strong position to modify behaviour patterns in line with its own objectives. Thus it will collect comparative data on doctors and hospitals in an attempt to monitor utilisation and track outcomes; it will refuse reimbursement for innovatory therapies until such a time as proof is available of medical effectiveness in alliance with economic efficiency; it will subject large claims to in-depth scrutiny in order to persuade providers to limit themselves to value for money. And it will experiment with the prospective payment that is a fixed fee for a given diagnostic group.

Where remuneration is retrospective, the supplier provides the service and then sends out the account. The claim might be settled in the first instance by the insured party (perhaps borrowing to smooth cash flow in advance of reimbursement) or it might be transmitted directly to the insuring agency (which will pay an indemnity up to the ceiling specified in the contract). More important than the first port of call is, however, the autonomy of the provider with respect to the magnitude. The provider determines the quantity and the quality; the provider establishes the fee per service; and the insurer is to a considerable extent at the mercy of the professional's judgement when it is asked in due course for a retrospective cheque. The insurer is somewhat less vulnerable where the payment is prospective and the scale of charges is the agency's own. In such a system the insurer states that it will pay no more nor less than a named sum for a specified intervention. The supplier, in accepting the offer, is clearly exposing itself to the risk that the procedure will unexpectedly exceed the burden budgeted: it is in that sense agreeing to act as the sub-insurer for the lump-sum hernioplasty that develops complications or the non-invasive scan that, being inconclusive, has to be followed up with exploratory surgery. Yet the supplier, in settling for the insurer's shilling, is simultaneously acquiring a strong incentive to be economical with its inputs: while any corner-cutting that transfers the risk back to the client will presumably jeopardise the relationship with the insurer, still the precommitted sum provides a reason, medical efficacy constant, to keep costs down and efficiency high. The moral of the story is effectively this, that if insurance matters, then so does the insurer. The insurer can make things happen and very often does so.

There is a concluding comment to make about the nature of health insurance; and it is in effect a warning against incautious generalisation. Insurance contracts can take a variety of different forms. They can also be issued by a variety of different bodies. Given the many in the one, the reader would be well-advised not to confuse the combinations with the permutations despite the superficial similarities that mask the very real differences.

Thus insurance contracts, kaleidoscopic and heterogeneous where unregulated by oligopoly or State, can take a variety of different forms. Some refund the fee for service, in whole or in part, without limit or up to a prearranged maximum. Others, dispensing altogether with fees and bills, simply supply the prepaid entitlement in kind, either employing their own closed panels or buying in outside services on behalf of their clients. Some contracts restrict cover to expensive contingencies such as hospitalisation, anaesthetics and surgery. Others protect against minor illnesses, sponsor antenatal care, refund preventive immunisation, encourage regular mammograms, and reimburse cures for alcohol dependency and drug abuse. Some contracts define medical need to mean physical malfunction; others are sympathetic to mental health as well. Some cover the chronic in addition to the acute (and may also incorporate a guarantee of income-replacement); others cover prescription charges and perhaps even fringe treatments but draw the line at nursing homes, wheelchairs and walking frames; still others cover dentistry and optometry but not blood bought for transfusion or organs purchased for transplantation. In some cases the employer pays the whole premium; in other cases the burden is shared with the employee; in other cases the tax relief contributes the public finance foregone; in yet other cases it is the taxpayer-citizen who supplies the revenues that finance the pool. Sometimes the economic ceiling is fixed and irrevocable: then the patients may die but the costs will not rise. Sometimes, alternatively, the standard package is no more than a foundation upon which top-ups can proceed unhindered to build: then some will insure for superior amenity (a choice of waits and schedules), others for superior quality (a surgeon of above-average eminence), others for superior quantity (a lengthy period of in-patient convalescence) and the insurer will have in consequence to pay the price of an inflation that insurance itself has fuelled. All of which is to say that insurance contracts can take a variety of different forms. Logically so; since different individuals tend to have different problems, different circumstances and different preferences.

Insurance contracts can take a variety of different forms. They can also be issued by a variety of different bodies. Thus it is, in the mixed welfare environment, that some agencies are run by the medical profession, others by the government, others by commercial organisations in pursuit of profits, others by charitable institutions with a public service ethos. Structures differ, motives differ; and a further complication is the fact that many if not most individuals are likely to hold a mixed portfolio of claims to care. An American with an occupational plan might, for example, supplement that cover with a private policy of his own against deductibles and co-insurance; he is reassured by the knowledge that there exists a State safety-net in the event of ultimate destitution; and he is, in short, the beneficiary of multiple protection provided for different reasons by different agencies situated in different sectors.

Situated in different sectors, but supportive and symbiotic as well. Agencies in the private sector frequently rely on governmental intervention for grants and subsidies (as where an insurance policy attracts fiscal concessions at the taxpayer's highest marginal rate). Agencies in the public sector often depend on commercial carriers for the execution of the contract (as where the State assists the absolutely-deprived by paying in the actuarial premiums on their behalf). It is by no means easy to identify with precision the exact point at which the privately-funded ceases and the publicly-funded begins. The truth is the whole: the warning cannot be treated too lightly as the private and the public sectors of health insurance are successively subjected to closer scrutiny in the two chapters which now follow.

5 The Private Sector

Insurance as an instrument is central to the broad topic of care. Its principal characteristics were considered in the previous chapter while the public sector will be the subject of the next. It is the task of the present chapter to examine the four modes of health cover that happen to be supplied in the private sector of the mixed welfare economy. The alternatives are the occupational plan, the individual plan, the prepaid scheme and the autonomous fund. The options are distinctive if not always mutually-exclusive. They will be considered respectively in the first four sections of this chapter.

The fifth and final section will be concerned with the State. Even where the State does not aspire to the high status of the funder of first resort, still it will often wish by means of legislation to play an active role in rendering the private sector of health insurance fully subservient to that which it defines to be the national interest. Stranded on the middle ground as is the normal situation in welfare capitalism, the intrusion of compulsion, regulation and subsidisation even into the consenting privacy of the dyadic contract should surprise no one who accepts that the public interest will frequently march alongside the private in matters of health.

5.1 THE OCCUPATIONAL PLAN

In some countries – the United States is one – private health insurance is typically arranged through the group contract which the firm provides for its employees as, like a company car, a fringe benefit. The system is not ideal, and Henry Aaron is only one among many to have expressed serious reservations: 'If the United States were designing its health care financing system from scratch, I do not think it would choose to base it on employer-sponsored insurance. But the investment in the current system is huge.'[1] Indeed it is: bygones may be bygone but still we start from here. Not that here is necessarily an intolerable place to be. The system is not ideal but nor is any other. Many beneficiaries are more than satisfied with the protection they enjoy under the occupational plan.

The firm may itself act as the insuring agency in the employer-sponsored system, itself holding the premiums and itself taking the decisions. In this way the plan makes a gain in the form of freedom and flexibility. An in-house fund is unlikely to be constrained by the same restrictions on investment practices that would apply in the case of an insurance company: while the possibility cannot be ignored that an unscrupulous employer will be tempted by the freedom to raid the fund, the flexibility with respect to the outlets may in the end prove the stronger argument. Besides which, of course, the in-house fund has the additional advantage that it is not obliged to cover the profits, the taxes and (doing its own administration) the overheads of an outside agency. This means that a higher percentage of the premium income can be paid out to the employees in the form of benefits.

Looking on the debit side, the firm that holds its own fund is undeniably vulnerable to a major catastrophe. An explosion at the works or an earthquake that devastates the locality can bankrupt the fund: where an exhausted fund acquires a first claim on the employer's assets, it might even bankrupt the sponsor as well. The firm is likely, recognising the contingency, to re-insure the risk with a commercial carrier. The insurance company would take over the exposure to large losses. In return for the fall-back guarantee it would be paid a small percentage of the premium income.

Possibly the firm that holds its own fund will wish also to farm out to an insurance company or to some other external agency the practical burden of routine administration. The services specified will presumably include the collection of payments and the processing of claims. The firm will offer the outsider a fixed fee but not a percentage or a commission. The reason is clear: the firm is here employing the external organisation for the execution of non-discretionary obligations but is retaining for itself the control, the decisions and the risks.

Sometimes the firm will itself act as the insuring agency in the employer-sponsored system. What is more commonly the case is that it will not. What is more commonly the case is that the firm will opt to hand over the premiums and the choices to an insurance company to which it delegates, for a named period, the control that has become a chore. The sponsor continues to monitor the performance of the fund on behalf of the employees. Dissatisfied, the sponsor will, in the long run, transfer the franchise to a competing bidder. For the duration of the contract period, however, the employer's *de facto* authority will be as minimal as that of the local representative who sends up the funds. That alienation of responsibility is, indeed, an important reason why the busy employer so eagerly espouses the option of fixed-term delegation.

In many ways, it would be true to say, all parties benefit from the system of fixed-term delegation.

The *sponsor* benefits. The existence of alternative insurers provides a competitive check on high mark-ups and excessive profits (always assuming that oligopolisation does not lead to collusive price fixing nor cartellisation to the suppression of product differentiation). The whole of the employer's contribution is normally tax deductible as a legitimate business expense (such favourable tax treatment making it artificially easy for the organisation significantly to boost *morale* by means of insurance cover more generous than the counterpart pay). The net cost to the firm can, in a buoyant economy, very often be passed on to the consumer in the form of higher prices. Unless, of course, the industry is too competitive (domestically or internationally) to permit of the price tags beings pushed upwards by the cost of the benefits that are provided: then, should the shareholders be unprepared to countenance lower dividends and the unions be equally intransigent about lower wages (or a slower rise in wages), the position of the employing organisation forced internally to absorb the net cost can be an uncomfortable one indeed.

The *insurer* benefits. The carrier's knowledge of the firm and the industry allows it to set an experience-related premium (a fee actuarially estimated on the basis of the specific claims the unique pool has made in the past and of the liabilities it may be expected to impose in the future). The risk of adverse self-selection is eliminated by virtue of the fact that the whole of the occupational group is automatically blanketed in (whereas the isolated individual applying for insurance must always be suspected, often unjustly, of deliberately purchasing cover not behind a veil of ignorance but rather in the full knowledge of above-average expectations). The economies of scale that arise in connection with the bulk deal have the effect of cutting the cost (a reduction, to be fair, in which a prudent employer with the power born of size will rationally seek to negotiate himself a share).

The *employee* benefits. Premiums are frequently funded exclusively by the employer's side (and even where they are not it will be the study of a go-ahead union to minimise the proportion that is contributory). The involvement of both the employer and the insurer gives the employee the protection in practice not of one but of two third parties (as opposed to the situation where an employer whose speciality is not insurance struggles alone to cope in-house, aided by consultants). The fact that the employer chooses and bargains on behalf of the group spares the employee the labour of collecting information, making decisions, monitoring quality, promoting efficiency. And there is strength: a single individual has little influence on the charges made by an insuring agency but the position of the group as a whole is that much more powerful.

The *spillover community* benefits. Intelligent choices and quality control are not, as Paul Feldstein points out, free goods like the sun and the rain; and thus it will often happen that

> some consumers make their enrollment decisions based on limited information. Other subscribers, however, are more knowledgeable; for example, unions and employers can afford to develop the necessary expertise and information to evaluate alternative medical care delivery options available to their employees. ... The greater selectivity of better-informed groups benefits the less-informed subscriber. [All automobile purchasers are not equally knowledgeable, yet automobile companies compete on the basis of quality (e.g increased warranty periods) as well as on price and styling, because *part* of their market is knowledgeable and willing to shift their purchases] .... The competition among health plans for the better-informed purchasers, those who are more likely to switch plans if quality deteriorates, will help those who are less well informed.[2]

Clearly, the spillover community committed to allocative efficiency will stand much to benefit, alongside the sponsor, the insurer and the employee, from the system of fixed-term delegation and from the occupational plan.

Yet there are disadvantages as well; and one of the most obvious of these is the potential repression of the employee's preferences. Where the employer represents, the employer decides; and (not least because the insurance companies quote lower rates for the unitary plan with the lower cost of administration) the employer will be strongly tempted to opt for the standardised product. The standardised product will have a definite appeal to the standardised consumer who feels no need for a range of choices. Its appeal will be somewhat less, however, to the non-median consumer whose perceived requirements are not identical to those of the other pebbles on the beach.

Thus a bachelor or a spinster might be broadly satisfied with the standard product but not so a husband or a wife. Where there is more than one earner in a family, each with cover for spouse and offspring, both are likely to see that the same individuals in effect enjoy duplicate cover; that the surplus is *de facto* a waste; and that felt welfare would rapidly be raised were the means to be found of channelling the unusable excess into higher pay or some valid alternative. The second policy could be used, for example, to top up the co-insurance provisions of the first (a procedure normally acceptable in law despite the fact that it defeats the economist's objective of deterrence through cost-sharing); or to double the value of the protection extended (an option, admittedly, likely only to be of practical use when each policy is subject to a ceiling limit and the actual cost of medical care turns out to be exceptionally high); or to shift welfare entitlements out earmarked health altogether (perhaps into neighbouring areas such as vouchers for school fees or additional pension rights). Given the standardised product, the consuming units will not enjoy the freedom to make choices such as these. Instead they will be forced into the fringe benefit paid to them in counterfeit money that is the health plan with surplus protection.

The unions can, of course, press for diversity. They can demand that the employee be offered a choice between the plans provided by a single insurer; or between those issued by competing insurers; or between those that combine insurance with delivery in different ways. Where the non-standard consumer is lacking in voice, however, it is by no means obvious that the unions will see the need to defend the powerless by demanding diversity on behalf of a minority. It is in a case such as this that the true complement to freedom of choice might indeed be the intervening hand of State compulsion.

Potential repression of employee's preference is one disadvantage associated with the group plan based upon the workplace. Impeded mobility of labour is another. A job change is often accompanied by transitional unemployment and the withdrawal (either immediately or after a grace-period) of the job-related health protection. Such an interim is a bad to fall ill, an anxious time lest one might. Employees will in the circumstances think twice before indulging in voluntary unemployment. Their reaction is entirely rational in the light of the disincentive. It is also to be regretted, where the outcome of the search impeded would have been higher productivity for the nation, higher income for the worker.

A new job, the change made, will entail a new occupational plan. Perhaps, where an unrestricted choice is not allowed, it will entail a new general practitioner as well. Not only does this mean the termination of a doctor–patient relationship which will often be regarded by both parties as eminently satisfactory, not only is repeated interruption a detrimental practice in a sensitive area of social life where continuity of responsibility is of considerable benefit, but it also imposes economic costs where it necessitates the repetition of basic tests and the taking on multiple occasions of a medical history. An existing complaint is a further consideration: covered by the old plan (perhaps because the condition was only diagnosed after the old plan had become binding), the complaint might be made subject to an exclusion clause under the new one. Even if the exclusion clause is no more than a temporary measure, a precautionary device intended to be suppressed once an observation period has elapsed, still it does leave the afflicted party in the short-run without any cover at all for the condition. Employees with such complaints will not unnaturally think twice before changing their job. Then there is the problem of the co-payment. A new contract means a new period for the purposes of estimating annual cost-sharing ceiling arrangements: irrespective of the deductibles (normally non-portable) already paid out, the clocks are put back to the starting point and the annual march to the frontiers of the individual's out-of-pocket commitment must begin anew. Even where the employees have no strong attachment to their old doctor and no on-going health problem, such a financial burden is an impediment to mobility.

As is *ceteris paribus* the differentiation in the cover provided. Tax relief on employer-sponsored insurance makes the fringe benefit more attractive than equivalent pay – an incentive to select an employer who promises a plan in preference to one who offers the sum in cash. The high cost of the individual arrangement makes outside cover a pricey option – a disincentive to select an employer who pays reasonably well but offers no package of benefits. A rational sponsor anxious to minimise turnover will offer entitlements above the odds in a bid to retain key staff by means of golden handcuffs. A rational union keen to recruit will treat expensive dental services and low co-insurance rates as trophies of success in the battle to demonstrate the relative value of its bargaining power. The outcome is differentiation of cover such as can in some measure restrict the willingness of labour to be mobile. Whether the restriction will be significant or marginal is, here as elsewhere, an empirical matter that cannot be resolved *a priori*. What is clear is that, like the repression of employee's preferences, it has the potential to produce a result that would not, carefully considered, be regarded as in keeping with the public interest.

The occupational plan has the further disadvantage that it is, like the textbook minimum wage, a tax on jobs and a possible cause (especially in labour-intensive industries) of reduced employment opportunities. Particularly vulnerable are the low-paid: even if the employer's contributions are related percentagewise to wages (and most of all if they are an unadjusted lump sum per capita), the worker who is unskilled is the worker most likely to be deemed expendable when overheads rise. Employers facing inelastic demand functions will probably seek to cost-push the burden on to the consumer. Employers facing price-sensitive demand relations will clearly be in a much weaker position to employ such a strategy in defence of jobs.

The occupational plan has the final difficulty that the insurance umbrella, however protective it may be of those to whom it affords shelter, is simply not large enough to cover the territory. Many citizens will be enrolled in a plan. Many, on the other hand, will not be. The unemployed and the retired cannot by definition form part of a workplace-specific insurance pool. Nor can the self-employed or those who are employed by more than one organisation. The part-timer under the threshold number of hours will enjoy no cover. Nor will the seasonally or the occasionally employed. Employees in risky trades will be especially exposed, where their employer cannot afford to pay the above-average premiums that experience-rating will dictate. Employees of small firms will also be at risk, where the insurer is unwilling to quote odds for a restricted sample and the sponsor is reluctant to band together with other businesses in a joint attempt to transcend the invisibilities of insignificance. New employees are often required to observe a waiting-period before the cover becomes binding: no problem for middle-class salary earners who remain in one job for an extended time, the waiting-period is more likely to leave without protection those workers (many of them black, or female, or under 25) who are particularly prone to starting and leaving employment. Dependants of employees are often stripped of cover when a death or a divorce deprives them of their entitlement: the law might specify a breathing space of, say, three months, but sooner or later they will have to make their own arrangements.

Presumably they would be well advised in such circumstances to seek out an occupational plan. Yet to do that they will have first to seek out an occupation; and that the household carers or the long-term unemployed will not be able to do. An alternative is to fall back on the traditional cover afforded by relatives and charities, past savings and future borrowings – and the individual plan.

5.2 THE INDIVIDUAL PLAN

There are two reasons why an individual might desire an individual plan. The first has to do with the total utility of the all-or-nothing. The second relates to the marginal utility of the little-bit-more. The second is, arguably, the more common and the more important.

The *first* reason relates to the situation where the individual regards the plan as his or her principal defence against hazard to health. In the American system of private insurance the principal defence is more likely to be group cover than personal cover; while in the British National Health Service that principal defence is more likely to be the collective facility than the consumer's purchase. Those who treat the private plan as their principal defence are in the American system therefore those who do not fit into the work-related scheme (the business consultant who goes freelance, for example); while those who behave analogously in British conditions will tend to be tourists and non-residents for whom the Service (in contrast to its practice in a more generous past) does not provide the free guarantee. In all countries it is the function of the individual plan to satisfy the needs of those who for some reason do not enjoy access to the mainstream option. In few countries, however, is the individual plan itself that option.

The *second* reason refers to the situation where the individual regards the plan not as the cake but as the icing, not as his or her basic cover but as his supplement and her complement. Thus an individual with the principal defence of a group plan but subject nonetheless to cost-sharing provisions might take out a supplementary policy of his own with the intention of freeing himself from the practical burden of deductibles and co-insurance. Such protection against deterrence may open the door to moral hazard and the wasteful overconsumption of a virtually free good, but it is also fully in keeping with the central premise of the free market that the consumer on balance is the best judge of interest. Besides that, the trade is virtually impossible to prohibit, where the purchase is multinational, the scale worldwide, and exchange control superseded by unfettered convertibility.

Just as an individual might seek top-up protection against deterrence, so an individual might take out a top-up policy to pay for additional services or incremental quality. Such would be the case where an individual with the basic cover of a national insurance system chose to purchase private insurance in order to pay for luxury hotel facilities while in hospital, the execution of discretionary tests that would not routinely be performed, the services of a full-time nurse, a costly surgeon not drawn from the panel, the amenity of a live-in home help during the period of convalescence. Depending on what would otherwise be on offer, there are any number of useful top-ups that might conceivably figure in an individual's contract: X-rays, ambulance services, blood, optical care, mental care, cosmetic surgery, convalescent homes, dentures, non-generic pharmaceuticals, anaesthetics of a superior nature, treatment for drug abuse or alcoholism, designer frames, contact lenses, appliances such as a replacement limb or a wheelchair – there is no obvious limit to that which the anxious can make the object of their additional or incremental insurance.

Including the major catastrophe that will often impose a long-lasting strain. Being a catastrophe, the eventuality rapidly exhausts all private cover where the prearranged limit is significantly less than infinity: the individual is then forced to run down his savings, to sell his home and property, to borrow from friends and commercial lenders, and ultimately to sink into personal bankruptcy in the absence of the major risks protection that is activated by just such an emergency. Where the potential burden is multi-period, moreover, the relevant insurance will have to be multi-period as well: the standard policy is for twelve months at a time (the mean length therefore being six) whereas the heavy costs of stroke, schizophrenia, serious accidents, major cancers often are long-term drains that in some cases become lifetime liabilities. The standard private contract carries no commitment to renewal. The top-up contract operative exclusively in the unusual circumstances of the medical catastrophe is different. It is a private sector promise of help even in hard times. By virtue of that promise the individual's mind is set at rest with respect to the continuing availability of funds in the worst-possible scenario.

The trigger threshold may be defined in the contract in terms of an absolute sum. Alternatively, the relevant burden may be defined to be a fixed percentage of the individual's normal income or the family's normal earnings. However it is defined, the fact is that the catastrophe is costly. Fortunately, therefore, the crisis is also a rarity: the catastrophe being the exception, the premiums for the cover need not be high, the probability of claiming on major risks being in the event so low. So low, indeed, that some insurers compete by allowing the individual subscribers to request the return of a portion of their payments where no extra burden is actually imposed upon the fund. The monies paid having been invested at interest or in shares, the subscribers requesting the withdrawal might even find themselves in the unexpected position of paying tax on a cash surplus when it had been their original intention merely to exchange a pecuniary premium for the consumer satisfaction of enhanced security.

Nor is it the healthy alone who stand to obtain benefits in cash as a result of having taken out top-up insurance against the medical catastrophe. The policy may well protect the catastrophically ill against serious loss of income (paying out, say, 75 per cent of previous earnings after a deferred period of, say, 26 weeks), if necessary until the normal age of retirement (provided only that the insured party remains medically unfit for his normal occupation or any reasonable alternative). Such income-maintenance (together with any invalidity benefits that might be available from the State) is a source of great reassurance, not least to the risk-averter with responsibilities and dependants: however catastrophic the unpredictable uncertainties of life will be to the isolated individual, they are many times more immediate a problem to the breadwinner with financial commitments and hungry children. Moral hazard is unlikely to be an important consideration in such a scenario. People do not deliberately cultivate cardiomyopathy or encourage atheroma merely in order to get out of work. The conclusion must therefore be that the social benefits will almost certainly outweigh the social costs in the case of the top-up cover taken out by the cautious against the contingency of the catastrophic.

There are two reasons why an individual might approach a private insurer for a plan. The *first* reason is that of the outsider who has no other access to the cake. The *second* reason is that of the insider who has the cake but wants the icing. Both reasons are as sound as revealed preferences can *ceteris paribus* ever be. Sometimes the cake, sometimes the icing, what is clear is that individual plans are often perceived by the individuals concerned as filling a gap which, left unfilled, would regrettably have left them vulnerable.

The fact that individuals desire cover does not mean, however, that they will be given cover; and it is here that the story which began with hope must inevitably turn sour and sad, All employees who are nominated for a sponsor's occupational plan normally enjoy a probability approaching a certainty that the sponsor's insuring agency will not refuse to take them on board. Not so all candidates who apply on their own. Such individuals will often find it difficult and occasionally even impossible to locate an insurer who is prepared to put them on his books. An obvious example is the employee who loses his job (and with it his cover) because of severe bad health. The individual may well continue to require regular and costly treatments, and will in all likelihood be turned down by the insurer for precisely that reason. An individual who is HIV-positive, or is in and out of problem-drinker units, or has multiple sclerosis, or is suffering from Alzheimer's Disease, is not so much a high potential risk as a high proven drain. The managers of private organisations have a duty of care to their shareholders and their policy-holders to keep out the high proven drain who will be an intolerable loss-maker for the pool as a whole. Compassion is compassion but business is business. Hard cases like the autistic and the anorexic are not good business but bad.

As with the chronically sick, so with the enfeebled old. The principle of preferred risk is a strong incentive in commercial conditions to maximise the numbers of healthy young professionals while minimising the participation of the senescent elderly virtually certain to take out more than they put in. The strict discipline of the competitive market dictates that companies wishing themselves to survive should, overcoming natural sentiment, have the courage to show the bedridden grannies and the confused whiteheads politely to the exit. Clutching at straws, the philosopher with a preference for the private might invoke the notion of lifecycle savings employed to finance lifecycle care. The idea would be that the young should deliberately save while in their prime so as to be prepared for the considerable medical expenditures that will almost certainly be occasioned by the wearing out of the body as the existence moves inexorably towards the soul's final release. Taking responsibility for oneself is always and everywhere a good thing, but the sad fact in the present context is that it is unlikely to be enough. Old people on low incomes might not have been able to build up adequate savings. Old people experiencing a run of bad luck might have exhausted such self-insurance as once they commanded. Old people, anxious like non-old people about health and money, might in the circumstances apply for cover to smooth their passage through life's seventh age. They might apply for cover but still not be given cover. Old people are expensive and competitive profit-seekers simply cannot afford consistently to rank charity above commerce when selecting their trading partners.

Sometimes individuals will find it impossible to arrange cover at all. Sometimes (the end result is the same) they will find it impossible to arrange cover at any premium that they can reasonably be expected to pay. Determined to impose some ceiling on the cross-subsidisation of the sickly by the well, the rational insurer deterred by transaction costs from individual risk-rating will have to fall back upon standard categories such as age, sex and occupation. Grouped experience is, however, a blunt instrument where the applicant is a one-off: it is unable, for example, to distinguish the non-drinking barman from his hard-drinking colleague or the healthy older person from her severely debilitated neighbour. Most of all is the actuarial base likely to be seriously suspect by virtue of the fact that it is the self-selected consumer who makes the first approach. Individuals who apply as individuals have made a calculated and conscious decision to obtain cover. They have made a rational choice to spend their own money on a risk-sharing scheme. They know what they know about their Saturday nights and their Sunday lunches, their throttles and their clutches, their friends and their enemies. They know what they know – and the insurer does not know what they know. Information-asymmetry is an actuary's nightmare; and thus it is that the wise insurer will add a mark-up for an individual plan that would not have been quoted in the case of a workplace scheme. A good-sized pool needs no hedge. A one-off applicant is, however, a different matter. The wise insurer, aware of its ignorance, will in the case of the one-off applicant prudently supplement the actuarial with the precautionary by charging an above-average premium in recognition of the above-average temptation to conceal material facts to which his would-be ward will undeniably be exposed. The wise insurer will in this way *de facto* be securing re-insurance of its own, by means of plucking an abnormally high number out of the air as the minimax alternative to being caught whistling the wrong tune in the dark. The net result is high premiums of individual plans and therewith a disincentive for individuals (even if not uninsurables) actually to pay the price.

Individual plans tend to be higher-cost plans. Applicants' characteristics are no doubt an important cause of the disparity; but so too are the economic and fiscal constraints of the institutional environment within which the contracts are written. Thus the higher administrative costs associated with the individual plan (the marketing and the selling, the corresponding and the explaining, the recording and the claiming) will tend to breed and form a higher charge than that which would be ground out by the economies of scale and the quantity discounts of the group arrangement. Besides that, there is a man-made differentiation in costs and benefits that is the engineered outcome of differential access to fiscal welfare. Specifically, individuals are not in most countries entitled to tax relief on the personal premiums they pay for an individual plan (such insurance being treated as a standard consumable and not an intermediate good) whereas employers are almost always permitted to deduct from their taxable income the cost of their occupational scheme (the benefit being treated as an input that promises productivity and not an output that produces satisfaction). The thrust of the skewness is clear enough: as a direct consequence of the uneven tax subsidy, a given sum of money purchases less protection in the individual case than it does for the group, a given bundle of undertakings costs more money in the former case than it does in the latter one.

So unequal a subsidisation of equal citizens, *prima facie* inequitable in itself, is that much more a source of perceived unfairness where it is correlated inversely with the income distribution. Such would be the case, for example, where an affluent executive with a group plan has *de facto* access to a Revenue contribution but an impoverished pensioner struggling to keep up an individual plan is simultaneously condemned to the *laissez-faire* self-reliance of responsibility without relief. Horizontal and vertical inequities of this nature could, logically speaking, be eliminated at a stroke were the tax concession either to be extended to embrace the individual provision or to be withdrawn altogether from the group contract. So great will be the other advantages of the occupational plan, however, that even the suppression of the fiscal privilege is unlikely to make its premiums the equivalent of those that will be charged for an individual plan.

Charged, certainly. Paid, perhaps not. Consumers given the opportunity to put their money where their mouth is will presumably welcome the autonomy and the consultation that personal tailoring through effective demand must inevitably bring with it. Consumers given the legal access but not the economic wherewithal will, however, almost certainly, be less confident about utilisation and choice, freedom and need. The fact is that not all individuals enjoy an equal status at the starting line; that the rich man's revealed preference is all-too-frequently the poor man's shut gate; and that the deterrence of the high premium can just as easily be the marginal person getting nothing as it can be the marginal purchase subtracted from an already generous package. It cannot be very pleasant to be out of work and ill in a society which expects the individual in such circumstances to search out his own insurance. And to pay for it.

The inability to obtain insurance is not, admittedly, a synonym for the inability to obtain treatment. Doctors and hospitals, apart from the bad debts and the uncompensated procedures, are known to practice price discrimination in favour of the uninsured. Such selectivity, such inequality, effectively reduces the gap between the care consumed by the insured and the care consumed by the uncovered. Also, much of unemployment being temporary and much of treatment being postponable, it must not be supposed that the well-founded fears of the uninsured will inevitably be matched by the pressing urgency of their unsatisfied needs: so long as future cover makes no rigorous exclusion of all pre-existent conditions, no great harm will necessarily be done where those between jobs decide rationally to put off the elective. It should be remembered in addition that one member in employment is often sufficient to secure the whole family occupational cover. Where one spouse has the security of the other spouse's blanket, the health hazard of personal unemployment is reduced by virtue of the continued entitlement to an employer-sponsored plan. The single person is not so fortunate.

The care purchased by the cover might, of course, be non-productive (the unwarrantably-protracted in-patient stay, for example); and it might even be counter-productive (as where the third-party guarantee facilitates an exceptional new procedure which is subsequently found to be unsafe). More insurance may mean more care but the link between an increase in inputs and an improvement in health is far more tenuous. The contribution of formal care should not be exaggerated. Nor should the insured party be lulled into the fool's paradise of thinking that miracle workers and wonder drugs can ever be a close substitute for devolved responsibility and personal vigilance. Yet occasions there will always be where formal intervention can make a significant difference to the quantity and the quality of life. It will be in acknowledgement of eventualities such as these that the representative citizen is likely to want to guarantee that the representative consumer will be granted unobstructed access to the requisite treatment. Much can be said in support of the individual plan, but it cannot reasonably be expected to supply such a promise.

5.3 THE PREPAID PLAN

Private sector organisations can and do develop which, analogous to a national health service, provide both insurance and treatment. The group which insures is the group which supplies. Unlike that private insurance which simply pays or refunds the fee of an independent supplier, here there is no independent supplier and no third party insurer. Rather, there is a unitary body committed at one and the same time both to finance and to provision. The central characteristic of the supplier-sponsored system is that the competing organisations collect an agreed capitation fee in advance from the enrolling units (individuals and/or their employers). In return the organisations undertake to cater for all specified health needs of the insured parties over the period in question without expecting any further contributions apart from the cost-sharing payments that may be specified in the contract. The best-known of the supplier-sponsored insurers are the health maintenance organisations (the HMOs) that have developed in the United States and other countries, most notably since the early 1980s.

Within the broad church of the supplier-sponsored system there is definite scope for variance. In some cases (the 'staff model') the doctor will be a salaried employee, providing care in premises supplied by the organisation. In other cases (the 'group model') the doctor will remain in outside practice and the organisation will either subcontract to him its capitation or (but less frequently) pay his fees in respect of specific services rendered to its members. In other cases (the 'network model') the organisation will have a series of contractual links not with individual doctors but with independent practices. Some organisations will have their own hospitals and their own consultants while others will be content to buy in the services of the institutions and the specialists, paying the charges on behalf of their subscribers. Some act as insurer of last resort; others reinsure with a commercial agency which underwrites either small risks (the hospital costs, say, of the individual members) or large losses (those caused, for example, by a national epidemic). In some cases the organisation is not profit-seeking; in other cases it is. In some cases the doctors are given a share in the operating surplus; in others they are confined resolutely to the employee's standard rewards of capitation, salary and (less often) fee. Some organisations are small and local (and exposed therefore to the vicissitudes that afflict a given region or industry); others are large and national (and able therefore to spread their risks by means of diversification and diversity). The pattern varies but the principle remains the same, that insurance is integrated with delivery, that the supplying organisation assumes the agreed risks in exchange for the prearranged fee, and that medical care is free or nearly free at the point of consumption to the patient who has prepaid his or her premium. Irrespective of the frequency of the visits or the quantity of the treatments, the patient has the welcome guarantee that the fixed charge, once levied, provides protection against subsequent drains such as might otherwise prove economically crippling.

Supplier-sponsored private insurance has the great advantage that it tends to keep down the average cost per patient-year. The burden of inefficient delivery or unnecessary treatment falling upon itself as insurer, the organisation has the economic incentive to encourage staffs to cut waste and to boost productivity. A similar incentive operates in the case of preventive medicine aimed, by keeping the patient well, at minimising the burden of expensive curative care at some later stage. The success of such a policy should not be exaggerated: there are limits to what doctors can do at the best of times, and a long-term benefit might in any case be heavily discounted on the basis that it might never arise or else be reaped by a competitor. All things considered, however, there is clearly much to be said in favour of any measures that might be taken to reduce the incidence of illness.

There is a further incentive to keep down costs in the form of pressures to treat simple complaints without referral for expensive hospitalisation. Not only is there an economic gain to be made in this way (where the general practitioner educates a diabetic in the art of self-treatment, say, or where she herself applies a local anaesthetic and removes a mole) but it also offers primary care a new lease of life and a more prestigious and *morale*-enhancing role. The pecuniary incentive to keep down average cost is evidently an integral part of the supplier-sponsored system. Whether the horse led to water has actually chosen to drink is less easily established. Even if the practitioner's incentive structure only *tends* to keep down the average cost, however, there can be little doubt that the saving on administration produces the economical benefit in practice: the minimisation of user-charges means that a multiplicity of bills (often very small ones) do not need to be processed, the centralisation of records spreads the overheads of diagnostic tests, the communication of information within the organisation reduces the frequency with which (even where there is referral to a specialist or a hospital) a full medical history must be taken. In these and other ways the average cost of the supplier-sponsored organisation is kept within manageable limits and its competitive position correspondingly improved.

Competition is an important characteristic of the market in which the prepaid plans have to operate: alternatives exist, rational consumers have freedom of choice, and organisations unable to match up to the opposition (whether from other prepaid plans or non-delivering insurance schemes or even the State) know that sooner or later they will sink without trace. Such competition puts teeth into pecuniary incentives and compels those teeth to bite deeply into costs. An organisation which is locked in rivalry is clearly more likely than one which enjoys the protection of monopoly to explore the possibility of cost-reduction by means of early detection: outpatients are cheaper to treat than those who require acute care. It is also more likely to avoid under-employment of capacity in the hospitals which it owns: it simply cannot afford low occupancy rates and idle operating theatres.

Competition compels suppliers to please consumers by paring premiums, but it also forces them to differentiate their package in such a way as to satisfy felt wants. Thus the suppliers will be led not by national plan but by their own self-interest to position their premises in locations that suit the convenience of their customers; or to match the supply of specialist services to the requirements of the region; or to adjust the bundle of basic benefits until it meets the specific needs of a targeted public. Competition evidently has a tendency to safeguard the interests of the consumer of insurance and provision by providing a stimulus both to lower prices and to satisfied demands. The very fact that alternatives exist gives the purchaser the incentive to shop around. That incentive generates an economic gain for the community as a whole where it operates in such a way as effectively to keep the insurers on their toes.

The unattractive side of such shopping around will be advertising and salesmanship (perhaps manipulative) and a determined touting for business (perhaps undignified). No one who has the patient's interest at heart can afford to neglect the threat to consumer sovereignty that is represented by any attempt at want-creation. Yet no one, equally, ought to forget that economic markets have long relied, not altogether unsuccessfully, on the commercial dissemination of factual information on the prices and specifications of the alternatives on offer. Competition involving supplier-sponsored organisations is, it must be added, unlikely to be the most frenzied or the most malign. The enrollment being annual (not daily or spot), subscribers have ample time to shop around prior to concluding a subsequent contract, either with the current supplier or with a rival, at the end of a specific year's prepaid cover. Consumers familiarise themselves with different bundles of insured contingencies and the different prices charged by means of studying the publicity materials issued by the different agencies. They complement such comparisons with newspaper articles read and issues discussed with friends and advisers. Consumers in this way have the opportunity to learn to be cost-conscious and to develop an appreciation of value for money. The fine print and the exclusion clauses will no doubt take time and educated intelligence to master; and there is always a danger that the non-specialist will miss something as crucial as a refusal to cover self-inflicted complaints such as unexpected damage to the stomach lining caused by the lethal poison that disappoints; but at least it is a great advantage that such choice under the prepaid system can be exercised in a quiet moment. It would clearly be difficult to be equally calculative in a genuine emergency. Ignorance and uncertainty remain obstacles to rationality. On the other hand, the choice of insurance is not the choice of treatment: for that the doctor's recommendation in the supplier-sponsored insuring agency remains the gatekeeper that allocates the access.

Apart from cost and choice, it is, arguably, a further advantage of the prepaid plan that it raises the standard of care. At the most elementary level, it does this by improving the quality of the doctor–patient relationship. Under the prepaid plan (in contrast to the fee for service) the practitioner has no pecuniary incentive to over-treat: this breeds trust and encourages the patient to have confidence in his faithful adviser. Also, where the doctor employed by the prepaid plan is on a salary he has no financial reason to resist the group practice: the capital overheads of expensive equipment can then be spread, division of labour within the multi-party coalition becomes possible, doctors are put in a position where they are able to discuss cases with other members of the team, informal peer-review comes to be practised on a continuous basis, and thus are positive steps taken such as tend to raise the standard of care. The prepaid plan is not, of course, alone in having what is likely to be a beneficial impact on the quality of treatment: a national health service, for instance, would be able to eliminate at a stroke both the economic incentive to oversupply and the economic resistance to group practice by seeing to it that all doctors were remunerated by salary alone. The fact that the same benefit can be provided in a different manner does not, however, detract from the fact that it can be provided by the prepaid plan.

The principal disadvantage of the private sector system of supply of finance in tandem with supply of provision is that of conflict of interest between the two wings of the multi-product firm. More specifically, the insurance wing will demand that costs be kept down while the delivery wing will press for patient-centred medical care. There is no reason *a priori* to think that the compromise struck will be any worse than under any other of the health alternatives, but the possibility nonetheless exists that corners will be cut as an organisation out to maximise the difference between revenue and cost opts to do so by cutting back. Conflict of interest is evidently present in the prepaid case, just as it is present in the insured fee-for-service system. The conflict is operative, however, in the opposite direction: the danger is not that too much care but rather that too little will be provided. The trade-off between the doctor's desire to help the patient and his equally real desire to conform to the organisation's guidelines will be particularly acute where the doctor has a share in ownership, or is promised a low-user bonus, or fears his contract will not be renewed if he exceeds the norm. Clinical freedom and medical independence pull him in the direction of generosity. Where savings made by suppliers are retained by suppliers, sheer greed pulls him back.

The objectives of the organisation might dictate that a ceiling on usage be imposed but so too might the actual quantity of resources at the disposal of the plans. The organisations are, after all, budget-constrained and therefore unable to provide more services than they can support from the premiums they have received: the money spent, and irrespective of generosity or greed, they have no choice but to curtail care. That it is why there is an implicit threat of default even when the contract promises 'all necessary' or 'fully comprehensive' cover. The supplier will seldom be brought to book for the consequences of budgetary limitation: the secret of the ceiling might never become public knowledge, and doctors enjoy considerable discretion in deciding what treatments are appropriate. Besides that, there is no reason to suppose that the agreed cover pre-specified in the contract will necessarily be infinite in value: the insurance exhausted, even the budget-constrained practitioner will often be able to save himself from litigation (most tragically where the patient happens to die) by pointing out simply that he had done no more than he had promised to do when he suspended the expensive treatments the moment that they reached the agreed upper limit. When in doubt as to how best to proceed, the budget-constrained practitioner faced with a high-cost challenge such as elective surgery often has the option of calculative procrastination: contracts are for one year at a time, there is seldom an obligation to renew, and the principle of voluntary exchange dictates that free enterprise as well as sovereign consumer be granted the right to choose.

Voluntary contracting can evidently damage the health. It will certainly be seen as so doing by the cohorts of bad risks who find themselves without cover, here as in other cases, for no greater crime than the statistical probability that they will require intensive and expensive care. Once in the club, the high users will find no disincentive to their utilisation of as much of the prepaid service as they can obtain. The problem is to persuade the rational maximisers to admit them as members, given that it is so much in the economic interests of the organisation to specialise on the more attractive propositions. The exclusionary mechanism is as Hydra-headed as Kali and often just as cruel. Sometimes the potential loss-makers are kept out by means of a flat refusal; sometimes the unhealthy are subjected to discourteous treatment and long waits; sometimes those likely to impose above-average burdens are made to feel unwelcome by a marketing strategy that sells an image with which they cannot identify. Differentiation of service is itself a mode of discrimination to which Enthoven among others has drawn attention: 'For example, a health care plan might recruit an outstanding pediatrics department, to encourage the enrollment of healthy young families, but offer a weak cardiology program, to discourage the enrollment of people with heart problems.'[3] Location of premises has a similar effect: concentration in middle class suburbs to the neglect of the deprived inner city is a means of ensuring that the burdens will be disproportionately low (and the surplus potentially high) while the conscious choice to site a practice on the fifth floor of a building without a lift is an entirely rational one for a costing, benefiting business that does not want to sell to the crippled. Last but not least there is the premium itself, always a barrier to the participation of the poor and *a fortiori* a burden when subscriptions are deliberately inflated in such a way as to discourage the less affluent. The deterrent of price is clearly one, but only one, of the reasons why prepaid plans will not develop in all areas of the country or serve the interests of all sectors of the population to an equal extent. So long as satisfactory alternatives exist, of course, the restriction of access in the specific case of the prepaid plan is unlikely to prove as unacceptable as it would were there to be no other game in town. Be that as it may, the acknowledged success of the plans in keeping down hospitalisation rates may be a tribute not so much to the clinical achievements of the organisations as to the expert selectivity they have practised in skewing their recruitment towards higher income consumers with a healthy life style.[4]

Even for those allowed to join the plans and able to pay the premiums, the range of choices may well prove disappointingly limited. There are limits to differentiation in the key areas of services and premiums. Services are likely to be subject to some variance (in terms of entitlements, say, or waiting-times for a specialist appointment, or the commitment to evening and weekend consultations); and so too are premiums (discriminating by age, ceiling of cover, family size, even income as approximated by place of residence as approximated by location of practice). Yet *de facto* diversity might still be constrained by the tyranny of the majority in the form of reasonably standard individuals unwilling to consume anything other than a reasonably standard package. Travelling times and geographical immobilities reinforce the demand-led homogeneity. They favour the emergence of the local monopoly and promote an imperfect market in which small numbers of oligopolists with a desire to suppress uncertainty can institute collusion and rely on price-fixing. Such imperfections frustrate both the choices and the efficiencies that are widely cited as the principal advantages of the competitive system.

Besides that, the subscriber to the prepaid plan is normally expected to choose his doctor from the closed panel provided by the organisation and is unlikely to enjoy cover if he selects an outsider such as, say, an eminent specialist recommended personally by a fellow sufferer. Generally, of course, the patient does have a free choice within the group (not much comfort if he strongly dislikes the panel's sole expert in a field); and occasionally there is provision for a limited indemnity where the customer elects to shop around (the limitation in itself a disincentive to choose the best). Also, at the annual enrollment the consumer always enjoys the opportunity to change his panel (but once a year in the market for insurance contrasts poorly with once a minute in a Third World produce market). None of which should, however, be allowed to obscure the fact that a closed panel is by definition not an open one. Here too, in short, the range of choices may well prove disappointingly limited.

Again, there is no consumer, citizen or community participation on the boards of the organisations. Perhaps dominated by professionals and administrators, perhaps controlled by the executives and the shareholders of huge multinationals, the decision-making bodies of the prepaid plans do not directly incorporate the user interest. They prefer that it should be represented instead via the competitive process. All of this suggests that the pluralism and the choice that are among the most attractive of the characteristics of the supplier-provided system might in certain circumstances prove somewhat less appealing than the textbook idealisation would suggest.

Not that the consumer will necessarily *want* to be offered a range of choices. Choice and change may be widely regarded as a threat to good care: young people newly arrived in an area may not yet have built up a vested interest in continuity of care but the position of the more settled population is likely to be different with respect to a service where the personal element looms so large. Bankruptcies of old firms and rapid entry of new frustrate the stability-seeker in his pursuit of more of the same: partricularly where providers make disproportionate use of inexperienced doctors yet to find their niche in the lucrative fee-for-service establishment, the revolving door nature of the High Street model will to many consumers appear inappropriate in the specific case of the ongoing relationship with the family physician. Also, intelligent choice and therewith effective competition are only possible if the patient is adequately informed as to his medical needs: asymmetrical knowledge and the sheer cost of learning about alternatives suggest that this condition will not inevitably be satisfied. At least, in the case of the prepaid plan, the consumer is given the option to get involved. Even if he decides not to exercise his option, presumably he will be pleased that he was asked.

5.4 THE AUTONOMOUS SICKNESS FUND

The friendly societies and the mutual aid funds of the nineteenth century were intended to be self-help groups and cooperative ventures. Their heritage lives on in the *Krankenkassen* of Germany and in other systems of health insurance that similarly rely on multiple loci of collective responsibility and large numbers of self-governing risk-pools. The funds are not commercial and do not set premiums with an eye to profits. Nor are they an arm of the State and the accountable agent of elected politicians, national or local. Rather, they are solidaristic and corporatist, a vestigial organ from the *laissez-faire* world that preceded the Welfare State and a reaffirmation that small groups with something in common (only a step removed from the love and duty of the consanguineous family) are the traditional units for the sharing of burdens. The common characteristic can be any feather that identifies the bird (place of residence, for example, or political affiliation or religious belief), but very frequently it is the occupational base that unites: trades unionists early developed so strong a sensation of a journey shared that they began to call one another comrade and even brother, and a friend indeed is a friend in need.

Membership of some fund is frequently made compulsory by law. Where it is, the funds acquire *de facto* the parafiscal power to levy a tax at a rate which they themselves often remain free to determine. The individual for his part retains the freedom to choose the fund that he wishes to join and to revise his choice at his own discretion. The range of options open to him should not, however, be exaggerated. Nor should the constraints be obscured by the plurality of funds (several thousand in Germany, for instance) that are registered in his country. Numbers are no proxy for competitiveness where access is contingent upon a qualifying characteristic such as occupation or place of residence, and virtually the whole of the benefits package can be standardised by means of State regulation. Besides that, funds apparently autonomous are often federated into national unions of funds: such a flocking together undeniably boosts the bargaining power of the small insurer *vis-à-vis* the medical professionals and the pharmaceutical companies but it also, where it leads to the adoption of a common package, reduces the range of choices that are open to the individual. The range of choices may be less than might be thought given the large numbers of funds in existence, but some choice there will normally be: a farm worker not wishing to register with a locally-based body might, for example, have the opportunity to join a body that covers the whole of the agricultural sector. There will normally be some choice in the decentralised system of independent funds. Not every member of a private sector occupational plan, not every subscriber to a public sector national insurance, will be quite as fortunate.

With respect to the assets, it is the task of the funds to set and to collect the premiums. Here, within the framework of such statutory maxima and minima as may have been laid down, the funds have scope to differentiate. Some will institute a flat rate subscription (and therefore a low one, lest the poorer classes experience genuine hardship or even be deterred) while some will have a preference for income-related premiums that are a percentage of pay (up to an agreed ceiling in some cases, without any upper limit in others). Some will require contributions from both employer and employee (the precise shares liable to vary, however, from 99%–1% to 1%–99% by way of the celebrated 50%–50%), others from the employer alone (the cost perhaps capped once a threshold is reached), still others exclusively from the employee (most obviously so when the employee is the *self*-employee). Theoretically, all benefits are to be financed out of premiums and there ought not to be an Exchequer contribution. In practice, the Government (central or local, depending on the degree of devolution) is very often a significant source of supplementation. In a sense such subsidisation is the inescapable counterpart of compulsory membership: if pensioners, the permanently disabled, the mentally ill, the unemployed are all obliged to join but not all able to pay, then it must be expected that the State, the impoverished duly means-tested to prevent abuse, will offer to cover their subscriptions and their co-payments on their behalf. The medieval guilds that were the forebears of the funds made it their business to look after their own. The modern funds, unafraid to look the gift comrade in the mouth, are more likely to turn to the polity for help.

The funds have scope to differentiate with respect to the assets. With respect to the liabilities as well; since, subject to the usual *caveat* that the statutory limitations must be observed, they are in a position to vary the menu in order to cater for a difference in tastes.

The *first* decision to be made relates to the bundle of entitlements on offer. The ceiling number of weeks of hospitalisation for the same illness in a given number of years, the opportunity (or lack of opportunity) for the individual to make as free a choice of dentist, optician, surgeon or other specialist as he can of his general practitioner, the presence (or absence) of a gratuitous annual check-up that includes screening for cancer, the presence (or absence) of co-payments and whether or not they cease once an agreed maximum has been reached – these and other heterogeneities can differentiate the benefits even where the law limits the variance.

A *second* decision to be made on the liabilities side has to do with the option to provide. The funds can and sometimes do supply their own health centres, hospitals, pharmacies, sanatoria and rest homes (a system which health care professionals normally regard with a not-unexpected lack of enthusiasm). More common, however, is for them, as financing agencies, to negotiate contracts with outside doctors and institutions provided by the private sector or by the State.

A *third* decision, going beyond medical care, concerns income maintenance. Thus some funds (but not all) will contract to pay cash benefits in compensation for loss of earnings: they will not cover full earnings but only, say, one-half or two-thirds of the previous basic rate; and they will not pay forever but only, say, for a maximum of one year out of three in cases of acute illness, a total of three consecutive years in cases of chronic. Needless to say, the money will only be provided where the employer has no practice of granting paid sick leave or maternity leave and where a medical practitioner is prepared to certify that the individual is genuinely unfit for work. Even within the framework of the statutory limitations, it is clear, there will normally be some freedom for the autonomous sickness fund in some way to differentiate its package.

Behind the funds stands the State; and thus it is that the *de facto* autonomy of the self-managing funds cannot be regarded as complete. On the one hand the funds are depoliticised and independent, exempt from cash limits and free from the rigours of national budgeting. On the other hand the funds require governmental approval at the stage of registration; their operations are circumscribed by regulation and their packages moulded by prescription; their resources are augmented by subsidisation and their membership assured by compulsion. On the one hand the funds are subject to no coordination but that of tradition and demand, to no planning structure more central than their own administration. On the other hand the funds have the reassurance that a beneficent State, armed with a health map of the nation and determined to assign a high priority to areas of deprivation, will make capital grants to private hospitals or expand the bed stock in the public sector in an attempt to ensure that provision will be forthcoming the moment that finance articulates a need. On the one hand the funds are self-governing entities, responsible only to the representatives of the insured (if directly consulted), to the medical professionals (if invited to the insurers' boards) and, most of all, to the managers and the bureaucrats who are charged with the day-to-day operations of the organisation. On the other hand the funds are the thin ice of autonomy that obscures but does not eliminate the deep waters of collective rights and public duties. The sickness funds, in short, have characteristics both of voluntary contracting and of the citizenship base such as situate them firmly on the middle ground of the modern mixed economy.

The benefit is the diversity. Not everyone can identify to an equal extent with all possible bases for banding; and there might accordingly exist a societal preference for differentiation which anyone but the most totalitarian of homogenisers would be prepared to tolerate. The cost of the diversity is, however, the exposure. The risk pool by area or occupation is, for one thing, not always a representative cross-section of the national population. Some funds are likely to be under particular pressure due to poor housing and the dietary deficiencies in a region, high unemployment and economic distress in a trade. Other funds will be able to cut premiums or boost benefits by virtue of their historical connection with healthy localities or low-risk professionals. Equitable or not, what is clear is the difference in the exposure of the funds. Nor should it be forgotten that the multiplication of small funds tends to raise the average administrative overhead and to reduce the effective bargaining-power of each. Federations of funds do, admittedly, go some way both toward spreading the risks and restoring the leverage. Yet the benefit is the diversity; and for that reason the unitary and the centralised must not be regarded as a frictionless panacea enviably deficient in side effects that inconvenience and harm.

5.5 FINANCE, CARE AND POLICY

It is often said that market mechanism and State intervention are substitutes and competitors. A more realistic approach would be to view them as complements and allies, each striving in its own distinctive way to raise the level of welfare in the community. The first four sections of this chapter have identified shortcomings as well as successes in the private sector of health insurance. It must be the task of the present section to establish to what extent a government wanting neither to supply insurance nor to provide care can, using the three policy instruments of compulsion, subsidisation and regulation, effectively assist that private sector to consolidate its successes while simultaneously eliminating those shortcomings that tend to call its good name into unwarranted disrepute.

(a) Compulsion

All coercion involves a welfare-loss to the individualist with a sense of self. Every person is to some extent an individualist with a sense of self. Every person to some extent values autonomy and independence. Every person to some extent resents being bullied and pushed around.

Yet sometimes it will nonetheless be the case that coercion will be consensually regarded as the undesirable means to some highly desirable end. In such circumstances it will exceptionally be the democratic choice that a moderate infringement of personal liberty should be ranked above a self-orientated myopia in which the free-for-all rapidly degenerates into the free-for-none. Two arguments in support of coerced conformity were presented in Chapter 4.2. Popularly accepted, those arguments would constitute a limited defence of moderate compulsion by general consent. Two arguments do not suggest that the citizen be required to sell himself into slavery. What they do suggest is that the citizen be required to purchase some insurance.

The minimum package mandated, no one would legally be left with less. In this way the group would be able both to protect the ignorant individual from his own myopic lack of imagination and to insulate the collective coffers from the depredations of the Atomic Bum who, wrapping himself in explosives and announcing 'Your money or *my* life', acts in the calculated expectation that the civilised society will not allow him to suffer and die. The compulsory minimum would be a matter for debate between (in consultation with the consumers) the politicians and the professionals. It would in that sense be a considered verdict on the adequacy and quality of cover.

The minimum package has the great advantage of clarity. Where policies are extensively differentiated from top to bottom the representative consumer may end up in some doubt as to the precise rights and entitlements that he holds. Where the core of the cover is compulsory, however, the purchaser is more likely to have become acculturated to the contents of the contract. Such a familiarity with the package considerably facilitates the best-judge task of intelligent shopping around. The existence of a standardised minimum makes it relatively easy for the determined consumer to make direct comparisons between the competing insurers. Over the minimum range, after all, the protection is made constant by law. Only the price will be a variable.

The minimum package may be supplemented by a top-up policy; and it is here that the individual retains the discretionary freedom to mix and match. With the freedom comes the risk. For the patient the danger is that superfluous insurance will be the trigger for unneeded intervention; while for the society as a whole the threat is of intolerable inequalities accompanied by care-cost inflation. Aware of the problems associated with a plurality of tiers, an intervening consensus might demand a ceiling as well as a floor in order that marginal cover be kept within acceptable bounds. In the limit the concerned consensus might demand that the ceiling should become the floor in order that each naked Adam be the equal of any other in the eyes of the doctors and of the hospitals. Compulsion in such circumstances will be somewhat more than moderate. It must not be expected that a concerned consensus will necessarily want to debate a compromise when it is able actually to annihilate a minority.

The minimum package will tend in any case to drift upwards over time. Partly this will be brought about by the interested lobbying of pressure groups (each coalition wanting one more service to be incorporated in the social minimum). Partly it is the inevitable concomitant of the political rent that is paid by the democratic electorate to the office-seeker who lengthens the list (an incentive to promise even the medically-marginal should it happen also to be glamorous and newsworthy). Such incremental drift is wasteful, in the sense that it is likely to reflect political expediency somewhat more than concern for health. It is also a threat to the freedom of the market: clearly, as the floor rises in pursuit of the ceiling, as the compulsory component becomes, percentagewise, ever more comprehensive, so the surviving range of differentiated bundles becomes that much smaller and less significant.

The minimum package will presumably be an attractive option to the administrator (who will not live in fear of unpaid statements) and to the clinician (who will be empowered to treat on the basis of genuine need without regard to effective demand). The package will be of less obvious benefit, however, to the employee who is mandated to contribute to the premiums but whose earnings are insufficient to support a burden that (not least because of the extension of coverage itself) is rising at a faster rate than pay. The position of the marginal employer will be no less uncomfortable. Particularly if mandated to blanket-in the organisation's retirees (a strong incentive *ceteris paribus* not to take on older workers, least of all women who in developed countries tend to live longer), particularly if a small pool in a risky trade (both factors being acknowledged causes of above-average premiums), the more vulnerable employer is likely to complain that the exposed competitor can be driven into the bankruptcy courts by a compulsory scheme which an oligopolist or a monopolist might easily be able to take in its stride. This is not to say that there ought never to be a compulsory scheme, only that persons who end every discussion by declaring 'there ought to be a law' ought themselves to be reminded of the infinite complexities of the human condition.

(b) Subsidisation

Mandatory insurance is only a practical proposition where the mandated can afford to pay. Sometimes they cannot, either because low pay has stranded the employee at the subsistence level, or because prolonged illness has rendered the unemployable medically indigent, or because shoestring operation has left the employer economically incapable of absorbing additional expense. In such cases one option will be free treatment in a charity clinic or a State institution but another will involve the community, through its government, exclusively in the provision of financial aid.

Thus, with respect to the beneficiaries, the State could undertake to pay the private-sector premiums on behalf of those citizens and residents who, means-tested, are found genuinely to be incapable unassisted of purchasing the minimum package. As the *quid pro quo* for the support, the paternalistic polity might demand the right to choose the carrier on behalf of the poor and the old for whose cover it has offered to pay. It might even incorporate a social engineering objective of its own, as where it registers its wards predominantly with protective institutions (health maintenance organisations, for example) possessing characteristics which it wishes actively to encourage. All things considered, the unemployed and the sick will probably prefer the billeting without consultation to the uninspiring next-best of no nannying but also no insurance. Even so, a public opinion sincerely committed to the notion of consumer sovereignty is unlikely to be entirely comfortable with any system under which the wards of the

State are rendered less eligible for freedom of choice merely because they are the recipients of legitimated transfers and not of earned incomes. A dependency culture is unpleasant enough. To impose a barracks mentality as well would be to go too far. It would spoil the identity of the underprivileged to an extent that the democracy is likely to deem unkind.

Thence the argument that the subsidy should in the first instance be directed not to the insuring agency but to the final beneficiary who would in this way be permitted to select the insurer. Such a devolution of function would do much to return the dread-disease patient or the disadvantaged single parent to the capitalistic market economy from which they would have been distanced and alienated in the absence of the aid. Homeless drug addicts and the helplessly alcoholic being only two groups which would be tempted to divert the subsidy to a purpose antithetical to that for which it was intended, a society committed to health as well as to dignity will probably want to experiment with the compromise procedure of insurance paid for not with convertible cash but with earmarked vouchers. The compromise is without a doubt an affront to the consumer sovereignty of the addict and the alcoholic. Their frustration is very real; but still they should be reminded that public opinion, here as so often the enemy of the minority, does not regard health insurance as income maintenance and nothing more.

As with all means-tested benefits, the insurance vouchers should taper gradually to zero as household income rises in the direction of the cut-off point: the alternative would be to rely on the *either/or* of a single threshold such as can all-too-easily impose upon low-income units the discouraging disincentive of the highest marginal tax rate in the nation. Yet stigma and low take-up are bound to inhibit the effectiveness of income-related payments, at least in achievement-orientated societies where the judgemental consensus openly holds the strong conviction that to succeed in a means test is simultaneously to fail in life. One solution to the problems of humiliation and under-consumption might be the automatic and impersonal allocation of the vouchers. Should the entitlement be distributed at the same time, for example, as a computer-assessed reverse income tax is paid out to the needy, the recipients of the insurance credit would be spared the inconvenience of having actively to opt in if they are to be given access to the social subsidy. Proper safeguards respected, selective subsidisation of certain premiums out of general taxation would seem to represent a useful halfway-house in the theory of intervention. The insurer can remain private (and need not be a public sector of last resort). The premiums can be actuarially-based (and need not be community-rated). Yet the State for all that can have an active role to play: judiciously and sensitively, it can see to it that subsidies are targeted on the persons and the families who are least likely to be able to pay for themselves.

Subsidisation from tax revenues transferred has its counterpart in subsidisation through tax revenues foregone. Thus tax relief for health cover has long been an acknowledged means of making a collective contribution towards the premiums that are paid for the insurance contract. The concession can be business-only (the case of the occupational plan) or it can be extended to the household as well. The relief can be selective (confined to the aged, say, or the bedridden) or it can be across-the-board. The exemption can be capped (limited by a ceiling lest excessive cover and cost inflation be the consequent diswelfares) or it can apply to the full range of the protection purchased. The deduction can be standard rate (denying to higher-band taxpayers the higher tax savings that would otherwise be theirs) or it can be allowable against any marginal rate, however elevated. Subsidisation through tax avoidance will clearly be a mixed bag and a multitude of possibilities. Generally accepted is the likelihood that the tax-offset will stimulate the consumption of the commodity. Less acceptable, of course, is the possibility that both equity and efficiency will come under threat where it is the goal of fiscal policy to subsidise worthy industries when it is needy individuals who are better deserving of the support.

Subsidisation via tax relief is the principal mode of public support to the employer who provides a company plan. It is not the only one. Small firms quoted prohibitive premiums will sometimes succeed in securing a supplementary grant from the State where they can prove that conformity to legislation would impose an intolerable strain. So will firms situated in high-cost localities (most of all where they can demonstrate that high premiums contribute to medical schools and spillover training). A special case will sometimes be pleaded by an employer with an above-average proportion of low-paid labour (workers, in other words, for whom the fringe benefit is an abnormal percentage of total remuneration); or by an employer with an above-average experience-rating (a risk-profile, needless to say, to be explained exclusively in terms of the hazards of the industry and not at all with reference to the negligence of the firm). Employers as a body will be especially quick to demand compensation from the State where a mandatory scheme deliberately incorporates wider social objectives: where occupational plans are required, for example, to promise continued coverage for the redundant and the retired, there the employers are likely to complain that, neither Medicaid nor Medicare, they cannot reasonably be expected to pay for such a *de facto* Welfare State out of their own limited resources. The government, sensibly wary of eloquent manipulators and vested interests, is bound to show an exceptional grasp of the employer's difficulties when confronted with a challenge such as that represented by the hiving off of welfare obligations to the employing organisations. The government in virtually all countries is itself the largest single employer of labour.

Just as State subsidisation of health insurance can be targeted on the individual consumer, just as public support can be channelled to the employing organisation, so the focus for the governmental grant can be the insuring agency. Thus the State might offer tax concessions and tax holidays in respect of the start-up capital that is committed by new suppliers. It might promise loan guarantees, token rentals and generous credits in a bid to stimulate novel competitors to experiment with innovative combinations of insurance and delivery. It might excuse not-for-profit insurers the burden of direct taxation on the moral grounds that a charitable orientation cannot be other than a good thing well deserving of the nation's thanks. Selective subsidisation, finely tuned, is clearly an instrument of considerable potential. Selective subsidisation without careful consideration, on the other hand, is an unquestionable invitation to the selfish and the blinkered to exaggerate the beneficial spillovers they bestow on the community while at the same time ignoring the market distortions and the inequitable diswelfares which State support is equally capable of generating. Subsidisation is the second of the three policy options open to a State wishing to influence insurance without actually writing insurance; but it will evidently have a greater appeal to the pragmatists and the eclectics than it will to the pessimists who, sceptical about sensitivity, argue instead for neutrality and constitutionalism.

(c) Regulation

Compulsion on the demand side will often prove toothless in the absence of supply-side regulation. The reason is obvious: the statutory obligation of the citizen to secure cover must sleep undisturbed in the library of unenforceable edicts where it is not accompanied by the counterpart obligation of the insurer to sell the contract.

The young and the healthy will have no problem in finding a vendor who is able and willing to reap the gains from trade with them. Not so the Creutzfeldt-Jacob patient or the victim of Parkinson's disease: what the young and the healthy can do, the high-risk and the high-use cannot, where one private insurer after another denies the obvious loss-makers any access at all to his fund. The State could, of course, itself become the insurer of last resort for the hard cases. Rather than unsurping the private sector's role, however, what the State might prefer instead to do is to opt for legal regulation specifying open access. Open enrollment would then ensue and all insurers would be prohibited from concentrating on the good risks while refusing to sell to the less attractive ones. In order to ensure that each carrier took its fair share of the uneconomic business, the State might even supplement its non-discriminatory legislation with a public body briefed to place the bad risks in such a way that no insurer ended up with a percentage that was inferior to the norm. Private insurers will no doubt object that their industry is not a public utility and should not be treated as an arm of the welfare complex. They are unlikely to be much reassured by the answer of the State that insurance has duties as well as rights; and that those duties, extending beyond the payment of taxes, must inevitably embrace the commitment to turn away no traveller on a December night.

Where the law specifies that all risks must be enrolled, the insurers may seek to compensate themselves by means of differential pricing. So discriminatory a practice is bound to attract the attention of the regulators; but that does not mean that they will necessarily intervene in order to suppress it. A gladiatorial sportsman, the regulators may well reason, is morally bound to pay a higher-than-average premium in recognition of the higher-than-average probability that the member of the craft will ultimately make use of the cover. The extra danger, long the legitimation for the extra income, may well be taken by the regulators as good grounds also for an extra premium. Even if they do intervene, therefore, the regulators may elect to do so no more than lightly. They may elect to scrutinise above-average charges in order to ensure that they are no more than proportional to the above-average risks. Once satisfied as to the actuarial legitimacy, they will thereupon allow those higher charges to be implemented without further controls. Such scrutiny works against the exploitation of the client. So, to be fair, would a competitive market and an informed shopping around.

Much more extreme than simple scrutiny is that interventionist regimentation by means of which the regulators outlaw altogether the differentiated contribution. In its place the regulators substitute the standard charge, invariant per level of cover irrespective of whether the risks are good or the probabilities horrendous. The actuarial tailoring of experience-rating goes out. The cross-subsidisation of community-rating comes in. The move is from the *I* to the *We*, from the individualised proportioning of costs and benefits to the non-selfish universalism of the nation that pools. The sickly are in this way protected from *de facto* exclusion through economic pricing. Attractive as their inclusion will undoubtedly be, it would be a mistake to neglect the extent to which the morally-informed orientation will also be acclaimed as an advantage in its own right by a generous community that instinctively ranks the shared above the personal.

The orientation is moral but the homogeneity for all that a source of difficulty and debate. A legally-specified minimum package accompanied by a nationally-determined constant premium is detrimental both to effective competition on the part of the insurers and to that differentiation of product in line with preference which is one of the strongest arguments in favour of consumer-led supply. Also, the identical bundle imposing different costs in different areas by virtue of differences in producers' traditions, institutional efficiency and input prices, equity to the insurer would seem to suggest local rather than national calculation where the carrier is unable to escape the community-based rating. Furthermore, low-income subscribers being subject to the same community-rate as the most affluent, a humanitarian desire to help the sick may prove unexpectedly to generate a regressive transfer. This would be the case, for example, where a low-risk poor person (prevented by compulsory membership from opting out into self-insurance through savings) ends up cross-subsidising a high-risk wealthy person afflicted with a long-standing medical complaint. The argument that the lower-income groups tend to experience more spells of illness, more accidents at work, than do the higher-income groups is, in the context of redistribution within pools, not entirely a convincing one. The actual take-up of benefits may be very different from the consumption that would be extrapolated from need. Should an inverse care law be in operation, low-income subscribers will have just cause to complain that they are unambiguously paying a subsidy to high-income individuals easily able to pay for themselves. Such a regressive transfer is not in itself a reason for rejecting community-rating (it might most of all be an incitement to proportion care more precisely to need). What is well illustrated by the transfer is, however, this, that the homogeneity of the standard charge, moral is orientation, must always be a source of difficulty and debate.

Yet a good case gains nothing from exaggeration. Legislated standardisation may be a novelty for the nation but it is a commonplace for the firm. The healthy member of an unhealthy group has long been involved, through the occupational plan, in cross-subsidising his or her representative colleague. Much of the discussion concerning the constant premium must in the circumstances be as aridly scholastic as the definitional disputation over whether pooling in the nation is significantly more socialist than is pooling in the firm. Perhaps the film actor experience-rated with the film stuntman enjoys a surge of fraternal solidarity that is sadly denied to ordinary men and women when they contemplate the costs and the benefits in which the community-rate will involve them. Perhaps, alternatively, the occupational pool based on the workplace or the industry has long been a maelstrom of intense resentments which nothing but a residual romanticism has prevented the outside world from identifying. Whatever the perceptions, and whether they differ as between the group based on labour and the group based on citizenship, the fact remains that sharing and redistribution, as old as insurance itself, can hardly be said to date from community-rating alone.

And there is more. The healthiest members of the unhealthiest pools would not lose but actually gain from a move towards community-rating in place of a costly association with peers more sickly than the national norm. Such a lessening of the burden that is borne by the healthy is likely to have an especial appeal where the good risks have consciously acted to defend their health status. Too much ought not to be made, however, of such a reallocation of responsibilities. Setting aside the extreme values such as the war correspondents and the dialysis patients, the casualties of pernicious anaemia and the sacrifices of Kaposi's sarcoma, what is striking in economically-advanced countries is not the dispersion in risk-pools but rather the convergence. A move from experience-rating to community-rating might not in such circumstances lead to as great a rupture with the structure of existing payments as concentration upon the obvious and identifiable problem cases would lead one to suppose: a reform rather than a revolution, the move from one pooled estimate to another will probably shift the average but need not do so to any significant extent. The impact of the change will be visible most strongly where the rerating in question involves a move not from an occupational pool but from an individual plan. Where the rerating in effect collectivises and nationalises a value that had previously been factored down, there, it is clear, the at-risk with the high premium and the obsessively protective with the low will experience a noticeable change in their contributions. In few countries, however, is the individual plan itself the mainstream option in the field of health insurance. We start from here; here is the shared; and the community-rate is in that sense no more than more of the same. No more than more of the same; and perhaps not very different either.

Even if the arguments in support of community-rating were on balance to be decisive, still it would be a mistake to assume that the adoption of the expedient must be regarded as inevitable by all concerned citizens anxious to ensure that actuarially-fair premiums should not be imposed by commercially-minded insurers in such a way as to frighten off needy clients likely to make disproportionate demands. An obvious compromise would be for the private sector to risk-rate as closely as possible to the individual optimum (account taken of the rising cost of increasing disaggregation) – and for the State sector then to rebate the higher premiums (in whole or in part) that are charged those organisations and those individuals that are statistically more likely to impose the above-average strains. In this way the private sector would not lose out financially when it enrolled clients drawn from high-risk categories; but the subsidy would nonetheless be the intentional outcome of the democratic calculus and not the haphazard result of undiscriminating cross-subsidisation. That the rebates in question could be made income-related rather than lump-sum would be a further point in their favour: the application of a sliding scale in the case of the individual plan would confer a particular benefit on the relatively deprived that a nation with a commitment to social as well as medical health will almost certainly treat as a definite welfare-gain.

Legislated regulation can enact open access and impose community-rating. It can do more. It can see to it that private insurers are solvent, responsible, in possession of proper reserves and re-insurance bonds, fully able to honour their commitments but not at the same time so restricted by licenses and inspections as to be prevented from taking innovative action that expands the client's freedom to choose. It can issue guidelines (binding or voluntary) to the insurance companies in an attempt to bend their investment policies to domestic priorities. It can oblige employers to offer not one but a choice of occupational plans (including, perhaps, a health maintenance organisation as an option). It can press sponsors to supply not schemes but money. Where schemes are supplied, the rational reaction of the employee (particularly if the plan incorporates no charges or fees) will be to select the cover that is the most comprehensive and the most costly. Where the sponsor's subsidy is a health-related fixed payment, however, the employee's incentive to search and economise becomes that much greater. Particularly is this social benefit likely to accrue where the shoppers securing the minimum package for less than the allocated sum are permitted by law to keep the surplus for themselves.

Legislated regulation, again, can allow the citizens of a mixed health economy the freedom to opt exclusively for private sector cover: it can, being specific, exempt them from the contributions and taxes that they would otherwise have had to pay for their share in a national health service. It can compel hospitals to admit and stabilise emergency cases without regard to insurance status. It can require delivery systems to promise the patients the right both to choose their general practitioner and to change their doctor as frequently as they wish. It can demand from licensed advisers that they utilise a standard *pro forma* in order to assist their clients to make intelligent comparisons of policies, packages and prices.

Legislated regulation can also involve the establishment of a watchdog body briefed to defend competitive practices in the insurance industry. Natural monopoly is unlikely to be a serious threat in an industry which, admittedly subject to the falling average costs of economies of scale, is also characterised by the shading and differentiation of a non-standard product. The restrictive practices of the collusive oligopoly are likely to be the greater problem. Premium-fixing and market-sharing, price-leadership and quantity-quotas, coordinated caution towards unfamiliar risks and predatory underselling of new entrants – these are allocative imperfections which will seldom be favourable to value for money. Legislated regulation and the watchdog body (accompanied by price formulae and even by price controls) might in the circumstances be the only way of protecting the consumer from a producer interest grown too powerful to be said to serve.

Legislated regulation need not, it is clear, be regarded as synonymous with the suppression of individuals'choice and the regimentation of producers' potential. Sometimes the impact of State upon health will be rather to expand freedom than to circumscribe it. Enthusiasts must always be reminded that the shepherd's definitions might not be those of the sheep; that the regulators, captured by their industry, might become the spokesmen for its interest; that the distortion of market signals might sow confusion to such an extent as to retard economic growth and the welfare it facilitaties. Clearly, if the social democrats are able to make a good case in favour of managed capitalism, then so too are the libertarian individualists able to muster strong arguments against it. Not everyone will want in the circumstances to go as far as Tawney when he declared without qualification that 'the mother of liberty has, in fact, been law'[5]. Tawney would have won more adherents to his manifesto for mix had he identified the father as well. Almost certainly the father is enterprise; and insurance is no exception to the rule.

6 The State Sector

Socialisation is a spectrum and not a point. Even where the State writes no cover and provides no service, still it can guide and direct by means of compulsion, subsidisation and regulation to such an extent that the *de jure* nationalisation of the property rights will frequently appear unnecessary to ensure the pursuit of public objectives by private organisations. Yet sometimes the public sector makes a conscious choice to expropriate or to duplicate the capitalist market in order the better to serve the public interest. National health protection is a case in point.

The public sector does not normally insure property against loss or damage. Sometimes it does (as where it seeks to stimulate exports through a guarantee of payments). More often it does not (taking the view that the contingencies are acceptable to commerce and the premiums acceptable to consensus). The private sector, on the other hand, is reluctant to insure income against incapacity or unemployment. Occasionally it will make a limited undertaking (as is done by the autonomous sickness funds that were examined in the previous chapter); but its more common position is that the replacement of income is not properly a task for the market mechanism. The loss of income is (unlike the statistical death) difficult to foresee: this is why the private sector is able to provide life insurance but unable to quote odds on the opportunity to earn. Besides that, income-maintenance is fraught with moral hazard: the temptations faced by the insured suicide with needy dependants are as nothing compared to the incentives to reconsider behaviour patterns that challenge the work ethic of the man or woman whose earnings are protected against idleness. Just as the public sector is reluctant to involve itself in the insurance of property, so, it is clear, the private sector does not normally insure income against the micro-losses and the macro-swings that can so tragically shipwreck the household's hopes.

The public sector and the private sector tend to be complementary rather than competitive where the gamble centres around property or income. Health, however, is different: both sectors there tend to be actively involved in the supply of protection. The overlap has not failed to attract the attention of Manicheans determined to rank the rivals and to name the champion. Even the most extreme votaries of the most simplistic *either/or* have a right to the intellectual tolerance of a civilised community. Being fair, however, it is unlikely that a single answer will emerge as to which sector it is that is more likely to do the better job. The objectives may overlap but they are not identical. The techniques may be similar but they are not the same. The two sectors being as convergent as two countries in Europe but also as divergent as Britain and Portugal, few things can make a greater contribution to debate than a willingness to avoid superficial generalisations that obscure the extent to which the preference for a sector must always be a matter of taste.

The present chapter does not score the two sectors as if they were two football teams in pursuit of the Cup. What it does is more modest. It opens the black box of public protection and finds that, just as private insurance can take a multiplicity of forms, so can its State equivalent. Specifically, and looking inside the black box of nationalised finance, there would appear to exist no less than four differentiated models of public sector involvement in the payment for provision. These are the self-funding model, the residual model, the universalistic model and the national health model. Each model will be examined in a separate section of the present chapter.

6.1 THE SELF-FUNDING MODEL

Insurance means the payment of a premium in exchange for a promise. In the case of the self-funding model it is a national agency that issues the insurance: it is a public body that collects in the contributions and sends out the policies. The agency is fully owned by the State. Crucially, it is rigorously self-supporting as well. Owned by the State, the agency nonetheless receives no grant in aid but finances itself entirely from the subscriptions of its members. In such a system the members in aggregate will be able to take out no more than that which they in aggregate have chosen to put in; and they will see this to be the case. More privileges mean more payments; less burdens mean less benefits; collective choice is the unique standard of optimality; and thus does the health budget emerge.

The earmarked charge makes an appeal to personal responsibility, in the obvious sense that the individuals who are entitled to the benefits are expected also to cover the costs. It makes a contribution to fiscal transparency as well: separate accounting reveals to all concerned precisely how much they are currently spending on their national health insurance, precisely what incremental burden they would have to shoulder in order to secure a given amelioration in the standard of service they are supplied. Besides that, the earmarked charge being a non-fungible payment, its significance for rational choice in the political democracy must not be overlooked. The operational independence of the State-owned agency from the directing, interfering State is a valuable guarantee to the sensible shopper that his preferences will indeed be respected. Discretion permits authorities to shunt funds promised for health into marginal constituencies and pet projects of their own personal choosing. Non-fungibility erects a constitutional bulwark to such taxation without consultation. One consequence might be additional resources being devoted to health: there is clearly less of an incentive to support extra taxes for extra care where the monies raised might easily be used for nuclear weaponry instead.

Earmarked payments relate actuarially to national pools. For that reason the charges automatically incorporate the cross-subsidy that is subscribed by the good risks and serves as succour to the bad. The charges would have to rise, needless to say, were the private sector permitted to indulge in the cream-skimming of the robust and the healthy while relegating to the national pool the infirm and the chronic whose needs are so likely to exceed the average. Thus it is that a national health insurance system will normally take the illiberal step of requiring comprehensive membership. Earmarking opens the door to exit: individuals who want to 'go private' will clearly find it easier to opt out of an identifiable charge than they would to contract out of a *pro rata* share in general taxation. Ironically, earmarking thereupon closes that door again lest the charge be higher for those who stay behind than was the charge before the health-conscious and the well-nourished were able to make good their escape.

Because earmarked payments reflect actuarial values, they tend to be lump-sum. Like the poll tax (to finance the local authorities), the road fund levy (to maintain the motorways), the radio licence (to subsidise quality broadcasting), the 'health stamp' tends to take the form of a fixed overhead that is invariant with respect to income. Income taxes are normally proportional (levied at a constant rate for all income bands) or progressive (levied at a higher rate in higher brackets). Lump sums, on the other hand, are always regressive: an identical charge must inevitably represent a higher percentage of a poor person's income than it will for the rich. As the same may be said of rail fares and tickets to the zoo, the price of fresh fish and the value added tax, the existence of an unequal percentage cannot reasonably be taken as *prima facie* evidence of an intolerable injustice without calling into question the very legitimacy of the capitalist market itself. Should health generally be regarded as a special case, however, then there is an obvious measure that can be contemplated by a society determined to alleviate the perceived hardship of inequitable inequality.

That measure would involve the substitution of an income-related for a lump-sum contribution. The hypothecated health tax would be a case in point. Perhaps levied at the same time as the normal income tax in order to facilitate coding and expedite collection, the flexible subscription would ensure that the rich paid more and the poor paid less. Because both the proportional and the progressive rate would have the discriminatory bias, a moderate society might want to impose a ceiling on contributions in order to protect tax payers on high incomes from excessive demands. A moderate society might reason, for example, that is acceptable for the rich to make twice the average payment in exchange for the common cover, but that anything more than twice would smack of malice. Whatever the attitude of the consensus towards the ceiling, however, far more predictable will be its attitude towards the floor. A compassionate society will almost certainly want to excuse the poor their payments, just as it normally exempts those on low incomes from the burden of direct taxation. No rational profit-seeker will be in a position to do as much.

Direct taxation is generally regarded as redistributive from the rich to the poor to an extent that earmarked lump-sums can never match. It is that redistributive characteristic which, more than any other, has caused egalitarians to reject subscriptions and to champion taxes. Aneurin Bevan was one of these. Thus it was, looking back after ten years on the health system which he while in Cabinet had done so much to revolutionise, that Bevan spoke as follows in the House of Commons of his early intellectual inspiration: 'The redistributive aspect of the scheme was one which attracted me almost as much as the therapeutical. What more pleasure can a millionaire have than to know that his taxes will help the sick?'[1] Bevan appears not to have waited for an answer. Perhaps that was wise.

6.2 THE RESIDUAL MODEL

In the case of the private sector policy or of the sealed State fund it is the protected parties who pay the premiums. In the case of the residual model it is the general taxpayer. Rich in need but poor in wealth, the residual unfortunates who treat non-contributory relief as the third party of last resort are in the unenviable position of requiring assistance without being able to afford insurance. Driven out of the mainstream, forced into the backwater, they know that some at least of their medical bills will be settled by their fellow citizens through an integrative State that does not want them to beg.

The outsiders might be the uninsurable, the tragic victims of chronic conditions and catastrophic illnesses to whom no drain-minimising, gain-maximising agency will be prepared to offer an entitlement. Alternatively, the also-rans might be acceptable to the market sector, but only at actuarially-fair premiums which the old, the unemployed and the impoverished might simply not be in a position to pay. Sometimes exhausted, sometimes refused, sometimes not affordable, sometimes not renewable, private cover is not attainable cover for a number of high-risk, low-income groupings within the population. Nor is self-supporting public insurance a realistic alternative for the penniless unemployable, the homeless migrant or the abandoned parent with a dependant family. The contributory principle, so successful in satisfying the demands of the affluent and the healthy, is self-avowedly a failure when confronted with the no-less-real requirements of the disadvantaged and the incapable. It is in the very specific circumstances of insurance failure that a caring community will look to the State for a residual guarantee. At least up to some minimum level of decency, that community will reason, all residents ought as a matter of simple humanity to enjoy adequate claims on medical resources. The access is legitimated exclusively by resident status and medical need. It is not legitimated by contributions-record or effective demand. Vagrants and immigrants, unemployables and incurables – few will seriously propose that those without contributory cover be allowed to die where they fall.

Safety-net protection is sometimes taken to be as minimal as the naked light-bulb and as basic as the clinic in which the patients are seen only by auxiliaries. That residual protection *can be* third-rate protection is not in dispute. Where a society regards those unwilling to achieve and unable to save as indolent pariahs who have somehow defaulted on the ethic of personal responsibility and earned reward, it is likely that the taxpayers will not be keen to donate more than is absolutely essential to assist the medically deprived who have in some significant way deplorably refused to assist themselves. That residual protection *must be* third-rate protection is more debatable. People do not plan or want to be struck down by a disease so crippling that, their job lost, their savings gone, they have no option but to fall upon the parish in a state of medical indigence. No sane person ever becomes seriously ill by deliberate decision, however numerous the careless who commit contributory negligence through slipshod prevention. Should the wider consensus regard the innocent bystander as the typical applicant for public benefits, the service authorised will probably be significantly more generous than where the typical applicant is considered to be a feckless free rider on the scrounge. The society is unlikely to authorise the private room and the full-time nurse that were the generous entitlement of the young executive before the multi-period wasting disease that prematurely terminated his private cover. Nor, however, will it necessarily restrict itself to the naked light-bulb and the treatment by auxiliaries that it might see as the just deserts of those who have only themselves to blame for their plight. Fault apart, the society will often be led by interest alone to err on the side of plenty. The social safety-net ultimately protects the representative resident; much if not most of serious illness is random in its incidence; and no one can say for certain that he will never himself stand in need of minority care supplied under the terms, mean or generous, of the residual promise.

The decision made as to whether to authorise the thin gruel or the thick steak, the community will have to face up to the challenge of identifying the eligibles. Deterrence through second-best is the traditional stimulus to selection through self-selection. Thus the offer of no more than the thin gruel is more than likely to frighten those who can possibly afford to pay into the expense of private cover that they might rationally have spared themselves had the public residual guaranteed the thick steak instead. Squeezing in the deprived is not the same, however, as crowding out the affluent; and that is why a caring State will act still more decisively to concentrate the residual protection where the need is believed to be the greatest.

The choice might involve blanket cover on a geographical basis (as where all residents of a depressed area such as rural Alabama are automatically registered for the insurance they are believed to lack). Alternatively, the characteristic targeted might be the age-group of the potential recipient: premiums rising when incomes are falling, an obvious group will be the old-age pensioners who are the ascriptive beneficiaries of American Medicare. Entitlement based on place of residence rather than on household income obviates the onerous task of form-filling while discrimination based on age-group and not on wherewithal is presumably as stigma-free as old age itself. No doubt these are definite gains, but it should also be remembered that they are purchased at a cost: resources intended for the impoverished will have to be shared with the affluent who happen to dwell in an area broadly classified as deprived or who happen to have grown rich even as they grew old. Whether to secure exemption from a statutory obligation to buy private or to demonstrate eligibility for the benefits that are State, what is clear is that no proxy can ever be as finely-tuned and as accurate as the careful examination of each applicant's unique circumstances such as underlies, say, the American Medicaid. In order that the safety-net authorisations be kept safe from the depredations of wealthy insurables, what is clear is that no bulwark can ever be as strong as the personal means test employed in such a way as to screen out the prosperous.

The residual model is an element in a wider welfare vision that embraces the actuarial and the non-contributory alike. On the one hand there is paid-for insurance, funded from stakeholders' premiums and unprepared to issue cover without the payment of the *quid pro quo*. On the other hand there is State assistance, dependent on general taxation and making no stipulation that to *take out* the beneficiary must first have *put in*. The actuarial principle is one which derives entitlements from purchase. The non-contributory principle is one which legitimates rights in terms of status. The one insisting on a contractual consideration, the other employing the Good Samaritan as its gatekeeper, there is a strong temptation to see insurance and assistance as radically different – and to treat the residual model as a case in point where the services are delivered on the basis of need alone.

Up to a point the temptation has some foundation in fact, if only in the obvious sense that general taxation is general and the residual sector is open to all in the event of authentic distress. Yet the distinction between insurance and assistance is by no means a clear-cut one. The borders are in truth blurred by complications that arise directly from the imaginative choice of the evaluatory perspective.

One such complication involves the inter-temporal dimension. Thus the young executive who both subscribes for an insurance package and pays general taxes to the State may well see himself as being the purchaser not of one protective policy but rather of two. In the short-run he knows that his earmarked contract, commercial or State, will cover his household's needs: he also knows that the share of his taxes that goes to the residual sector will be devoted exclusively to the health care of unknown others. The long-run is, however, a different matter. Even young executives grow old (the lifetime progression into high-premium, low-income retirement being one of the strongest probabilities in the highly uncertain world of health). Even young executives can be afflicted with a multi-period illness so severe that it leaves them unemployable and uninsurable. Even young executives might, therefore, regard that portion of general taxation that is used to finance the residual sector not as consumption (in the sense of compassion shown to strangers) but as investment (in the sense of multi-period protection upon which even young executives might be compelled themselves one day to draw). In paying for assistance, the young executive may see himself simultaneously as purchasing insurance. Where the other members of his ongoing social organism share his perception of a binding social contract concluded between the spot and the future, it will make little sense for the fullness of time to complain that he paid his *quid pro quo* for explicit cover but purchased no entry ticket whatsoever to the privileges of residualism. Such an entry ticket, he will say, he most assuredly did buy; but that he opted for continuous prepayment and made his contributions in the past.

He made his past contributions in money. Other individuals will say that they made their post contributions in other forms. Unpaid citizenship involvement introduces an additional complication and blurs still further the distinction between insurance and assistance. The argument is well illustrated by the example of the single parent who contributes five children. Reminded that she has never paid income tax in purchase or prepurchase of her residual authorisation, she will want perhaps to maintain that her contribution to the organic whole was indeed made, but was made in kind and not in cash. Because she took no job outside the home, she undeniably earned no income and paid no tax. Because, however, she devoted her career to breeding and rearing, her nation has in consequence been enriched to the value of the five hulking navvies who came to add their marginal productivity to the growth of an economy that might otherwise have been prevented from expanding by a labour-supply bottleneck. When the young executive applies for a residual authorisation despite the fact that he is currently paying no tax, he will make much of the multi-period insurance that his past contributions represent to him. When the single parent applies for benefits which she insists are entirely compensatory and not at all gifted, she will make much of her five children. Few arguments in social philosophy are as persuasive as the sight of a grey-haired old mother accompanied by five hulking navvies. Leaning on their shovels. Smiling benevolently.

6.3 THE UNIVERSALISTIC MODEL

A third approach to public insurance is (in common with self-funding and in contrast to residualism) to take State cover as the norm but (in common with residualism and in contrast to self-funding) to ensure that the appropriate revenues are drawn extensively if not exclusively from the general public finances. In such a case the individual may or may not be asked for a small subscription. Irrespective of whether or not a token contribution is required, however, what is of primary significance is its relative lack of importance: the individual under the universalistic umbrella has access to benefits far in excess of those supportable through earmarked contributions alone.

This property in itself tends to render the system intensely politicised. Citizens press for greater entitlements; politicians release the reins on public spending in an attempt to win votes; and there is also (turning from demand-led expansion to an unexpected contraction in the supply of service) the extraneous threat to health care that is represented by budgetary cuts in response to macroeconomic pressures. The self-funding alternative has at least this in its favour, that it is insulated from the piecemeal pragmatism of such instabilities. Especially where underpinned by a constitutional prohibition on tax-financed subsidisation, the self-funding system has the attractive characteristic that it is protected from politicisation by the visible and exclusive link between individual burdens and individual entitlements. Exchequer-funded universalism enjoys no analogous prophylactic against the politicisation of a sector so vulnerable to excesses and economies. Perhaps, of course, none is needed. The universalistic model grants to democratically-elected governments the discretion and the freedom that they require if they are sensitively to lead, to react, to coordinate and to adapt. Authority that is strictly mandated is authority that cannot respond rapidly to popular preferences or supplement contributions out of general revenues that the citizenry is keen to allocate to health. Undeniably a threat where irresponsible office holders satisfy their own ends through rigidity and inflation, nonetheless there is no reason to think that politicisation will always and everywhere prove antithetical to the public interest. It is the conviction of the advocates of flexibility that the potential excrescences can adequately be contained by democratic checks such as a free press and an opposition party – and that the advantages of a politicised system are likely on balance to exceed the harm that the option is clearly capable of causing.

Redistribution through the tax system is widely regarded as a characteristic of the universalistic model. Many, indeed, believe the superiority of public finance over private contribution to lie in precisely this propensity to levy the heavier burden on the more affluent contributor. The propensity is a fact. Still, however, it would be a mistake to exaggerate the importance of the bias. The redistributive argument, for one thing, is more persuasive when the graduation of income tax is steep than when the rate bands are so bunched as to approach the proportional. Also, egalitarians tend to be so attracted by the progressive bias of direct taxation that they often neglect the regressive incidence of the indirect taxes that contribute as well to the State's revenues. Aggregating the taxation of units (the personal and the corporate income tax) with the taxation of things (the value added tax, the stamp duty, the purchase tax, the excise levy), Phelps Brown reached the conclusion, relying on evidence presented to the Royal Commission on the Distribution of Income and Wealth, that the bias of the one tends in effect to cancel out the bias of the other: 'Taxation, when the direct and indirect forms are taken together, does little to change relative incomes.'[2]

Phelps Brown's result, derived from British data, is replicated in a number of countries including the United States, of which Pechman and Okner have written as follows:

> Regardless of the incidence assumptions, the tax system is virtually proportional for the vast majority of families in the United States. Under the most progressive set of assumptions. . . . taxes reduce income inequality by less than 5 per cent; under the least progressive assumptions. . . . income inequality is reduced by only about 0.25 per cent. [3]

No doubt the levelling egalitarians and the social engineers will express regret that general taxation is so lacking in the ability to alter relativities. Even so, however, they will clearly rank proportionality above the marginal contribution that, like the earmarked charge, must always be regressive: even where the overall incidence is percentagewise a constant, after all, still it will be the case that the richer person (the person in receipt of the higher taxable income and spending more on taxable goods and services) will pay a greater absolute sum into the general revenues than will a poorer one. That inequality many reformers will regard as eminently equitable. The rich being better placed to pay than are the poor, the argument will run, it is only right and proper that they be asked to pay the surcharged subscription. The rich will presumably reply with the counter-argument that there is neither justice nor logic in the derivation of the duty to pay from the simple ability to do so. Being in a minority, it is unlikely that their reply will arouse much sympathy on the part of their fellow citizens. Complaints concerning discrimination are always better received when they originate with the less-favoured than when the complainant is privileged and powerful.

The extent of the economic redistribution that takes place in the universalistic system is a matter for debate. Not so the extent of the medical redistribution: whatever the status of the subsidy that is paid to the poor by the rich, there is no dispute about the cross-subsidy that is the transfer from the good risks to the bad. It is that cross-subsidy in itself which is regarded by many as a significant advantage of the large-scale public sector scheme. Where the membership is as compulsory as the Revenue and as comprehensive as the nation, there the club is the citizenry and the risk profile of the pool is the same as that of the society taken as a whole. What full universalism will mean in such a case is that the contingencies shared will be fully representative of the national collectivity and that the insurance provided will be truly social in its coverage.

Collective cross-subsidisation of the worst by the best would not be possible in a multiple-pool system. Where State insurance is one option and private insurance its competitor, the certain result will be the cream-skimming of the young and the healthy by the commercial carriers, the relegation of the costly and the chronic to public sector residualism. The segregated system is far from unknown; and it does keep down premiums for those robust enough to be offered private protection. Yet it also means that there will inevitably be a bottom-dog pool made up almost exclusively of net liabilities bound to take out more than they put in. Universalism is different since there the gains are expected to march with the drains, the basically healthy to pay a cross-subsidy in support of the basically sickly. At least the burden need not be an exceptional one. Premiums would be high in a commercial scheme that opened its doors to the old and the ill; and the same prediction may confidently be made concerning a self-supporting fund situated in the State sector. Universalism, however, makes no claim to be actuarial: financed almost entirely from general taxation, hardly at all from individuals' contributions, it is the taxpayer and not the premium-payer who in the last analysis supports the bulk of the burden associated with the pooling of risk.

Universalism defines the nation as the pool. This broad perspective, the embodiment of perceived citizenship handed on from the past, may well serve as a further stimulus to social integration in the future: all members of the community are granted the identical status and the common entitlement, after all, irrespective of whether they are rich or poor, male or female, young or old, urban or rural, embarrassingly fit or terminally ill. Even those unable to pay contributions and taxes have their rights preserved and their payments credited in. The problems of catastrophes and multi-period drains simply do not arise. Neither does the need for the victims of life's greater vicissitudes to withdraw from their friends and neighbours to the ghetto that would be assigned them under the residual model. Where State universalism has become the norm, it is if anything the private sector that is the fringe, the margin and the exception in the context of commonwealth.

However generous the public scheme may be, it is in the nature of health-conscious human beings frequently to desire more. Thus it is that there will always be a demand for a private-sector safety-valve at the upper end of the services spectrum, just as there will always be a need at the lower end for the justly-celebrated State safety-net. No commitment of resources can ever be infinite; while some facilities (special menus and private telephones, for example) will tend always to be given the low priority of the discretionary luxury. There would appear in the circumstances to be a strong case in favour of a private penumbra such as supplements the universalistic guarantee of the therapeutic hard core.

Private supplementation enables the citizen whose valuation of care is abnormally high to transfer to top-up benefits the resources that he would otherwise have committed to some less-preferred purchase: in that sense the freedom to shift spending from alcohol and cigarettes to doctors and hospitals leads to a net welfare gain that a prohibition of such contracting would have prevented the citizen from securing. Since people in a pluralistic society will often be non-median in their preferences, the possibility is real that the opportunity to contract for the non-standard and the non-uniform will be regarded by the differentiated (who must have some money but who need not be rich) as a valued enhancement in their personal liberty. The State cake augmented by the private icing would be a compromise with especial attraction where the individual, broadly satisfied with the medical essence, would like nonetheless to enjoy extra choices at the margin.

Complaints of excessive conformity in the politicised sector are, admittedly, often matched by similar complaints concerning commercial insurers become insufficiently competitive. Profit-seeking carriers might target an all-but-identical package at the typical consumer (since minority tastes are seldom so lucrative as are concentrated agglomerations). Oligopolistic competitors might substitute collusive sharing for aggressive marketing (since organisational bureaucrats are frequently motivated to repress novel departures in order to protect stable conditions). Indifferent employers might offer but a single occupational plan (since business executives are normally pressured by more urgent concerns than the multiplied wishes of differentiated staff). It would clearly be an error to entertain too idealised a view of the alertness, the sensitivity and the adaptability that obtain in the real-world private sector: if public insurance can be weak on choice, then so too can private. Assuming the private sector can somehow be persuaded to differentiate, however, there is an undoubted attraction in the mixed insurance economy. There the consumer would enjoy the freedom to shop around for commercial top-ups but would simultaneously enjoy the universalistic guarantee of the therapeutic hard core.

Always provided, of course, that the essential cake and the discretionary icing can properly be distinguished. In some cases they can be: most people would accept, for example, that immediate treatment for cardiac arrest is a necessity, a private television or an outside fax a luxury. In other cases, however, the dividing-line is more difficult to draw. Medicine is about comfort – a good reason for treating as cake and not as icing the shorter waiting time that abridges the anxiety accompanying even the non-urgent intervention, the private room that spares the upset of a sudden death in an adjacent bed. Medicine is about survival – and while the access to an individually-manipulated pain-control drip may not influence expected life-years at the margin, the position is different in the case of the access to a named surgeon with experience far in excess of the average. Medicine is about integration – and the tiered standard therefore *per se* a threat to the common culture and the common condition that many regard as the nation-building contribution of a health system that unifies as it heals. It would most decisively be wrong for any community to level down by means of prohibiting outright the voluntary purchase of top-up amenity. Levelling up is, however, a horse of a different colour. Where genuinely exercised about comfort, survival and integration, an equalising collectivity will sensibly eschew the easy option of spiteful destruction in favour of a generous augmentation of universalistic entitlements. The effect will then be a diminished demand for private supplements, but the reason will be an increased supply of public benefits that is to the tolerant universalist likely to be the more attractive choice.

Universalism provides benefits, clinical and social. It also does so in a manner which is frequently described as economically efficient. Large numbers combined with standardised contributions breed economies of scale with respect to computerised record-keeping and other administrative overheads. Wasteful duplication and excess capacity are minimised; while at the same time the recourse to monopoly suppresses the marketing deadweight of zero-sum competitiveness that in the limit can serve significantly to push up premiums. The large pool facilitates the task of predicting claims. The sheer size means that the fund has exceptional power in bargaining prices with the drugs majors and the equipment manufacturers, the professionals and the institutions. Universalism will not always go hand-in-hand with efficiency: evidence on bureaucratic structures with a tendency to become secretive and complex, suspicious of innovation and reluctant to change, suggests that the effect of nationalisation will sometimes be rather to raise than to reduce the average cost of cover for care. That universalism can in the right circumstances prove conducive to efficiency is, however, less open to dispute.

Thus universalism sets medical personnel free to concentrate on medical matters. Suppliers make administrative savings by sending their invoices to a single agency. Then there is the public good dimension of health and care. A national system of health insurance is no barrier to mobility (whereas a plan based on a workplace or an industry will often be): one consequence will be unimpeded allocation and therewith a faster rate of economic growth. Comprehensive cover extends even to those who would otherwise have under-invested: the humanitarian spillover and the unwelcome contagion both suggest that the community which wants the benefits will rationally offer to contribute to the costs. Cash-contained universalism provides a brake on cost inflation and a buffer to moral hazard: some protection being a good thing but competitive escalation being a source of excess, there is much that is productive in a single State budget, coordinated, capped and subject to a ceiling which a multiplicity of independent rivals would have an incentive to bid ever upwards. In the light of externalities such as these, what is clear is the extent to which public insurance can properly be defended with reference to economic efficiency and economic advance.

6.4 THE NATIONAL HEALTH MODEL

Finance is finance. Provision is provision. The topic of care is always two. Demand is demand. Supply is supply. The reader who believes the two blades of the scissors to be only one will do badly in economics and worse in sewing. The reader who cannot tell the difference between the finance and the provision of care will by the same token find himself talking nonsense about insurance and rubbish about delivery. The topic of care is always two. Two it must always remain.

Sometimes the twins are separated in time and space. Sometimes, however, they are not. In the private sector, as noted in the preceding chapter, the separation is to be observed in a case such as that of the occupational plan (where the member of the scheme is simply given a transferable entitlement that he can then encash with the competing supplier of his personal choice) but not in a case such as that of the prepaid plan (where the health maintenance organisation arrogates to itself the double duty both of accepting the financial risks and of treating the medical complaints). In the State sector too the rule holds true that sometimes Tweedledum and Tweedledee are observed in isolation but sometimes unreservedly as a pair. Finance and provision are observed separately in the case of a State insurance fund that (either paying the bill directly or reimbursing the client for having done so) leaves the member free to select doctor and hospital in accordance with personal preference rather than property rights, public or private. Finance and provision are, on the other hand, observed together in the case of a national health service that, like the private sector's prepaid plan, is predicated on the notion that purchase and delivery should come already mixed. The State that protects is in such a system simultaneously the State that supplies. Thus is the citizen's right in effect a double entitlement.

A double entitlement, one hastens to add, which, being provided in kind, only promotes maximal felt satisfaction where most citizens entertain broadly similar desires. In David Collard's words:

> Whether 'health care' should be merely subsidised or allocated directly depends almost entirely on the closeness of the underlying consensus. If it is not very close, the simplest thing is to guarantee some minimum level of health care for each and then allow trade to take place at a 'subsidised' price. If consensus is pretty close (as was assumed at the time the NHS was set up) one might as well adopt the consensus allocation straight away on a 'free' basis. ... The less consensus or agreement there is, the more pressure there is to move from 'free' provision to market prices.[4]

Not that it will necessarily prove easy to measure the consensus or spot such pressures as may arise: Chapter 3 has already demonstrated the extent to which public opinion may be said to be more nearly a topic in metaphysics than it is in social science.

Consensus is problematic but it is also important. The economies of size often imputed to the unified network will not have as great an appeal to citizens who value diversity and choice as it will to consumers who, clustered around the mean, welcome long production runs because of the cost-saving that homogenisation engenders. There are no standard patients or off-the-peg doctors but there are nonetheless real limits to the range of alternatives that a national health service is able to validate without imposing intolerable administrative costs or sacrificing the economic gains that go with the uniform procedure. So long as consensus is satisfied with the trade-off there will be no problem. Where consensus demands differentiation there may well be. As Galbraith has observed, concerning the 'drabness of life' in the centrally-planned economy, variety lends itself badly to the coordinated matrix: 'This may be the problem of socialism. Planners can provide for everything but color.'[5] Should such variety enjoy a high income-elasticity of demand, then it is possible that the micro-planning of a national health service will ultimately be frustrated by the same pressures for tolerant pluralism that have imposed so heavy a tax on the macro-planning of the centralised totality. Buchanan is only one among many who would predict that it must and that it will: 'If socialism fails in the large it also fails in the small.'[6] Others, more agnostic, will not want to give up on the micro-collectivisation of the health service unless and until it can be shown that the gamut of preferences genuinely cannot be satisfied by a unified network prepared wherever possible to be flexible.

Consensus emanates from the common culture and in turn reinforces it. This defence of a national health service as effect and cause of social integration is bound to have a strong appeal to reformers who, democrats as well as engineers, will praise not only the medical care but also the shared experience that common institutions can deliver and segregated facilities will not. Sceptics complain that not all individuals, not all regions, not all minorities will want to be forced by welfare in kind into a common culture that they find incompatible with their own. Cynics insist that it is dangerously to paper over the cracks of alienation and conflict to manipulate popular consciousness into a euphoric one-nationness that myopically fails to notice the significant divides. Supporters, on the other hand, make much of the unifying tendency that they cite as an important advantage of collective provision. Rich patients and poor patients occupy adjacent beds in a nationalised ward, just as black boys and white girls share a single teacher and a united curriculum in a comprehensive educational system. Topping-up limited, opting-out minimised, the intended outcome is a warm feeling of belonging and togetherness that makes nationhood that much more meaningful than agglomeration.

The commitment to common institutions is a commitment to equal access. In that sense it is a commitment to social equity as well. A national health service undertakes to make available to all members of the national pool a common standard of medical treatment that promises best quality even to the most deprived. In order to attain this objective the coordinators plan provision in such a way as to incorporate the specific requirements of areas that are under-bedded and under-doctored, groupings that are supernormal in morbidity and mortality. The network of professionals and plant forming a united whole, sensitive targeting and selective discrimination become possible to an extent that atomism and random disposition would find difficult to match. State educational policy complements State health policy and ensures that skilled manpower with complementary expertise will be in stock but not in surplus at the time when the system articulates a demand for a service. And there is the payment, the *sine qua non* for the provision. The public commitment to finance, guarantees that the seamless web can safely be woven without any regard to the possibility that the consumer at the end of the day will not be in a position to pay for the product.

Enthusiasm about the seamless web must not, however, be allowed to proceed to the point where it effectively blots out the rents, the tears and the stains that the prudent shopper would do well take into account. Large bureaucratised monopolies unchallenged by competitors tend to develop organisational slack and internal ('x') inefficiency that reduce the real value of the health care supplied by the unnecessary cost of expensive carpets and over-staffed offices: this deadweight element deriving from salaried management's pursuit of job satisfaction is every bit as serious as the advertising and selling overheads that are so often mentioned in criticism of the private sector's market rivalries. Inflexible structures do not find it easy to incorporate new techniques into old routines and have a propensity to treat the patient who makes a request as a problem to be solved. Civil service contracts can make it difficult to adapt to change until such a time as colleagues in sunset specialities reach retirement age. Nationwide pay settlements circumscribe the scope for selective recruitment and limit the freedom of the unique institution to implement productivity-raising schemes such as the performance-related bonus promised to a technician who accepts single-man working. The concession that a national health doctor may undertake a limited amount of private work is open to abuse by the consultant who opposes shortened waiting lists because (apart from the symbolic support that waits provide to his sense of self-importance) he knows that he can cash in on desperation by selling a safety-valve for a fee. Unlimited expectations combined with unspecified entitlements are a cause of frustration where consumers, denied written-down contracts and vulnerable to national priorities, develop the perception that no legal right is guaranteed them save that of access to a general practitioner. The patient refused life-saving treatment in the private sector knows that she can seek redress against professionals employing criteria that stigmatise. The patient in the public sector, told that he has rights but not what these are, has no similar protection against rationing by social standards in a world of constrained availability and unsatisfied demand.

All of which is to say that the enthusiasm about the seamless web must not be allowed to become excessive. Yet no one can demonstrate that the cross-subsidy and the coordinated response do not after all promote good health, that compassion plus science do not in the last analysis add up to State. The truth speaks with many voices. Not least when it speaks about the national health.

Part III

Provision

7 The Individual

In some cases the finance and the provision of care are combined. Conceptually, however, the two pillars of the arch are entirely separate. It is with the supply of service that we shall be concerned in this part of the book, just as it was on the multiplied sources of effective demand that the previous part chose to concentrate. There are four principal agencies that are charged with the delivery of health-furthering attention; and each will form the subject of a separate chapter. Thus Chapter 10 will discuss the hospital, Chapter 9 the doctor and Chapter 8 the community. The present chapter considers the individual whose health is at stake.

No discussion of market and health can ever be complete which treats the health-holder as no more than the supplier of problems for which it must be left to wiser heads to supply the solutions. The individual is in truth something more than the passive bearer of symptoms which neither he nor she can identify and over which the insuring bodies and the treatment centres alone must hold the decision-making power. The individual, mind as well as matter, is in a position actively to influence his or her health status – or consciously to abstain from so doing. The individual, it must be emphasised, is no mere consuming unit in a medical manual but rather an autonomous producer of great potential. That potential is usefully examined under the twin headings of prevention and cure.

7.1 PREVENTION

In some cases the medical contingency can only be regarded as random and unforeseen, unpatterned and unpredictable: there is not a great deal the rational individual can do by way of conscious action to purchase himself full advance protection against an airplane crash, a hallucinator's assault or a drunk who recklessly exceeds the speed limit. In other cases, however, the medical contingency sends a proper warning before it such as enables precautionary steps to be taken in good time. Thus individual action might ensure that the threat never actually became a reality (as where cirrhosis of the liver is avoided by means of excessive drinking foregone and the peptic ulcer prevented through the selection of a low-stress occupation); or it might at least render the consequences of a calamity that much less serious (as where motorcyclists wear crash-helmets even when there is no compulsion and car owners voluntarily insist on fitted airbags that inflate in a collision). Given proper warning, the informed individual is clearly in a situation where he or she can frequently act to promote good health, frequently intervene to prevent bad.

Thus the health-conscious citizen might avoid sugar and sweets in an attempt to stem tooth decay and obesity; he might decline high-cholesterol foodstuffs and the inactive lifestyle in favour of fresh vegetables, vitamins and jogging such as are good for the heart; she might forego the risky excitement of surfboarding in order to devote her leisure time to the safe option of whist; he might reject the hazardous but lucrative calling of coalminer in favour of lower remuneration but better health as a postal clerk; she might wear an anti-pollutant mask in the street and fill her home with green plants such as absorb carbon dioxide. In these and in other ways the informed individual who wants good health can personally take action in defence of that status. Good health is not, in other words, to be likened to a secret potion that is produced *ex machina* by mysterious magicians and passively consumed by discrete health-holders who haven't a clue. Rather, good health is to be likened to a good marriage: the psychoanalysts and the counsellors no doubt render a very fine service but it is in the last analysis down to the individuals themselves to take the responsibility.

Or not to take it; since, just as the partners to a marriage might decide that the continuance does not repay the effort, so the health-holders might conclude that the health clubs and the health foods, the mackerel eaten and the chocolate refused, do not really add up for them to a particularly rewarding or merry life. Strange as it may seem to the health conscious, there actually exist members of the community who, either aware of the risks or inadequately interested to become informed, become dependent on psychotropic drugs to cope with their emotional stresses and strains; or obtain pleasure from dangerous and addictive substances such as gin and cocaine; or substitute promiscuous sexuality for the absolute protection against abortion, childbirth and venereal disease that is afforded by the single bed; or state without hesitation that they prefer television to exercise, competitive driving to orderly boredom, chips to bran, the medical risks of cosmetic surgery to the social risks of looking old or unattractive or both. Such members of the community are observed to reveal preferences which are clearly at odds with the value system of the most health-conscious of their fellow citizens, who will perhaps find it difficult to believe that anyone but a madman or a child could possibly be prepared to economise at the margin where health status is concerned. Strange as it may seem to the most health-conscious, however, the fact is that not everyone will refuse to trade some probable health for some anticipated pleasure; and that not everyone who makes such a swap can reasonably be dismissed as a madman or a child. There being no single definition of the optimal health-status, the discretionary remit of individual responsibility must evidently be allowed to extend to the risky options as well as to the safe ones if the preferences observed are indeed to be authentic, genuine and meaningful.

Smoking is a case in point. Objectively speaking, there is little doubt as to the numerous indicators of mortality and morbidity (including bronchitis, emphysema and cancers of the mouth, lung and throat) that are closely correlated with the common cigarette. As Joy Townsend explains:

> It is now estimated that one in every four smokers dies prematurely because of smoking and on average loses about ten to fifteen years of life and often twenty, thirty or forty years. ... In Britain 100,000 people a year die from smoking, that is one in seven of all deaths. It is the major epidemic of this century and greatly outstrips any other cause of premature death. ... The average smoker loses about five and a half minutes of life for each cigarette smoked.[1]

Assuming that individuals want good health, one obvious way of taking responsibility for that status would accordingly be not to smoke.

Yet people do smoke: perhaps because they find the activity pleasurable and relaxing in itself, perhaps because they learn from experience that it has the desired effect of boosting self-confidence and securing social esteem, the evidence indicates that a large number of persons do appear to enjoy the consumption of what is undeniably a dangerous substance. Interestingly, those consumers would seem, in the United Kingdom at least, to be found disproportionately in the lower occupational groups. The result is that smoking-related deaths and illnesses are in that country disproportionately a lower class problem. Thus Joy Townsend concludes, after an examination of the relevant British data, that

> an unskilled working man (social class 5) is seen to be three times more likely to die of lung cancer as a professional man and 25 percent more likely to die of ischaemic heart disease. These differentials are not all explained by smoking differences, but smoking is a major contributor and also multiplies the risk of other diseases such as pneumoconiosis, bronchitis and asbestosis for which lower-class workers are already at greater risk.[2]

Such an imbalance in the amount of self-supplied preventive care might in some cases be explicable in terms of the important causal variables of income and education. Thus a good income is a valuable asset for a consumer determined to eschew all pesticides and additives in favour of a healthy diet rich in organically-grown pulses; while a good education is a great help to an individual wishing to read and digest information on nutritional balance, proper hygiene, the benefits of relaxation techniques and the costs of immoderate sunbathing. In the case of smoking, however, it is not entirely convincing to explain the differential in self-infliction and self-prevention in terms either of purchasing power or of intellectual awareness.

With respect to income, it must be remembered that the action of smoking is subject to the deterrent of price. Unlike illness brought on by overwork or occupational hazard (where the counterpart of the strain and the peril is the pay and the promotion), illness brought on by smoking is accompanied by the supplementary diswelfare that the consumer is expected to make a pecuniary sacrifice before he is allowed access to the threat. It is clearly not lower incomes that cause the lower classes in Britain to consume more cigarettes per capita than do the wealthier groups. Nor is it education: so massive has been the State-sponsored campaign to publicise the dangers of smoking (a campaign relying on posters in schools, the selective or blanket prohibition on advertising, the health warning printed on each packet of cigarettes) that no rational citizen can remain unaware of the health hazards involved.

In the case of smoking it is probably not income and education that are the principal explanatory variables, but rather cultural and subcultural standards. The classes who smoke are likely to have shorter time-horizons than do the classes who do not: they are therefore more likely significantly to prefer the *now*, heavily to discount the *later*. Their more immediate attitude to time-preference is likely to be reinforced by their greater passivity: noting that only one smoker in four dies prematurely because of smoking (and that three, statistically speaking, do not), the operatives who routinely carry out the orders will probably be more prepared to trust in luck than will the entrepreneurs whose study it is to turn blind fate to their own advantage. Such cultural and subcultural standards are inculcated at an early stage (not least by the example of parents and other authority figures). They remain the focus of peer-group pressures throughout the unfolding lifecycle (not least in the form of acceptance or ridicule on the part of contemporaries who happen to smoke). The orientation in question is not the most favourable possible orientation with regard to the objective of maximal good health: irrespective of social class, the simple fact is that the smoker who smokes is the supplier of less preventive care than is the smoker who gives up. Pro-health or anti-health, however, the orientation is a social fact that must be taken on board the well-captained ship of state: not everyone identifies maximal good health with optimal good health, not everyone wants to provide extensive prevention at the cost of significant other benefits – and people do smoke.

Tolerance of diversity is of the utmost importance in a pluralistic society, but it is also a principle that is beset with a problem. On the one hand, there is much that is attractive in the doctrine that the discrete individual ought to be permitted independently to decide on the precise quantity of preventive care that he or she wishes to supply. On the other hand, it is undeniable that individuals do not exist in isolation and that one person's choices have definite and unavoidable consequences for his fellows and his community such as legitimately render his behaviour their interest. Freedom of choice is tolerable only insofar as it leaves as much freedom and as good for others. In the area of health-related choices this condition is not always met; and the imperative is then not simply to *defend freedom* but to *reconcile freedoms* as well. Two instances of interdependence will serve to illustrate the broad proposition that the non-isolated individual's supply of preventive care is a social fact of immediate and personal concern to all those members of his collectivity upon whom the spillovers and the externalities would *ex* prevention inevitably fall.

The *first* instance relates to insurance. Private or State, the system depends on a pooling of risks and a sharing of burdens. Yet any scheme which takes as its objective the redistribution of financial liability to the healthy from the ill is by its very charter intensely vulnerable to abuse. Thus it is that the smoker in the private sector not only imposes a strain on his own heart and lungs but also raises the premium that must be paid by the average subscriber in consequence of the smoking subscriber's above-average consumption of care. Again, and in the State sector, the freedom of choice of the committed alcoholic to rank the glass of wine above the cup of tea carries with it a similar threat not merely to the drinker's own mind and liver but to the tax burden of the free services and the availability to others of hospital beds as well. Had the drinkers and the smokers only indulged in the socially-average *quantum* of self-supplied preventive care, one is compelled to reflect, the premiums and the taxes would have been lower and the waiting times shorter. The freedom of choice of the less responsible is evidently capable of proving a costly luxury to the representative who share the pool.

Certain palliatives can nonetheless be found such as go some way towards internalising the externalities. One of these is the differentiated contribution that seeks to proportion personal (premium) costs to expected personal benefits: self-control would clearly be encouraged were a risk-rated surcharge to be imposed on the smoker and the alcoholic (to say nothing of those who indulge in dangerous sports or have a record of road accidents) and a similar incentive to look after oneself would be afforded by a low-claims bonus offered to those who, avoiding negligence, make only very moderate demands on the insurance funds. Another palliative is the high user-charge that would tend like any other price to reduce the quantity of ill-health consumed: where the marginal cost of smoking or drinking is known to include the marginal cost of doctors and wards as well as of cigarettes and alcohol, there the calculative citizen will have a private reason, overcoming moral hazard, to reduce the burdens shared with the insuring agency by means of a personal investment in self-supplied preventive care. A further palliative is the special health levy imposed on all commodities the consumption of which imposes a disproportionate strain on the pool: even if the swingeing tax does not reduce the burdensome abuse, still, it is argued, the earmarked nature of the payment means that the guilty industries are in effect themselves being required to make a supplementary contribution towards the cost of the care. The insuring agency may rely on the levy or the charge or the surcharge or it may simply make use of moral exhortation (not to drink and drive), targeted subsidisation (the provision of complimentary contraception or free exercise centres), educative advertisement (not to inject illegal substances with unsterilised needles) and savage prohibition (the ban on reimbursement for false teeth for the under-50s in an attempt to encourage proper care). What it cannot reasonably do is to do nothing: pooling means interdependence and fairness therefore dictates that rewards must not come without responsibilities attached.

The first instance of interdependence relates to insurance. The *second* relates to physical diswelfares imposed on innocent others. One illustration is the infectious disease that is passed on by the cook who is suffering from a respiratory complaint, by the blood-vendor who conceals a history of malaria, by the stricken actor who continues to play the romantic role. Another illustration involves smoking.

The freedom of choice of the smoker to enjoy a standard of health inferior to that which he knows to be attainable is a freedom which most tolerant persons would wish to defend. Cigarettes could be prohibited altogether; or sold only after midnight; or sold only subject to punitive excise duties intended to discourage; or sold only in isolated premises located at least one hour's journey from the nearest town. Clearly, they could; but most tolerant persons would probably regard such extreme paternalism as a well-intentioned but nonetheless ill-considered attempt on the part of a community calling itself caring to ride roughshod over the unique individual's preferred lifestyle. Yet smoking in isolation is different from smoking in society; and most tolerant persons would also say that, just as the smoker has a social right to go to Hell in a hand-basket if that is what he wants to do, so the non-smoker who is his neighbour has a right to be spared the contagions which are the uncompensated consequence of passive smoking.

The common compromise is to allow the smoker to smoke but to ensure that he does so only where the health and sensibilities of the non-smoker are not jeopardised. This is the argument for segregated sections and compartments in public places such as trains; or for the total ban in offices and factories (including the civil service, often called upon to set a good example) from which the non-smoker has no acceptable means of escape. The compromise scenario has a strong appeal to most tolerant persons; but they should also keep in mind the frequency with which peaceful coexistence will fail to provide any non-confrontational solution that is equal to the challenge.

Consider the case of the segregated section. The non-smoker's body is protected from the smoker's fumes. Not so, however, the non-smoker's living standards from the smoker's days off work and premature death. The social organism functions that much less efficiently where the discrete cell opts to ignore the needs of the integrated whole. Economic growth proceeds that much less rapidly where the rugged individualist dismisses as totalitarian the notion that the player has an obligation to the team. The non-smoker's new television becomes that much more likely to prove a mirage where the smoker's ill-health retards the advance of his company and of his country. It is arguably the case, therefore, that the smoker's freedom to smoke is more circumscribed even than the segregated section: sometimes the recipient of an expensive education financed by the public's sacrifices, sometimes the beneficiary of the free-on-demand services of a non-judgemental national health system which only looks the non-brushing sweet-eater in the mouth when it carefully fills his teeth, always the beneficiary of his neighbour's contribution to collective prosperity even when he makes no immediate contribution of his own, the smoker has in a sense no greater freedom to make himself ill through nicotine than he has to make his child a debilitated wreck dependent on public health and social services because of improper diet and inadequate rest.

The right to participate in the social game thus carries with it, in this perspective, the concomitant duty to keep in proper repair the powerful machine that is obliged to serve the All. In the words of the eminent but prudent social democrat T.H. Marshall: 'Your body is part of the national capital, and must be looked after, and sickness causes a loss of national income, in addition to being liable to spread.'[3] Marshall treated the right to enjoy the economic and welfareist privileges of citizenship as being inextricably linked to the personal duty of self-maintenance. Given such interdependence, the man who misses his yoga class or fails to eat an apple a day may properly be likened to the free rider who abstains from paying a tax; while the woman who binges on fatty calories when she ought to be eating wholemeal bread may perhaps be compared to the farm-labourer who makes conversation while the sun shines. Given interdependence, in short, self-supplied health care is everyone's business.

The eater of apples may be said to be manifesting a pro-health orientation, the smoker of cigarettes to be manifesting an anti-health one. Pro-health or anti-health, what cannot be denied is the impact of the individual on the outcome. So great is that impact that McKeown is only one among many to have assigned to the individual in the richer society the key role in the determination of the health status. In the poorer countries, McKeown argues, there is a premium on collective action to stem the transmission of water-borne diseases such as typhoid and cholera; to improve hygiene through the purification of drinking water and the effective disposal of sewage; to ensure that malarial swamps are drained and rats, mice and lice not allowed to breed plague. At low levels of national income, McKeown says, environmental health is crucial and the collectively-sponsored infrastructure of an importance only to be equalled by the rising living standards that more than anything else combat the nutritional shortcomings of poverty and the overcrowded housing that is the natural habitat of tuberculosis and infection.

Preventive action is largely a shared thing in the poorer countries, McKeown says. Different, however, are the affluent ones in their present stage of economic development: 'Personal behaviour is now relatively more significant than food deficiency and environmental hazards'[4], and thus 'in the advanced countries it is on modification of personal habits such as smoking and sedentary living that health primarily depends'[5]. As poor countries evolve into rich ones, McKeown believes, so self-supplied care must relatively wax and other-provided care relatively wane: 'The influences which result from the individual's behaviour (smoking, diet, exercise, etc) are now relatively more important than those which depend on action by society.'[6] The individual is the primary provider in the richer countries, McKeown says, the environmental infrastructure combined with per capita upgrading the principal source of improved health in the poorer ones—and the therapeutic intervention of the doctors and the hospitals, in the one case as in the other, no more than 'tertiary'[7]: 'Health is not determined mainly by medical intervention'.[8] Both the eater of apples and the smoker of cigarettes will find McKeown's protestantisation of the Kingdom of God to be of immediate personal relevance.

McKeown writes: 'I believe that the solution or partial solution of the problems of lung cancer, coronary artery disease, chronic bronchitis and peripheral vascular disease is more likely to come from avoidance of smoking than from medical treatment.'[9] The Health Officer's diagnosis is shared by the economist Fuchs, who says that, nowadays, 'it is the patient rather than the physician who has the major influence on his health'[10]: 'The notion that we can spend our way to better health is a vast oversimplification. At present there is very little that medical care can do for a lung that has been overinflated by smoking, or for a liver that has been scarred by too much alcohol, or for a skull that has been crushed in a major accident.'[11] There is very little that the doctors and the hospitals can do *ex post* to correct the avoidable pathologies of individuals' self-indulgence, ignorance, carelessness and misjudgement – but very much, Fuchs emphasises, that the individuals themselves can do *ex ante* to prevent the pathologies from ever arising.

Not all individuals, Fuchs admits, are today prepared to go out of their way to protect their health: 'The chief killers today are heart disease, cancer, and violent deaths from accidents, suicide and homicide. The behavioral component in all these causes is very large, and until now medical care has not been very successful in altering behavior.'[12] In the United States accidents, suicide and homicide account for three out of four male deaths in the 15–24 age group; heart disease (where genetic propensities are known to be exacerbated by self-destructive conduct in the form of excessive smoking and unalleviated stress) is the main killer of men over 35; and cirrhosis of the liver from alcohol actually exceeds lung cancer (itself in no small measure a self-inflicted pathology) as a cause of male morbidity in the 35–44 age range. Medical care can often detect the risks (say, by tracking and screening) and sometimes it can even reverse the outcomes (as in the case of the mugger's victim who might without intervention have bled to death from the wound). Yet too much should not be expected from the doctors and the hospitals; and more therefore, perhaps, from the individuals themselves. Suicide claims as many lives among white American males of 15–24 as do cancer and heart disease combined. There is not much that the doctors and the hospitals can do about that. They can talk to the downhearted and patch up the botch; but even the most wondrous of wonder drugs is no substitute for the genuine miracle and the *ex post* corrective infrequently as effective as the *ex ante* avoidance. Thence the conclusion, that individuals have consequences and that no discussion of the provision of care can ever be complete which does not assign an exceptional importance to the potential contribution of self-supplied prevention.

7.2 CURE

It is often said that an ounce of prevention is worth a pound of cure. The figures are suspect but the intuition for all that is sound. The king's horses might not possess the medical skill to make Dumpty the Humpty he was before the fall; the king's men might find it wasteful that resources should be used to bend a bent rod than need never have become bent in the first place; the king himself might express the opinion that no one but a silly goose crosses the road without looking to right and left or visits his doctor with constipation if his food lacks fibre. The general view in the palace and the stables is likely to be that people who sit on fences ought to see to it that they sit safely as well. Prevention might not be precisely sixteen times as valuable as cure, but, due weight assigned to medical failure, economic inefficiency and moral fibre, there must be a strong presumption that it remains the more valuable nonetheless.

More valuable or less valuable, however, few observers would wish to say of cure that it had no value at all – or to deny to the individual an active role in the supply of curative care such as he enjoys at the preventive stage when he guards against dysentery by brushing away flies. Non-professional medication is useful in that it reduces both the time-cost and the resource-cost that would have been incurred had outside expertise been required. It can also mean the difference between life and death: when a child swallows his tongue in the course of aerobic exercise, when a woman experiences an electric shock while putting up shelves, when a man severs a vein on a jagged plate broken in the washing up, then the premium is on speedy reaction and the time lost before the ambulance arrives is often time that cannot be spared. Most accidents happen in the home, and so do a number of epileptic fits, bee stings, and sudden faints. It would clearly be of considerable value if each household were able to boast at least one trained first-aider, able to deal quickly both with simple treatments and with medical emergencies.

Much curative care is supplied on a non-professional basis. There is much to be said in its favour: not only does it economise on the use of doctors and hospitals (as where the household itself circumvents high-tech medicine by employing tweezers or a sterilised pin to take out a splinter) but it also reduces the passivity of dependence on others (a useful contribution once it is recognised how variant are patients' attitudes to pain and anxiety). It is important, of course, that the individual be prepared to call for second-aid when he believes there to be a need for skilled treatment. The do-it-yourselfer's undoubted successes in stopping a nosebleed with an ice-cube or treating a burn with cold water might make him both overconfident about his own abilities and ashamed to ask the doctors to decide. The consequences in such circumstances could easily prove preverse. Thus he might treat a stomach ache with chicken soup and a cup of camomile tea when the proper diagnosis might be a grumbling appendix, the proper treatment an immediate operation; while she might laugh off a fall with a swig of brandy and a lightly-boiled egg when in fact she is experiencing internal bleeding necessitating hospital care. The problem with self-medication is always to know when to go to bed and call the doctor and when merely to go to bed. The problem is a very real one, partly because the patient does not necessarily possess the medical knowledge to be able to tell the trivial from the life-threatening, partly because rapid recourse to the trained expert will in some cases make the difference between recovery and death. No one should exaggerate the importance of self-supplied curative care, but nor should its constructive contribution be neglected: whether in disinfecting a cut or applying a cold compress to a sprain, whether in drinking cocoa when he feels sleepless or pulling herself together when she feels disorientated, the individual has the opportunity to play the role of the doctor and in that way to free the trained experts to treat symptoms less amenable to devolution.

Self-medication can take the form of bed rest, orange juice and a piece of steamed fish. It can also take the form of non-prescription compounds available on an over-the-counter basis from pharmacies, supermarkets, health shops and newsagents. Aspirins and painkillers, cough mixtures and headache tablets, lotions to soothe the sunburn and creams to calm the rash, substances to quieten the upset stomach and liquids to firm up the bowels – through these well-known preparations and others, it may be argued, the pharmaceutical manufacturers and their retail outlets fulfil an enabling function by helping people to help themselves.

Yet not all drugs are freely available. Some are placed on a controlled list, obtainable only with a professional's permit; while others are prohibited altogether, supported or not by a practitioner's prescription. Thence an imbalance in the mixed economy of yes-but individualism, that the consumer in the semi-protective society retains an absolute right to poison himself with vitamin A, laburnum, oleander, holly berries and paracetamol, a discretionary right to destroy himself with steroids, barbiturates and methylmorphinan monohydrate (also known as $C_{17}H_{19}NO_3H_2O$), and no right at all to go laughing to the grave with heroin, cyanide, arsenic and krypton-85. The commanding economy, hostile to deviants who mistake selfishness for a virtue, will take a dim view of the internal bleeding and the kidney damage that can be caused by an overindulgence in aspirin. The liberating economy, on the other hand, will express concern not at the ease with which penicillin can be obtained but at the frustrating obstacles which the paternalistic community raises up between the sovereign consumer and the chemical hallucinogen. On the middle ground between the wise leadership and the permissive tolerance stands the mixed economy of yes-but individualism that divides the labour of choice.

One reason for denying to consumers the final say might be the familiar problem of inadequate knowledge. Thus it might happen, science being complex, that the uninitiated require the guidance of the trained precisely because the uninformed are not in a position unassisted to decide. Not all persons, it is argued, will be willing and competent to devote time and energy to wide reading and careful study: many patients will be uneducated or confused, very young or very old, and thus a world away from the economic man's ideal of the rational calculator. Besides that, responsible evaluation is more difficult even for the most alert of consumers once an illness has struck; while few if any consumers, alert or indifferent, will see a need in good times to study pharmaceutical texts as a precautionary investment in a low-probability rainy day. The experts, on the other hand, have the background knowledge that enables them rapidly to match the chemicals to the symptoms and that simultaneously keeps them on their guard against hidden risks. The experts have the impartial intelligence that the consumer lacks. From that asymmetry then follows the argument that it can only be the trained who can identify the optimum.

The legitimation of authority in terms of unequal information is a time-honoured defence. It is properly a defence of advice, however, and not really a defence of restriction at all. Prudent patients will generally solicit counsel: orthodox or fringe, Western or traditional, many respected superiors will always exist and will always be approached in different circumstances by different individuals. Few opponents of coercion would want also to ban consultation. Some advocates of freedom would, indeed, go so far as to support liberalisation precisely because of their conviction that is likely to multiply the channels and the funnels through which the guidance is transmitted. Yet prescription and proscription are a world away from the simple description that the prudent solicit. People who approach authority for advice must not be assumed also to be asking authority for restriction. To the extent that they are not, their felt welfare would actually rise were the bundle of joint products effectively to be broken up.

Some consumers will perhaps not want authority even to supply advice.

Negatively speaking, those consumers will be aware of the dependence of doctors and pharmacists on the publicity campaigns and incomplete documentation of the pharmaceutical majors: while the vulnerability of the experts to manipulation and interest will presumably be less than that of the uninitiated (not least because of background knowledge reinforced by medical journals), still some patients will take the view that generalist advisers provide insufficient protection against exaggerated and misleading claims. Positively speaking, therefore, some consumers will set themselves the task of generating their own countervailing power and of serving, often or always, as their own best judge. The magnitude of the undertaking need not be insuperable. Individuals would not need to collect information on all drugs, only on a few drugs, since no one person would ever require more than a small number of drugs at any one moment in time. Individuals, as David Green points out, would have a strong incentive to ensure that they do collect adequate information before they make their choice of drug: 'Indeed, the patient has a stronger incentive than the doctor, for it is the patient who will suffer any side-effects.'[13] It is the patient who will face the risk of bone marrow suppression leading to anaemia if the drug is taken – or the probability of earlier death from autoimmune failure if it is not. It is the patient who will experience the drowsiness or the sneezing, the constipation or the cough, the insomnia or the anxiety. Given the personal incidence of the side-effects, there would seem to be much logic in Green's assertion that the patient will have an especial incentive to become informed.

Yet individuals there will undoubtedly be, even in the health-conscious society, who yield to the temptations of the moment and choose to leap before they look. Impetuous by nature and bored by calculative servitude to a future that might never come, the spontaneous are seen to economise on advice, to laugh at restriction, when they swallow amphetamines and sniff powders that liberate the mind from the contemplation of the heatstroke and the hyperventilation, the epilepsy and the paranoia, the kidney failure and the withdrawal symptoms that are the addict's curse. In pain or in a hurry, even the normally rational will sometimes show much of the addict's weakness of will when they knowingly fail to read the instructions on the label, or when they deliberately exceed the recommended dosage, or when they recklessly opt for short-run relief of symptoms even at the price of long-run physical or psychological dependency. A tolerant society that believes there to be something in some sense good about revealed preference will not necessarily wish to stigmatise as ill-informed and random all choices such as these merely because they deviate from the mainstream's health-orientated norm. A tolerant society will be understandably reluctant to visit with sanctions and directives any subculture that values uppers that lead to downs that lead to suicide, any minority that worships slimness to such an extent that it wastes away to nothing on manufactured appetite-suppressants. Tolerance is tolerance, and even the self-destroying are entitled to the community's respect.

A compromise solution in such circumstances might be to decontrol all drugs but also to ask all purchasers to confirm in writing that they are reasonably aware of the consequences and implications of the medicines in question. In Green's words:

> One way of cautioning citizens without legally banning access to drugs would be to require them to sign a statement at the chemist's shop before they could receive items on a given list. The statement would verify that the patient had taken advice or obtained information and fully understood the likely effects of the drug he was buying and its possible side-effects.[14]

A minority, impetuous or impatient, might, of course, prefer the false declaration to the responsible collection of information that is by definition so out of keeping with its nature. Short of administering an *ad hoc* quiz, there is no way of establishing whether the patient who puts his money where his diazepines are has genuinely taken the trouble to convert licence into liberty. The alternative to allowing an ill-informed minority a greater freedom to articulate incomplete preferences might, however, be to constrict a well-informed majority into avenues of consumption down which it knows that it does not wish to travel. People cannot be compelled to make themselves wise: that is an argument for good government instead of representative government. Yet the ill-informed tail ought not to be allowed to wag the well-informed dog: that is an argument for freeing the rational from a restraint that was designed with the non-rational in mind. The compromise solution of decontrol accompanied by confirmation may not be ideal but at least it recognises the pull of principles. The prescription-only solution does not.

Interestingly, however, there will be circumstances in which the rational, neither madmen nor children, will make a conscious decision to support the doctor-knows-best system of autonomy alienated to an outsider. It is easy enough to understand why the rational would want to seek advice: curious as to whether hormone replacement therapy is likely to prove addictive, uncertain as to the speed with which antibiotics build up a resistance, anxious as to the long-run effects of anti-depressants on libido, it would seem to have all the logic of the division of labour that the patient with the symptom should approach the doctor with the training for the explanation and even the recommendation that would have entailed the higher transaction cost had the patient had to search out the answer for himself. More difficult to grasp is why the rational would enter the market in pursuit of restriction as well. Hiring a counsellor is the hard core of modern life. Hiring a jailer, on the other hand, is likely to raise a few eyebrows at the Dog and Duck.

Perhaps it is; but still the decision can be as rational as was that of the risk-averting Ulysses when, afraid of himself as much as of the Sirens, he instructed his crew to secure him against temptation lest, unbound, he calamitously steer his craft on to a reef. Ulysses employed a crew to protect him from himself. Modern man will be tempted to cast the doctor in the same role. Thus it may be seen by the patient as being in his own best interest that the morphine and the tranquillisers should be subject to some check on the easy over-medication of the desperate, the suffering and the confused. The patient when well will here be ranking the protection of restraint above the momentary relief that might ill-advisedly be chosen by the patient when unwell. Even the patient who is intelligent, educated and rational when in his normal state of good health may nonetheless reveal a general preference for medical supervision in the abnormal circumstances of the sick role and the reliance on medication. Active, autonomous and independent when in the healthy state of office or factory, the patient may nonetheless reject liberalised access (in the limit, open access) in favour of the passivity of the doctor-knows-best orientation that he believes the more suited to the needs of the at-risk. Loosely aware that different drugs have different side-effects (not least when consumed in combination with other drugs), conscious that regret can be irreversible where the drugs damage the thyroid or eat away at the stomach, the patient might decide when well that it makes sense to emulate the wise Ulysses when ill and to bind himself voluntarily to the one-to-one directive of the practitioner with the prescription. The patient will not say that the alienation of the freedom of choice in this manner ought to be the standard practice of the sovereign consumer. What the patient will say is that ignorance mixed with temptation is too dangerous a cocktail to be left to the discretion of madmen and children – or of the patient himself once the Siren of illness has befuddled the judgement.

Even if the patient should stubbornly cling to freedom, however, still the public might point to spillovers and plead for control. A nation with a health service will not look kindly upon unrepresentative health-averters who irresponsibly opt for short-run intensities despite the long-run expense that the diswelfares engendered will one day represent for their fellows. A society with a strict morality will not welcome the over-the-counter sale of a drug capable of producing an abortion or a contraceptive that encourages promiscuity. An economy with a commitment to growth will regard as deadweight the quack aphrodisiac that wastes social resources better deployed elsewhere. A government with a revulsion to rising cost will prefer rather to impose indicative ceilings on prescribing doctors than to allow patients to pay large sums for marginal preparations. The public, in short, has an interest and a consensus such as render the individual's drugs a collective as well as a private concern. Liberalised access might have to be rejected expressly because of that collective concern.

Prescription-only is one extreme, off-the-shelf is another. In the middle stands the pharmacist, whose involvement in advice and restriction will to some represent a useful halfway-house between conservative authority and unfettered exchange.

Where the patient (perhaps because he is poor) treats the pharmacist as his first line of defence, there, it is clear, the pharmacist will be exposed to a conflict of interest: the pharmacist will often find himself in the unattractive position of having to decide whether to push the high-profit drug when he knows the low-price medicament to be no less effective. The pecuniary interest of the commercial pharmacist trading from his own shop is a problem and even a risk; and so too is the limited nature of the counsel that is provided. The chemist takes no medical history such as would assist him to decide if the headache might be a tumour and the heartburn an infarct. Sometimes in a position to check the blood pressure or the cholesterol level, the retailer is never able fully to examine the patient or to conduct extensive tests. The pharmacist does not monitor for under-use in order to ensure that a course of treatment is completed. Nor does he have the time or the knowledge to fine-tune his response to a differentiated patient's unique requirements. Off-the-peg rather than tailor-made, the advice given by the pharmacist will tend to be general, the restriction represented by the pharmacy-only list to be selective. The patient who buys by the gross a cough mixture containing codeine will rightly be suspected of melting and coining. The patient who is moderate in his demands, on the other hand, is more likely to make his purchase without any greater impediment to his freedom of choice than would be the case were he to be buying an umbrella or a camera and not a tablet or a pill.

Some observers will no doubt infer from the above that the pharmacist cannot be expected to provide an intermediate service of any particular value. Other observers, however, will be more positive about the complementarity of the local pharmacy to the sovereign consumer's enlightened choice. Many simple complaints can effectively be treated by means of a standard preparation: provided that she asks key questions about duration of pathology and accompanying symptoms, the chemist is unlikely to be exposing the sufferer to intolerable risks when she takes it upon herself to prescribe for sunburn, laryngitis, indigestion or catarrh. Besides that, the local pharmacist may be less costly and more cost-effective than the highly-trained practitioner: expense is an important consideration, both for the uninsured individual and for the delivery-system as a whole. In difficult cases, moreover, the pharmacist will show common sense and counsel the patient to seek a proper consultation. Such screening and filtering reduces the number of minor problems that reach the practitioner while ensuring that serious problems detected by the pharmacist will be referred on. In this way the pharmacist can make a useful contribution to the smooth functioning of the medical system without at the end of the day dethroning the prescription which will remain the intermediary that restricts the access.

The argument for the prescription is the need to protect the patient. In that sense the consumer enjoys double protection, since even before a new drug comes into the shops or is placed on the ethical list it must first be vetted and approved by the representatives of the State. The purpose of such regulation is to ensure that the drugs dispensed to the public are known to meet certain minimum standards of quality and safety. Such a governmental go-ahead is a source of great reassurance to the consumer who, aware that he cannot perform his own tests, values the view of the State's scientists that the drug in question is believed neither to be harmful nor to be useless.

Toxicity and fraud are real threats, but so too is the preventable illness that is demonstrably not prevented when the introduction of a new (perhaps a life-saving) compound is delayed until such a time as it has been tested against every possible shortcoming. To delay is to raise the cost of the drug when eventually it is patented (partly because time is money, partly because of the risk that a research-intensive innovation will in the end be denied a license). To delay is in that way to restrict the introduction of new drugs and also to impede the entry of new firms capable of underselling existing oligopolists. Most important of all, needless to say, is the nature of the help on offer to the client. To delay might be to curse the potential beneficiary with morbidity and even with mortality – but not to delay might mean standards so low that the permitted consumer is abruptly summoned to follow the same sad road to the knacker's yard. In Milton Friedman's words: 'As is so often the case, one good objective conflicts with other good objectives. Safety and caution in one direction can mean death in another.'[15]

On the one hand there can be no doubt that looser regulations might lead to more disasters such as that of thalidomide: such errors of commission would be particularly a danger in the case of latent ill-effects with a long fuse such as are often said to accompany the use of anti-depressants, tranquillisers and the contraceptive pill. On the other hand a safety margin that is spectacularly cautious might lead to just as many pathologies if not to more: extended postponements are less publicised than are spectacular failures but novelty repressed and innovativeness stifled is none the less regrettable for all its anonymity. Bureaucrats in regulatory agencies will have more to lose from the spectacular failures than from the untreated complaints: they, it may therefore be predicted, will have a bias for meticulous scrutiny and lagged introduction. What is less easy to predict is the bias of the public itself when confronted with evidence such as that presented by Wardell, who has calculated that the delay of five years in authorising the use of benzodiazepine sleeping tablets in the United States meant the loss of 1200 lives: the barbiturates that had to be prescribed to the Americans even as the Europeans were phasing out their consumption were an invitation to suicide by overdose whereas the diazepines presented no similar threat of self-poisoning (deliberate or unintended).[16] More drugs would in this case have meant a safer service. Fewer drugs meant more deaths.

Regulation is *ex ante* protection. Legal redress is its *ex post* counterpart. In that sense the consumer of the prescribed drug that has also been approved enjoys treble protection, since the pharmaceutical company contemplating the marketing of a new drug is fully aware that heavy penalties will be imposed on it by the courts (to say nothing of the financial damage that will be done to its brand name) should its product be found to cause genuine harm. Thalidomide speaks for itself. As Friedman explains: 'The manufacturers of Thalidomide ended up paying tens of millions of dollars in damages – surely a strong incentive to avoid any similar episodes. Of course, mistakes will still happen – the Thalidomide tragedy was one – but so will they under government regulation.'[17]

The threat of such expense is a stimulus to the firm to internalise the task of protecting the consumer. Thus it will, in recognition of its liability, do extensive testing in advance of the product launch and continue thereafter the process of surveillance and monitoring (not least in cases where tests on animals give no dependable guidance as to the effects of the compounds on humans). It must also be recorded, however, that the deterrent of recourse to law is far more effective in the case of serious abuse than it is where the deficiency is limited. The reason is the cost of litigation: particularly where the litigant is an isolated on-off and not the member of a class, the financial implications of an unsuccessful action can have the effect of deterring not the *feasor* of the limited *tort* from failing the consumer but rather the victim of the limited deficiency from pressing his suit. Nor should it be forgotten that much of negligence is shrouded in a haze of ambiguity: the rights of the consumer of hormones or antihistamines in an off-the-shelf system are by no means clear and it is difficult to know how the courts would react to an unexpected allergy. Presumably the same rule would be applied that is applied when the consumer of a car threatens to sue the manufacturer because the temptation induced him to drive at risk. All of life has side-effects. All of life is not banned.

Concluding this chapter on the health-holder as a provider of health, the possibility must be admitted that the voyage may have been undertaken in vain. Individuals could be afforded much protection in states of good health and much care in states of bad were the responsibility for their health status to be transferred from their ignorant selves to their sensible leadership. Madmen and children are seldom asked for their opinions but rather made the dependent wards of more rational counsels. In the confusing area of preventive and curative attention, it might be argued, even normal individuals who know themselves to be adult and believe themselves to be sane ought to be accorded a similar measure of leadership and wardship lest *de jure* freedom to choose degenerate inescapably into *de facto* enslavement to lack of knowledge and weakness of will. In the confusing area of the preventive and the curative, it might even be maintained, each naked Adam will be not unlike the madman or the child when expected to make carefully-considered choices but not given the wisdom that would render the decision anything more health-furthering than random.

Thus the naked Adam might live to thank the sagacity of his keepers where the compulsory take-up of the dental check-up is validated in later life by the freedom from extractions and dentures. No less might Adam, unaware that an insect bite is about to turn septic but not keen for all that to be incapacitated by a fever, one day express the deepest of gratitude to the doctors who poked him with a needle and told him to drain the contents of a phial. The naked Adam might reason that freedom loses its attractiveness where the economy is anarchic and the trains do not run on time. Alternatively, however, Adam might express the opinion that efficiency is seldom a strong argument for compulsion precisely because it is in man's nature that he likes to be asked what he wants.

Such is the view of Fuchs, who warns that there is little point in saving the body if in the process it is the soul that must be sacrificed: 'In our zeal to raise health levels ... we must be wary of impinging on other valuable 'rights', including the right to be left alone. Strict control over a man's behavior might well result in increased life expectancy, but a well-run zoo is still a zoo and not a worthy model for mankind.'[18] This is not to deny that the well-run zoo has a certain appeal; and René Dubos is entirely right to conclude that, 'to ward off disease or recover health, men as a rule find it easier to depend on the healers than to attempt the more difficult task of living wisely'.[19] Yet autonomous involvement has a certain appeal as well; and for that reason there is much to be said in favour of the individual health-holder who squares up to the twin tasks of prevention and cure.

8 The Community

Few individuals are reclusive hermits who live in total isolation. Most individuals are social beings who interact with others. The health status of the isolated individual is entirely his own to determine, but not so the health status of the social individual: adversely affected by the smoking of his neighbour as well as by his own personal intake of alcohol, positively affected by a relative's willingness to provide domiciliary care as well as by her own independent insistence on organic foods, the social individual senses what the isolated individual cannot, that the members of a community have no choice but to share their germs – and their warmth.

The community can be as small-scale as the nuclear family or as macroscopic as the nation. Always characterised by perceived interdependence, it complements the individual's autonomy, supplements the doctors and the hospitals, and makes a significant contribution to the provision of care such as is best considered under three headings: the family, the social services and the environment.

8.1 THE FAMILY

The family provides both preventive and curative care. At the preventive level it educates children in the rudiments of hygiene (the washing of the hands before meals, for example) and the principles of nutrition (if only in the sense that most parents show some interest in a healthy diet). If teaches children the value of self-discipline (as in the case of not eating between meals) and the importance of deferred gratification (the basis for early investment in health capital to prevent decrepit old age as it is for regular saving to prevent financial embarrassment). It provides an outlet for the relief of stress (witness the psychiatric services of one supportive spouse to another) and generates a stable framework of integrative routines (a cocoon the importance of which is dramatically illustrated by comparing the much higher incidence of deaths among single and divorced men with the statistics relating to their married counterparts). At the curative level, meanwhile, the family provides the services both of short-term doctoring (as where the parent dresses a cut or sees a child through a migraine) and of long-stay supervision (as where a handicapped child or an aged grandmother is looked after in the family home); and it also supplies the informal sanctions that are so significant a safeguard against a relapse (as in the case of the child coming off heroin or the adult drying out from alcohol).

It would, naturally enough, be incorrect and misleading to see the family in too rosy a light. The baby-battering and the child abuse, the chain-smoking role-model and the psychological complex, the obsessive hypochondria that results from an over-drilled childhood and the careless habits that result from an over-permissive one, the extra risk of adult asthma where the child is brought up exposed to unvacuumed house-dust and the heightened danger of premature death where the child is rendered obese by sweets and HIV-positive by bad blood – phenomena such as these serve as a useful reminder to the excessively idealistic that the family can be a cause of bad health as well as of good. On balance, however, most observers would probably hazard the guess that the protection is likely far and away to outstrip the harm. In the absence of statistical evidence more robust than the anecdote, it is not possible to prove them right or wrong.

The family may be conceptualised as involving two adults of opposite sex whose conjugal union has been legally solemnised by church or State; or as involving two adults, unmarried save in their own eyes, whose stable relationship and cohabiting commitment is founded in implicit contract and exchange of consent; or as involving a network of kinship that goes beyond the nuclear unit; or as involving one adult responsible for at least one child. The inter-generational dimension is normally taken to be a distinguishing characteristic of the family. One person living alone is known as a one-person household. One person living with a dependent child is known as a one-parent family. A non-traditional and a non-conventional family, admittedly; but a family nonetheless.

The principal threat to the family in the poorer countries is early death (including death in childbirth). The position in the richer countries is somewhat different. For one thing, marital dissolution through early death having become so much less likely, a new threat to the stable union has arisen in the form of voluntary cessation: divorce may or may not affect the psychological health of the partners and their children, but it clearly has financial implications that can all too easily breed material diswelfares. Also, women's sense of self having become so much more acute, the wife and mother can no longer be relied upon dutifully to put family responsibilities above personal earnings and professional advancement: where care points one way, career the other, there the outcome of the conflict of objectives can potentially be as deleterious to health as the steady diet of convenience foods consumed by a latch-key child left alone when ill. Divorce rates on the one hand, the two-career household on the other – the family is the oldest known welfare state but it is also exposed, in the richer countries, to a dual threat that represents a challenge to its health-furthering functions.

The family being widely regarded as a constructive force, the State is often asked to rise to that challenge. It cannot reasonably do so, putting the clocks back, by decreeing that marriage must be regarded as a commitment for life or insisting that daughters and sons are the natural carers for their aged parents. Such measures would be out of step with the consensus of opinion and therefore unsuitable in a Western democracy that prides itself on consultation. What the State can do in the quintessentially private area of family life must be neither Draconian nor intrusive but rather sensitive and pragmatic.

The State can provide generous child benefits or income tax allowances in order to ensure that no child need grow up undernourished and cold in absolute poverty. It can see to it that the father of a child (irrespective of marital status) be made to accept some share in the costly liability. It can make high welfare payments to the unmarried mother and guarantee her a place in a public housing estate: the *largesse* rewards irresponsible attitudes (in the sense that those not yet able to support a child ought prudently to abstain from so exceptional a commitment), and the system is open to abuse by the scheming minx (the teenager, say, who makes it her study to acquire the status symbol of adulthood, the unearned income and the subsidised accommodation, all by means of a single act of non-wedded conception), but the alternative to assisting the irresponsible and even the blackmailing is to condemn the innocent to squalor and deprivation in the form of insanitary plumbing and inadequate heating such as are hardly compatible with a healthy life. The State can also reinforce the family by means of an expansion in public sector nursery places (accompanied, perhaps, by regulations, tax relief and subsidies that give the employer an incentive to provide non-contributory workplace childcare and flexible working hours): women wishing to take jobs would in that way be spared the burden of guilt and reassured that their child was receiving proper attention. The State cannot decree that the husband share in the housework or insist that the grandmother babysit a handicapped child. Clearly, however, there is quite a lot that the State can do to protect an institution that arguably does much to protect the nation's health.

8.2 THE SOCIAL SERVICES

Social services can be provided by central government, local government or the voluntary sector. Sometimes, indeed, they are as informal and as *ad hominem* as the support of a neighbour who shops and cleans or of a friend who sympathetically and compassionately provides reassurance and advice. Interwoven into the very fabric of the social skein, the non-market services that separate the *quid* from the *quo* are a living embodiment of the community's commitment to the good health of its constituent parts.

The non-market services reinforce the positive contribution made by the other players in the drama of care. In doing this, the social services work sometimes as complements and sometimes as substitutes. Thus they are complements to individual responsibility in the case of meals-on-wheels and home helps that assist the independent elderly to look after themselves; or complements to the family in the case of the health visitor who takes temporary charge of a long-term convalescent in order that an overburdened son or daughter might have a rest; or complements to environmental regulation in the case of a citizens' advice bureau that supplies reliable information on the disposal of asbestos. The social services, similarly, act as substitutes for the doctors where a community nurse provides antenatal advice and monitors pregnancy; or as substitutes for the hospitals where a social worker equipped with psychiatric skills facilitates the transfer of the mentally ill into the non-institutionalised setting. Sometimes complements and sometimes substitutes, the social services can clearly do much to promote good health in the caring community.

The voluntary sector is of considerable interest in any discussion of market and health. In some instances the voluntary organisation will take as its objective the assistance of unknown others suffering from a named complaint: one illustration would be a charitable trust formed to provide a hospice for patients terminally ill with cancer. In other instances the voluntary body will be expressly mutual aid, a self-help club established not to assist anonymous strangers but rather to staunch its own members in their individual resolve. Alcoholics Anonymous is one example of such a problem-solving collective; the discussion group convened by compulsive overeaters is a second. Be it outward-looking or be it an interest pool, what is striking about the voluntary association is the intermediate nature of its orientation. On the one hand the association is non-State: its presence in the private sector serves as a salutary reminder that welfare State and welfare society need not be the same. On the other hand it is non-profit: non-commercial in its success indicators, the fact that its activities so frequently duplicate those of gain-seeking business powerfully underscores the warning that private and public are not perfect synonyms for market and State.

The social services disseminate information about health and care. In that way they make a useful contribution to the important process of health education. They are not alone in being in a position to make such a contribution. Of obvious value will be the work of a fiscally-funded health education council that advertises against saturated fats and excessive carbohydrates, that goes public in its criticism of substance abuse and circulates pamphlets discouraging the inhalation of glue. Then there are the schools, which stimulate health awareness through lessons taught on biology and physiology, nutritious cookery, home economics and (more controversially) the facts of sex and contraception. No doubt much of such education can and should be provided in the home. Parents are not always assiduous or informed, however; and the consequences of the uncorrected deficiency can be serious indeed. Condom is a village on the road to Toulouse – even the most protected child knows that. Less appreciated in the playground might be the latest evidence on whether a woman, drunken, is absolutely protected against possible pregnancy. The school which provides that evidence is not encouraging promiscuity but merely seeing to it that the truth is known.

The media too can usefully disseminate information about health and care. Whether in publicising the dangers of narcotic solvents or in warning against the importation of rabid animals, whether in clarifying the risks from chemical fertilisers or in providing a forum to a politician concerned about salmonella, the radio, the television and the newspapers clearly help to make health-furthering intelligence a common property. Not, of course, that their contribution is an unalloyed benefit. Advertisements for cigarettes are often accused of manipulating the innocent into a lifestyle that will damage their health: while the media often maintain that the campaigns relate to brand-rivalries and not to smoking *per se*, sceptics take the view that the only sure preventative is the total ban.

Yet it is not only the advertising of tobacco that can be a threat to the health. All advertising in a sense embodies such a threat, if only because all advertisers can promise to withdraw their business where a news story detrimental to their commercial interests is not disregarded. A dependence on the pharmaceutical manufacturers must logically be an incentive not to expose a cholesterol-suppressant suspected of weakening the muscles. A dependence on the soap industry must, similarly, be a disincentive to put in the dock a washing powder that is believed to trigger contact dermatitis. The conflict of interest is an undeniable tension, but still the competition of the media provides a private-sector solution. Health news sells newspapers and encourages viewers to switch on: that simple fact is the reason why the commercial objectives of the private-sector media will ultimately cause them to champion the consumer interest by publishing a controversial revelation before a competitor darts in to do so first. Market capitalism in that sense compels the private-sector media *de facto* to fulfil a social service function that is very similar in nature to the intelligence-diffusing role of the traditional social services, narrowly defined. The social worker on the one hand, the commercial channel on the other – here once again, it would appear, the functions that overlap tend in effect to obscure the break in the spectrum.

8.3 THE ENVIRONMENT

The individual can defend his or her health by means of eating sensibly, exercising adequately and resting frequently. The family can contribute (if not through the transmission of pathology-retardant genes) through the inculcation of a propensity neither to worry too much about a sneeze nor too little about a lump. The statutory services can provide information (the anti-smoking campaign), guidance (the leaflet on child health) and support (the trip to the seaside for the elderly deprived). The voluntary sector can extend protection to addicted clients unable to help themselves and, acting more democratically, provide a structure for reciprocal gifts. The provision of care, it is clear, simply cannot be regarded as nothing more than the masked men carrying knives, the sterile theatres supplying soporifics, to which it is so often confined. Health care, like the environment, is in truth all around.

The environment being all around, it too can be mobilised in the service of care and shaped in such a way as to promote the good health of the community. Two dimensions of environmental health would seem in this context to be of particular importance. The first is stimulatory: a basic infrastructure of facilities should be put in place. The second is defensive: the regulation of harmful spillovers should be assured.

With respect to *infrastructural investment*, there is unlikely to be any real disagreement that effective sewers and clean drinking water are conducive to public health whereas stagnant swamps and uncollected refuse are not. Little disagreement is likely to surround the need for the facilities: 'Either lice will defeat socialism or socialism will defeat lice', said Lenin in 1919. Lenin's accurate diagnosis would have been even more accurate if he had added that capitalism is also put at risk by the threat. More contentious than the danger of radon gas escaping from fissures or rats spreading plague from kitchen to kitchen is, however, the answer to Lenin's perceptive query of 'what is to be done?'. More contentious than the need is, in other words, the optimal mode of sanitisation through investment.

Observers convinced by the doctrine of market failure will say that the transaction-costs of collecting user-charges and the economic overhead of excluding free riders would be so high as to render infrastructural investment commercially unattractive to private business. Water mains purified of aluminium and lead, fluoridation to reduce tooth decay, chlorination that combats bacillary dysentery, the eradication of open drains that make a public show of hazardous toxins and contaminated wastes – desirable projects such as these, it is argued, will never voluntarily be undertaken by profit-seeking enterprise. *Ex* the State, it is concluded, these projects will almost certainly not be undertaken at all.

Other observers are less convinced, however, that markets are inevitably exposed to failure, that the State must therefore be prepared to act the residual supplier by default. Much of the apparent failure, such sceptics will say, is not so much a deficiency in the market for health as it is a severe lack of imagination on the part of social analysts afraid to think creatively. The consumer will often be in a position actively to find his own redress: witness the bottles of mineral water and the domestic filters that are purchased by health-conscious households unsatisfied by the minimum standards that some at least of their fellows are more than prepared to accept. The employer will often be prepared to treat as occupational health that which he would naturally prefer to see a public responsibility: consider the draining of a swamp at the cost not of the non-judgemental nation but of the wealthy landowner whose labour force is daily exposed for his profit to the risk of illness. In cases such as these, clearly, a part of what is loosely called market failure might in truth be no more the failure of individuals to get involved – or the failure of the State to encourage them to supply good health at the margin.

De facto privatisation need not, of course, mean a financial burden borne exclusively by the market sector. Compelling the conversion to unleaded fuels, the State could provide a grant towards the elimination of the polluting emissions. Concerned about skin cancers and eye cataracts resulting from ultra-violet radiation, the State could provide a subsidy towards the phasing out of ozone-depleting aerosols, refrigerators and insulating foams. Committed to competition even in the face of the natural monopoly, the State could franchise the sewers to the licensee promising maximal improvement while at the same time offering a tax holiday in order to make the spending economically worthwhile. There are, in short, a significant number of combinations and permutations that love the dance in the open space that separates pure market from total State. Less contentious than the optimal mode of delivery is, however, the need for the infrastructural investment.

With respect to *regulatory control*, the same agglomeration of combinations and permutations, still whirling and jigging betwixt private and public, is yet again to be encountered. On the one hand there is much consensus that the consumer should be protected through sound sell-by dates (set perhaps with the supplementary objective of speeding up the distribution process) and truthful labelling of food additives (including pesticide residues and antibiotic sprays); that no individual not considerationed by a contract should be exposed to air, rivers and beaches (let alone fish sold as fresh) contaminated by radioactive waste and industrial effluent; that sheep tissues and growth hormones should not secretly be fed to pigs, cattle and poultry where the purchaser has been given to understand that his food chain has remained scrupulously unthreatened. On the other hand there is some dissensus as to *who* ought properly to bell the cat and as to *how* the aforementioned feline ought properly to be belled.

Clearly, the State could assume responsibility for the stringent monitoring of vacuum-packed sliced ham, pâté and soft cheese. Yet so too could the manufacturers (to prevent the debasement of their brand name through an association with listeria) and the retailers to boot (so as to outrival less health-conscious competitors, to keep up sales, to preserve their reputation, to ward off legal claims). Even the commercial sector, it would appear, can have solid market incentives not to undermine health but rather to protect it.

Nor should it be forgotten that not all consumers will want cast-iron protection if it unduly puts up the cost of the product. Pregnant women, cancer patients and the vulnerable elderly might welcome a guaranteed standard, either from the State sector or the private, but the representative consumer, trusting in the healthy body's normal capacity to resist disease, might be somewhat less enthusiastic about the financial burden of regular checks and the administrative back-up. In such as case, the legislated minimum and the environmental health officer will appear a necessity to some citizens, a luxury to others; and there might not be any single course of action that appeals equally to all.

Thus A, a worker, will recognise that the employer has no economic incentive to invest in the durable capital asset represented by the long-term health status of workers who are seldom with a single employer for life: nervous A will accordingly demand that the State legislate for occupational safety lest a self-seeking exploiter be tempted to skimp on prevention. Yet B, also a worker, will oppose such a regulation: aware that high pay will be jeopardised by new entrants the moment that the employer is forced to install expensive air conditioning, convinced that good compensation will be awarded to workers suffering industrial injury, greedy B will argue that the State ought not to intervene but that A ought simply to find himself an employer who promises the standard of prevention that A desires. To please B is to harm A. To please A is to harm B. The same regulation would please both members of the community provided only that both thought alike. But they do not.

9 The Doctor

Some doctors are generalists (the family doctor or general practitioner) while others are specialists (the hospital consultant, the expert surgeon). The normal system is for primary care to be the first step, and for the family doctor then to act as the gatekeeper who refers the case upwards if it requires attention more sophisticated than he or she personally can provide. Sometimes, however, the patient goes in the first instance directly to the specialist (a familiar scenario in the case of the dentist, the optician or the psychiatrist); and sometimes, too, the general practitioner has some specialist expertise (to such a standard, indeed, that he might himself be capable of treating the patient in hospital). There is no hard-and-fast rule that the generalist and the specialist should be separate breeds, but this is the most common system.

The fact that primary care doctors are the primary decision-makers is a mode of protection for the consumer: ill-informed about medical matters, unlikely to have the same operation so frequently that he can learn from experience, the patient has much to gain from the impartial advice of the family doctor. The general practitioner ideally has background knowledge of the patient and a shared medical history extending backwards so far that he is able quickly to detect changes in appearance, psychological state and other indices of health and illness. Such stability, such continuity, is a great asset, permitting as it does an assessment of the whole person in a way that would be impossible if, say, the first line of defence were to be (as it so often is in under-doctored areas, or at evenings and week-ends) the local hospital's busy outpatients' clinic. The general practitioner will ideally have some knowledge of the patient's home and family circumstances and frequently the patient's economic status as well. Even the most complete of medical histories will seldom record a bedroom that is damp, or a protective partner willing to serve as a domestic carer, or an income high enough to cover optional services. This information can nonetheless be of considerable value where the objective of the medical encounter is to treat the person, not just the person's disease.

The general practitioner will make it his business to screen and filter the petitions that are put to him by the patients who initiate the process of therapy when they treat his offices as their first port of call. His diagnosis will not always please, but at least it serves to protect the anxious and the ignorant from unnecessary treatment and (where the care bears a user-charge) from avoidable cost. It also defends the health system as a whole from ruinous burdens that would have little impact on the hypochondriac's symptoms. The principal variable cost of the primary consultation is the practitioner's time. However protracted the visit, the cost to the system of that time is likely to be far less than where the patient is unnecessarily referred to a state-of-the-art hospital for unwarranted tests and perhaps even for marginal treatments.

The diagnosis made, the general practitioner will then ideally outline the various possibilities and explain why he is calling in supplementary counsel. In discussing the malfunction and the cure, he will in effect be inviting the patient and the family to have an impact on the decision that is made. Even if they choose to waive their rights, they are likely to regard as desirably democratic a procedure that allows them to register an opinion should they wish to do so.

The treatment selected, the general practitioner might involve himself directly in the process of delivery. This is especially likely where the case is simple or where the doctor is a partner in a group practice that encourages each member of the team (which may enjoy the valuable back-up of a chiropodist, a counsellor, an ethnic community link-worker) to keep up his or her expertise by specialising on a particular therapeutic procedure. Alternatively, the general practitioner might shop around for care on the patient's behalf. The general practitioner knows the medical reputation of the specialist professionals. They in turn know that if they are unreliable or do not provide value for money they will not secure further referrals.

The intervention delivered, the general practitioner makes a *de facto* evaluation *ex post* of the quality of service and monitors the patient's recovery: the availability of such back-up doctoring in the period of convalescence is a stimulus to early discharge, where ambulatory care then economises on costly hospitalisation. The general practitioner, it must be concluded, is a valuable part of the network of care. That is why it is to be regretted that in some countries the generalist regards himself (and is so regarded by others) merely as a would-be specialist who couldn't make the grade. Lower incomes and lower prestige cause the pool of family doctors to contract. The result is a service medically and economically inferior to that which is supplied where the generalist doctor and the specialist doctor are fortunate enough to enjoy a symbiotic relationship.

This chapter is concerned with the provision of care by the doctor, whether specialist or generalist. It is divided into two sections. The first, dealing with price, considers the alternative ways in which doctors (either in the private sector or where paid by the State) might be remunerated. The second, dealing with quantity, examines entry qualifications and manpower forecasting.

9.1 REMUNERATION

The payment of doctors raises important issues of public policy. Remuneration is active; and different modes of payment potentially introduce different biases into the behaviour patterns of the professionals. The economic bias can, of course, never be more than potential. Professional ethic and personal decency, the desire to use advanced skills and the opportunity to contribute to research, a commitment to patients' health and a love of peer group recognition, these and other countervailing incentives will normally interact with income-maximisation and workload-minimisation. They will render the precise force of the more mercenary motives that much difficult to model and predict, even at the margin which is the natural habitat of the orthodox economist. Yet the economic bias remains for all that a real possibility: sometimes more serious (as where the doctor happens also to be part-owner of the profit-seeking hospital in which he operates), sometimes less serious (as where the doctor is paid by results, however uncertain and probabilistic), the potential bias remains a real threat that must be kept in mind as the three principal modes of remuneration of medical professionals come to be considered.

(a) Fee for Service

In some cases the doctor is an independent contractor, often with his own premises, who is paid a fee by the patient (or the patient's insurer) in respect of services rendered. The temptation that he then faces is an obvious one: to expand the services in order to multiply the fees.

Sometimes the conflict of interest will be muted: thus additional check-ups, diagnostic tests, injections and consultations might be recommended which, irrespective of the pecuniary benefits to the doctor, could conceivably yield medical benefits to the patient as well. At other times the operation of the perverse incentives will be less subtle: this is the case where visits are abridged in order to pack more patients in, or where preventive medicine is deliberately ignored because the real profit lies in curative, or where the doctor elects to perform an unfamiliar procedure in which he has little expertise because to refer would mean to lose a fee. In more extreme circumstances the abuse of confidence will be blatant: thus the doctor might unnecessarily prolong the patient's stay in a convalescent home of which he is a co-proprietor, or overuse specialist equipment in order to ensure rapid depreciation, or overprescribe drugs to be dispensed at a profit by a pharmacy in which he holds an interest, or charge significantly more for injections than he himself paid for the medicines, or expect fee-splitting and commissions in consequence of referrals made to particular surgeons or clinics. The traditional illustration of asymmetrical information exploited for money is the unneeded tonsillectomy or the groundless appendectomy, where optional surgery is recommended exclusively because of the fee-seeker's greed. The general lesson is that *ceteris paribus* the economic burden tends to rise and the standard of care to decay once humane trustworthiness is undermined by financial interest. As Abel-Smith points out: 'Where under the fee schedule extra payment is made for undertaking procedures, the emphasis in the consultation can be distorted to doing rather than observing and listening. The quicker the doctor decides to act, the higher the remuneration and the more he acts, the more he can claim.'[1]

The doctors faces an obvious temptation to act, but so too does every shopper to steal. Temptation is no proof of commission and no one but the most mean-minded of misanthropists will want to assume that it is. If it is the custom in a country for the general practitioner to act as adjunct hospital doctor for his patient, it cannot necessarily be inferred that he is supplying the service wholly or mainly because he is hungry for the fee. If it is the case that the patient who has paid for the consultation will not come away satisfied without at least a prescription, it would arguably be wrong to attribute the resultant over-treatment exclusively to the avarice of the supplier and not at all to the consumer's demands that the competitor is under great pressure to satisfy. Besides that, any attempt at quantity-discrimination or price-discrimination on the part of the practitioner must be blunted by the doctor's own ignorance of what the patient can afford. The doctor will employ proxies such as profession, place of residence, family responsibilities, education, but none of these is ever as reliable as the authentic data on income and wealth to which he seldom has access. One should, one suspects, always take great care not to impute evil motives to others without making due allowance for all the relevant circumstances.

Yet there is no denying the temptation faced by fallen man to neglect time-consuming tasks that generate no extra income while erring on the side of caution by over-supplying for gain. Nor is the patient himself likely to deny it. Aware that more services mean more fees (and aware too that all surgery means risk as well as cost), the patient might decide to defend himself against a doctor whose advice he fears might not be impartial by means of seeking a second opinion – and paying a second fee.

(b) Capitation Fee

In the case of the capitation fee the doctor, once again an independent contractor, is paid an annual sum by the patient's insurer (or by the patient). The doctor agrees in exchange to supply all specified services (notably those of primary care) to all registered for the duration of the negotiated time-period.

The doctor's income being a function of fee per person and not of fee per consultation, it will clearly not be in his financial interest to pyramid services, some of them unneeded. Instead, economically speaking, he will have an incentive to maximise his revenue while minimising his trouble. Thus the doctor, economically speaking, will have a preference for a long list over a short one (even if the result is lightning consultations, faceless bodies and unnoticed pathologies) and for healthy patients over sickly ones (even if the clients refused by one doctor are subsequently rejected as high-burden frequent-presenters by a succession of others). The family doctor in such a system will have no particular reason to treat time-consuming complaints himself: referrals to specialists will cut his workload but his own remuneration will not be affected. With respect to preventive medicine the prediction is less clear. Much depends on the doctor's own trade-off between extra work now and extra work later, weighted by the probability that the patient will be in the care of a different practitioner by the time the uncorrected condition ultimately develops into diagnosis and treatment.

Theoretically one would expect professionals on capitation not to congregate in highly-doctored areas but to spread themselves in a more or less even manner over the population that is the source of their business. In practice there tends to be a surprising measure of concentration among the competitors. Urban areas and their affluent suburbs offer psychic income in the form of amenities that compensate for any tendency towards shorter lists; and it is also the case that a supplementary practice on a fee-for-service basis is easier to build up where the catchment is wealthy than where it is poor. That is why the funding body (particularly where it is the State) will often opt to pay a differential capitation fee in under-doctored areas. An increased local availability of hospital beds and health visitors would no doubt make the neglected regions that much more attractive as well.

A funding body wishing to employ a more sensitive instrument than geographical weighting alone might, of course, opt to relate the differential capitation not to places but rather to persons. Where the capitation fee is standard within the area, there arises a horizontal inequity (even where practitioners' lists are of equal length) as between doctors whose patients make unequal demands. Doctors in such an undifferentiated system will tend to welcome healthy locals but will be reluctant to register difficult clients likely to make disproportionate claims. Where the capitation fee is not uniform but adjusted upwards for high-use categories, however, the standing of the old, the infirm and the occupationally at-risk is bound to rise in consequence of the institutionalised recognition that above-average consultation rates merit above-average financial rewards. Should the high-need groups turn out to be geographically concentrated, such discrimination by persons will have the same tendency to attract professionals to under-doctored areas that is enjoyed by capitation differentiated by place. In the one case as in the other the offer of the differentiated capitation is a clear admission that doctors, at least at the margin, are sensitive to the monetary incentive.

On top of the capitation fee a small number of additional fees might usefully be offered to stimulate the provision of discretionary services. Thus doctors might be invited to claim payment by piece-rate for cases treated without referral (minor surgery, immunisation, antenatal care) or for preventive work (smears, screening, contraceptive advice), or for treating out-of area patients not on their list, or for home visits and night visits, or for travelling long distances in rural areas, or for attending short courses on new developments. Perhaps also a ceiling limit should be imposed on the list to discourage doctors from accepting more patients than they can conscientiously treat without exposing their clients to the risks that are inevitable when the practitioner is overworked and in a hurry.

With respect to abuse of the capitation system not by a supplier but by the consumer, there might be an argument for rationing by waiting times and the deterrence of user-changers: the doctor on the capitation fee has no incentive to over-provide (as he does where paid by fee for service) but he is clearly vulnerable to his patients, who might seek unashamedly to over-demand in the absence of any incentive to limit their wants. Yet the rationing and the deterrence might in truth prove perverse and malign where the consequence is that the genuinely ill fail to obtain the treatment they require; while the imposed ceiling to the list might reasonably be criticised on the grounds that the individual doctor alone is the proper judge of the workload that he or she can handle. Nor should it be supposed that the supplementary fee is an unmixed blessing: productivity rises (since more ears are syringed) and accountability is promoted (since the community is given an itemised bill) but the counterpart of these benefits is administrative complexity (since the invoices must be processed), medical selectivity (since the incentive relates exclusively to a subset of services), mass production (since the rate per piece is seldom quality-controlled) and even over-production (since the fee for service is potentially the trigger for the unnecessary procedure). It must therefore be concluded that additional fees and maximal lists, waiting times and user-charges, can usefully be employed in an attempt to fine-tune the capitation system but cannot for all that be regarded automatically as conferring benefits not accompanied by costs.

(c) Salary

The doctor could receive his fee for service or his capitation directly from the patient as well as from an insuring agency, but only a very rich person could afford to retain a doctor on salary. The salary is at any rate the third payment-option. It is in Britain the standard payment-option for the hospital doctor. Not so in the United States, incidentally, where large numbers of hospital doctors are 'attending physicians', independent fee-earners not on the full-time salaried staff of a single institution.

Payment by salary is remuneration that is not proportioned either to services rendered or to patients registered: it is in the nature of the salary scale with its annual increments that length of service is employed as the proxy for performance. At least the scale normally incorporates salary bars, discretionary points, distinct grades and therewith the principle of promotion based on merit. The career structure offers in that sense a financial incentive to maintain a reasonable standard of service, to combine quality control with requisite economic awareness, to keep up-to-date with new treatments, new drugs and new developments such as will stand the promotion-seeking practitioner in good stead when faced with the challenge of the peer-review. The employer can encourage such upgrading of knowledge by providing in-service training; by subsidising refresher courses offered by medical schools or professional bodies; by permitting paid sabbaticals to perfect old skills or to acquire new ones. The opportunity to learn without loss of income is far less common in the fee-for-service or the capitation system. Less common but not for all that unheard-of. One of the advantages of a national health service is often said to be that it sets itself the objective of encouraging in-service education even for the nominally independent. It can afford the risk of doing so. Approaching the status of a monopsonist with respect to the services of general practitioners, the likelihood that a national health service will lose its investment to its rivals will seldom be very great.

Doctors will welcome the guaranteed income for its own sake. They will also welcome the guaranteed income for the beneficial impact that it has upon their professional relationships with their fellow doctors. Unlike fee for service or capitation, payment by salary means that other practitioners, no longer dangerous competitors, will be seen either as permitting extra work to be performed or as sharing existing burdens without also eroding living standards. Similarly with the formation of group practices: doctors on salary are not rivals for the same pool of business and are therefore more likely to collaborate and to cooperate.

The paymasters too will find much to admire in the salary scale. Unlike fee for service or capitation, the precise budget for doctoring is not demand-determined but rather fixed in advance. Also, the criteria applied in the promotions exercise can be such as stimulate cost-effective conduct alongside technical expertise. Nor should it be forgotten that differential pay (where scales are not rigidly national) can be utilised to encourage mobility into less-popular areas (the neglected inner city or the under-doctored countryside, say) and out of over-subscribed employments (the prestigious post in the teaching hospital, for example). Pay correlated with local scarcity is not the same as pay legitimated by peer-assessments; but that is no reason for the social planner to dismiss the local differential as a substitute for other norms when in truth it can complement them well.

Payment by salary is, however, subject to a certain number of disadvantages. Not the least of these is the danger that doctors, concentrating on promotion-related criteria, might opt for the under-supplying of valuable activities (including unorthodox procedures) that do not show up in appraisals. As with omission, so with commission, and thence the further perverse incentive that promotion by demonstrated competence might cause doctors to perform unnecessary operations merely in order to acquire proof of experience. Again, promotion by merit may conflict with promotion by seniority and in that way leave the bureaucratised incentive-structure somewhat over-determined. There is much to be said for the traditional defence that length of service is a reasonable proxy for quality of workmanship. Yet the age-related system does undeniably break the direct link between pay and performance.

Poor performers who remain in the system but fail to win promotion constitute a further problem. They may become demoralised and lacking in assiduity. They may substitute on-the-job leisure for work (say, by extending in-patient stays so as to reduce the throughput of surgery). They may reserve their real commitment for the small private practice that the system normally permits. They may even serve as paid locums to more successful colleagues offered high fees outside the hierarchy. Successful performers, meanwhile, suffer from anxiety as well as overwork, aware as they are that their career can be blighted by a mistake. Such anxiety may cause them to prescribe a stream of expensive tests and marginal interventions first and foremost as a means of insuring their future career prospects at a zero financial cost to themselves. Since the doctor on salary has (unlike the doctor on fee for service) no economic incentive to supply more than the minimum it may, of course, be the case that the additional services that are supplied by the self-protective practitioner do no more in the end than to correct a preexistent imbalance.

The position of the consumer where the doctor is on salary is an exposed one. The patient clearly has no economic sanctions to deploy against rudeness, unfriendliness, poor bedside manner or lack of human contact: the fee-for-service or capitation patient who changes his doctor in disgust will penalise that doctor with loss of income but the salary-system patient who goes elsewhere only reduces the offending doctor's workload. Where pay is not correlated with clients' assessments, the consumer will always be vulnerable in this way to a measure of neglect. While neglect is not the same as professional abuse or serious misconduct (against which the lawsuit provides the ultimate defence), still it is clear that much would be gained by the decision-makers if they went out of their way to let the patient speak.

At the very least the consumer should be encouraged to reveal his preferences by means of choosing and changing his doctor until such a time as he settles upon a practitioner with whom he feels comfortable. Such choices and changes should be carefully monitored and, in order to protect both the consumer and the feedback, contracting and recontracting should be free and easy despite the inconvenience to the administrators of customers who stubbornly prolong their search. Yet many unsatisfied consumers, either out of inertia or because they are ignorant of what other suppliers are able to deliver, simply do not vote with their feet. Thus it is that inspection of figures on choices and changes ought ideally to be complemented by an independent inspectorate, by a complaints procedure, and by questionnaires and surveys such as spotlight the apathetic and pinpoint the irresponsible.

So direct a mode of consumer consultation will be vulnerable to the obvious difficulty that the medically ignorant are being asked to evaluate the medically informed. Some critics will dismiss it out of hand as an invitation to inveterate hypochondriacs and chronic complainers. Others will go so far as to condemn it as wasteful of resources to the point of being counter-productive. Thus it might be asserted that the doctor, required to please the consumer to win his promotion, will act against his own better judgement (basing himself on wants rather than needs) by referring a persistent and troublesome patient purely in order to protect his assessment. The same point reversed suggests that there might be discriminatory neglect of the self-effacing who do not complain: self-interest dictates that the elective should be reserved for the difficult whose critical comments would otherwise look bad in the file. Disadvantages such as these undoubtedly reduce the value of the subjective information that is obtained through questionnaires and surveys – but do not imply that the feedback has no value at all. Ideally supported by the objective checks of medical audit and in-service monitoring, the subjective input will be of considerable interest to anyone who believes patient's opinion to be in any way relevant to the vexed question of how the doctor ought best to be remunerated.

9.2 ENTRY

In few countries is practitioner's performance made subject to continuous assessment. Understandably, therefore, it is to stringent checks on the professional calibre of new entrants that the potential patient most frequently looks for protection against the depredations of the frauds and the quacks, the charlatans and the incompetents. Asymmetrical information leads uncorrected to market failure, it is argued; while rigorous testing provides the consumer with the assurance that the supplier has attained a specified standard of proficiency. The licensure may be the prerogative of a professional body or it may be the charge of a State board but its purpose, in the one case as in the other, is avowedly defensive: entry controls protect the consumer who lacks the knowledge to protect himself.

Controls that screen and filter confer the benefit that they block off market failure arising from unsubstantiated claims. With the benefit comes, however, a cost. The narrow gateway means limited access and restricted competition. The higher standard of service means a lower number of practitioners admitted. The harm would be less if the job description of the doctor were unambiguous or the optimal doctor–patient ratio the object of consensus. Yet they are not, and thence the problem that one person's safeguard is another person's exclusion. Not every consumer will want the same quality of service; the average level of competence can be too high for Jack even as it is too low for Jill; and some patients might actually welcome the chance to pay less for less. To deprive them of the opportunity to reveal such preferences – and to reap the associated gains from trade – is in effect to reduce their felt welfare. As Frech puts it: 'The argument that licensure benefits the public by raising quality is faulty. If consumers choose a lower quality level than they really desire, they lack adequate information. If licensure raises quality above the level that consumers actually prefer, a cost will result, not a benefit.'[2] And that tax the self-aware best judge will not necessarily be keen to pay.

Imposed standards can be too high. They can also be too homogeneous. A unique gateway means a uniform specification. Different consumers, however, might want different things. The existence of the alternative sector is a case in point. The supply of fringe and complementary practitioners offering non-orthodox treatments such as homoeopathy, osteopathy, hypnosis, herbalism, reflexology, iridology, aromatherapy or acupuncture must be indicative of an unsatisfied demand. Yet such practitioners (even when equipped with certificates from their own professional bodies that prove their professional categorisation not to be fraudulently claimed) are generally regarded not merely as differentiated from the mainstream but as inferior to it. Non-orthodox practitioners are seldom classified as approved outlets for purposes of national or private insurance (consultations being therefore on a non-reimbursable fee-paying basis). They are not normally entitled to prescribe dangerous drugs or to issue a death certificate. They are seldom if ever allowed staff privileges in hospitals (a denial occasionally extended as well to orthodox practitioners employed by non-orthodox agencies such as health maintenance organisations). Alternative practitioners are, in short, the subject of a number of discriminatory measures that restrict the range of choices (both actual and potential) that are on offer to the consumer of care. So monolithic an approach to occupational self-definition is difficult to reconcile with variety and diversity such as the self-aware best judge is seen so often to value in markets where, admittedly, uncertainty and ignorance on the demand side do represent a threat to rational choice, and perhaps even to survival itself.

Nor is the traditional gateway always easy to reconcile with the invention and innovation, the discovery and change, that are the essence of medical science. The intended objective of the conventional standard being the screening of the new through the filter of the old, the bias is bound to favour the *status quo*. The purpose of the bias is to maximise the likelihood that past successes, however moderate, will be repeated in the future – and to minimise the likelihood that something truly dreadful will happen as a result of inadequate professional discipline. The conservative's bias will be shared by all who believe that there is medical consensus on standard treatment, that the disinterested ethic of non-commercial conduct would come under threat were professional practice to be heterogeneous, that deplorable spillovers such as epidemics could easily result were the ill-informed patient encouraged to make an unwise choice, that prestigious professional lobbies genuinely have the public good at heart. Yet medicine is not an exact science; and there will therefore be some observers who will argue in defence of a less self-satisfied approach to the standards imposed in the course of occupational licensure.

Occupational licensure always means that the new entrant has demonstrated his knowledge and expertise through satisfactory performance in qualifying examinations. The license is in that sense a written guarantee to the uncertain and the ignorant. It confirms that the practitioner followed an approved curriculum at some time in the past and that he was tested competent by his peers prior to being permitted membership in their mystery. The guarantee is depressingly date-stamped, however, where the information it conveys relates exclusively to knowledge and expertise at the moment of entry and not at all to knowledge and expertise at the time the consumer is contemplating the consultation. Past examination successes are no real guarantee of present-day competence, no real proof that the practitioner remains in touch with new developments. Yet the probability is low that the doctor once on the register will be struck off for anything less than gross misconduct or flagrant dishonesty – anything, say, like simply not being very good. A profession genuinely anxious to retain popular confidence would therefore insist, logically speaking, not just on strict standards at the time of admission but on compulsory in-service training and periodic relicensing as well. Particularly where a primary care doctor is self-employed (and thus escapes the statutory retirement age), particularly where he trades as a one-man practice (and thereby escapes the continuous monitoring and collective discipline of the medical partnership), there it is genuinely possible that his learning will have ceased half a century before his treatments. Such a possibility few of his patients will contemplate with true indifference. Thence the argument for regular relicensing, perhaps once every ten years.

It is a matter of record that professional bodies are normally opposed to such reviews. No doubt their hostility is partly to be explained in terms of the vested interest of a closed shop that restricts entry through high standards while simultaneously concealing the traces of incompetence among the incumbents: a parallel may perhaps be drawn with the professional pressures that prevent one doctor from criticising another in public. Yet vested interest is by no means the only explanation of the professional bodies' opposition to re-examination. For one thing, they might maintain, evaluation can and does proceed by means other than examination: thus medical audit collects comparative data on diagnoses, treatments, achievements and failures while inter-personal contact (as where more than one surgeon is active in an operation) serves as a potent force for continuous inspection. Besides that, it is by no means clear what sort of questions ought to be included in the relicensing test. A general practitioner ought, after all, not only to be able to identify diseases and name drugs but also to be prepared to shop around on behalf of his client. The patient's ignorance with respect to specialists and approaches ought not to be compounded by that of his adviser (a lazy agent, say, whose standard procedure is automatically to refer to the same individual or institution), but few observers would for all that want to see a doctor publicly stigmatised for being unable to answer questions relating to the business side of the practice. Even more difficult to assess is the human dimension of the doctor–patient relationship. For some people the general practitioner replaces the priest or the friend as the confessor of last resort. What the patient most requires in such a case is not medical care, narrowly defined, but rather the pastoral role of the listening ear combined with the welfare function of putting isolates in touch with non-medical services. Few if any relicensing schemes will pick up the valuable but non-technocratic side of the medical encounter. Opponents of relicensing may therefore conclude that such schemes are both unnecessary and unworkable.

Occupational licensure is a mode of certification: it confirms to the consumer that the practitioner has successfully passed certain examinations. Normally, moreover, occupational licensure provides a supplementary guarantee as well: not only does it confirm that the new entrant was found by examination to have attained a pre-specified level of knowledge and expertise, it normally also indicates that the entrant acquired the excellence as the result of completing an approved course of study in a recognised institution. The two hurdles of testing and training could be separated, as where attendance at a medical school were not made the precondition for taking (and passing) the licensing examination. In practice they tend to be combined. The consequence is that the existing generation of practitioners is given not one but two opportunities to pre-specify curriculum content and to control numbers.

It would be wrong to accuse the profession of excessive traditionalism combined with excessive greed when the truth might be that greater ease of entry would genuinely threaten the standard of excellence. What might reasonably be proposed as a compromise, however, would be for the profession to retain its hold over licensing and standards but to release its grip on medical education. Educational liberalisation would then lead to a proliferation of medical schools differentiated by entry requirements, teaching methods, fees charged, recommended length of study such as would replicate at home the position that has long obtained worldwide. Unknown graduates of foreign medical schools have long enjoyed a considerable measure of international mobility (even without global free trade in doctoring). Their successful integration despite their differentiated training would seem to suggest that the professional monopolisation of domestic schools might usefully be called into question. The hurdle of training devolved, the corporatised profession could then concentrate its energies on the hurdle of testing in order to ensure that no practitioner, however trained, would enjoy a licence to practice who had not attained a pre-specified standard of knowledge and expertise. The factual knowledge is easy enough to examine. The practical expertise is more of a problem: few readers of this or any other book would want to be the patient who underwent the operation on the basis of which the would-be doctor failed to win his credential. Be that as it may, the broader point is clear enough, that training is training, examining is examining, and there is no reason to expect that educating and licensing must inevitably take the form of a single bundle. To break up that bundle, to pluralise the education while centralising the licensure, would arguably do much to ensure that greater freedom of entry would not lead to a diminution of respect or trust.

Occupational licensure is a mode of certification. As a means of labelling it is one option among many: the range extends from alternative paper qualifications to word of mouth, personal recommendation and established reputation. The guidance which the license provides to the consuming public is without any doubt of considerable value. As a means of excluding from practice all but those who have followed a single path and espouse a single norm it is, however, somewhat more controversial. It is one thing to certify calibre and quite another to deny entry to the uncertified, the less certified and the differently certified. This is not to say that certification by professional bodies or by State boards should be terminated, only that the consumer's freedom of choice would be expanded if legal barriers to the practice of medicine by those without the single standard certificate were to be removed. Certifying examinations could be retained as a means of providing the consumer with a standardised yardstick; and the voluntary selection of a traditionally-certified practitioner would, naturally, remain an option even in a deregulated system. What would happen under deregulation is not that existing choice-sets would be closed off but rather that the range of alternatives would be expanded. New modes of certification would emerge (not least on the part of consumerist and commercial organisations: 'This' Friedman says, 'is something the private market generally can do for itself'[3]). New forms of provision would arise (including paramedical doctoring in simpler cases such as the setting of a broken arm). The result would be a spectrum of standards rather than a single gateway.

The State in so open a market might, restriction of entry and certification of competence swept away by pluralism and decentralisation, decide that it has no further role to play apart from the enforcement of the law of contract that guarantees to the consumer the right to sue for redress in case of breach. Alternatively, it might decide that the minimal option of simple registration is called for lest untruthful practitioners, as Milton Friedman indicates, take advantage of unequal information to frustrate the spirit of the agreement: 'I do not think that one can rule out on grounds of principle the possibility that there may be certain activities that are so likely to give rise to fraud as to render it desirable to have in advance a list of people known to be pursuing this activity.'[4]

Thus the State (perhaps devolving the actual operation of the scheme to a private-sector databank) might decide to require of all those defining themselves to be the practitioners of a health-related craft to put their particulars on record for inspection by their prospective clients. The data on the register would vary from traditional qualifications to tabulated outcomes to customers' testimonials, and it would be difficult to exclude diplomas of dubious intellectual worth (some of them all but purchased for money); but at least the prospective client would have the full facts before him – together with the name and address of the practitioner in case something went wrong. The client would then make his own choice according to his own criteria. Some, thoroughly confused by the possibilities, would no doubt wish most sincerely for the restoration of professional self-regulation that, even if unaccountable power and a restrictive practice, at least was prepared to tell them the nature of their needs. Such persons are to be reminded that traditional advisers will almost certainly be available even in a liberalised system: a belief in choice is not antithetical to a belief in custom, and most consumers are also profoundly conservative.

Liberalised entry affects more than choices. It also influences numbers. The entry controls that are implemented by the medical schools and the professional bodies on behalf of the State have the effect of shaping supply in the image of the manpower plan. The relaxation or removal of those controls inevitably conjures up the spectre of shortages and surpluses, bottlenecks and lags. No one will view the non-optimal balance between practitioners and needs with any real enthusiasm (even when one reflects that vast excess demand for places in medical schools does suggest that liberalisation is more likely to mean *too many* than it is *too few*). Yet no one will find it easy to propound a single definition of optimality and balance capable of appealing equally to all three of the intellectual constituencies that hold strong views on the appropriate standard.

The *first* constituency relies on professional judgements. It seeks to forecast the incidence of medical needs at some date in the future and to translate those needs both into medical services and into doctor hours as estimated by leading consultants. It then formulates normative guidelines as to the mix of expertise that will be required at the target date and the precise numbers of practitioners that ought to be equipped with the disparate skills appropriate to each of the manpower categories.

Manpower policies informed by professional judgements will be weak on substitution, whether of capital for labour or of less-qualified for more-qualified staff: professional rigidities and the tyranny of the *status quo* will be a positive disincentive to the rethinking of functions, even if the organisational realignment were to be capable of saving the skilled practitioner for the genuine challenge by means of hiving off the more routine tasks to machines, drugs and auxiliaries. Nor do such manpower policies make much allowance for cost: professional judgements made of the ideal doctor–population ratio would be the same if the remuneration of the doctor were to be doubled as they would be if the payment were to be cut by half. The economic rent associated with entry restriction is unquestioningly accepted as the necessary price of best-possible practice; little interest is shown in the minimisation of burdens (including the travelling-time and waiting-time of the patient); and no technique is proposed that would facilitate comparison between spending on health care and other claims (that of education, say) on scarce social resources. Manpower policies informed by professional judgements will evidently have the greatest appeal to those members of the community who are prepared to set aside substitution and cost. They will be convinced that, when all is said and done, it is the expert and the expert alone who can specify the professional optimum.

The *second* constituency is administrative and extrapolative in nature. It does not rely heavily on the advice of doctors (which it treats as subject to the bias of vested interest). Instead it proceeds by means of projections based upon the present practices either of the country in question or of some comparable country – a country that either has different ratios somehow judged superior or that is, simply, situated at a higher stage in its economic development.

The projections will relate to the ratio of practitioners to population (allowance made for expected changes in key demand-side variables such as income and age structure). They will also incorporate the ratio of one specialism to its complements (surgeons to anaesthetists to nurses to midwives to radiographers to physiotherapists, in other words, in a coordinated matrix that is the sworn enemy of the wheel that lacks the crucial cog). Future demand predicted, arrangements can then be made to educate the appropriate supply by means of regulating the capacity of the medical colleges. The planners will no doubt aim at a small overshoot in recognition of probable losses due to premature death, emigration, transfer to administrative positions, withdrawal into non-medical employments. The planners will strive nonetheless to keep costly over-supply to the safe minimum: *too many* means a waste of specialist training even if *too few*, arguably, means a waste that is, morally speaking, that much more serious.

The planners will have to make some allowance for putative changes in medical technology over the lifespan of the training (although no one can foresee with any real accuracy what these will be). An estimate will also have to be incorporated of the impact on doctor's productivity of a better educated and more affluent community (although the contradictory pull of *longer* consultations due to *embourgeoisement* and *less frequent* consultations due to improved nutrition suggests that a guesstimate utilising the entrails of a representative fowl might be more appropriate). The planners will have in addition to satisfy themselves that the ratios they employ as their base are not concealed by frustrated demand (the problem of the under-doctored area unable to find suppliers and the uninsured household unable to pay); or boosted by unwarranted manipulation (the case of producer-led consumption in communities where the doctoring stock would *ex* the endless tests and the frequent check-ups be conspicuously in surplus); or distorted by market imperfections (not least among them the rigid conventions and fixed coefficients promulgated by the professional bodies). The planners will not in short find their task of projection an easy one. It will be their belief, however, that present conditions (suitably corrected) give useful guidance as to future needs; and that the medical schools (adequately coordinated) can therefore safely use such extrapolations as the basis for their admissions policies.

The *third* constituency adopts a position that is essentially economic. Unconvinced that the expert knows best what the patient requires or that the administrator is able to predict the future course of needs and wants, this third group of thinkers maintains that optimality of doctoring and nursing has no meaning independent of gain-seeker's supply and utility-seeker's demand. Entry barriers and restrictive practices would have to be abandoned; inflexible lines of demarcation would have to be erased; remuneration would have to become individualised and competitive. The free market made, this third group of thinkers tends to argue, the correct number of medical professionals will emerge automatically, as if guided by an invisible hand that equates marginal returns from alternative occupations (allowance made for non-pecuniary benefits) and ensures that all services will be supplied at minimum cost (allowance made for travelling times).

The most radical scenario would be to allow unrestricted admissions into medical schools and into the medical professions. The patient would then decide if he wanted to pay more for a more personalised service (or, indeed, less were he willing to be treated by a paramedic). The practitioner would select her specialism in the light of alternative returns to her human capital (and might want to move to some other graduate job were those returns to appear to her to be too low). The greater reliance on price competition would mean that the State could renounce its countervailing bargaining power in the medical labour market (a power which has far more logic in its favour when the professional bodies hold a monopoly position). The unpredictable outcome would in free markets then come to reflect individual choices and little else.

Yet free markets are often accompanied by cobweb oscillations and multiplied instabilities: given the length of time it takes to train a surgeon (let alone to increase the supply of his co-workers) the cost of the lag might be the death of the patient. Thus it might be desirable for market pricing to be adopted as the ideal but for the State to see to it that *coordinated* choices are made by isolated individuals. The *ex post* pay would not diverge from the *ex ante* value, given the assumption, as Newhouse explains it, that the manpower planner would 'seek to train the number of physicians that would be forthcoming in long-run competitive equilibrium'[5]. How the planner can know the market-clearing price in advance of his decision to regulate the quantity supplied is not, however, entirely clear. It is always easier to leave it to the price mechanism to eliminate the surplus gains of restrictive rent-seekers than it is for the planner himself to estimate what quantity of manpower would in the long-run produce that non-monopolised equilibrium.

Besides which, there remains the question of the qualification – and here it must be admitted that the idea of the planned market equilibrium, like the *dirigiste* proposals of the professional and the extrapolative constituencies, is compatible only with authoritarian licensing, not at all with indicative certification and simple registration. Entry qualifications might evidently point in one direction but entry quotas in another. In such circumstances the advocate both of many gateways and of capped access will have no choice but to opt for one but not for both of his two objectives.

10 The Hospital

In-patient treatment is expensive as compared with primary care. Costly on an individual basis (it is normally cheaper for the same complaint to be treated in the home than in the hospital), it is costly as well in aggregative terms (the hospital service accounts for a large and disproportionate share of a nation's health budget). Expensive or not, in-patient treatment is often crucial where the problem, too complicated for the community nurse and the family doctor, requires specialist care and institutional back-up. Once upon a time the rich could be treated at home and the hospital was the refuge of the poor. The medical division of labour and the increasing capitalisation of procedures revolutionised the traditional pattern; and nowadays even the affluent are prepared to go into hospital for their health. Inclusion as well as expense evidently renders the hospital an important topic in the provision of care.

The hospital is the subject of this chapter, which is divided (as was the previous one) into two sections. The first of these sections examines remuneration given motivation. The second examines entry given cost.

10.1 REMUNERATION

In some cases the property rights in some or all of the nation's hospitals will lie with the central government, which may then delegate routine administration to a national health service. In other cases the ownership of a given hospital will lie with local government, or with a trades union, or with a university, or with an occupational or professional body providing a service specifically for its members. Sometimes hospitals are owned by ethnic communities committed to mutual aid and sometimes they are owned by religious groups anxious to foster the gift relationship. Some hospitals are the assets of insuring agencies (including those health maintenance organisations which make it their business to supply both primary care and in-patient treatment); others belong to a single doctor or group of doctors; still others are the investment of unsentimental businessmen responsible to partners and shareholders for profits. The range of possible modes of ownership is clearly an extensive one. Generalisation about motivation is for that reason fraught with difficulties. The mission hospital is likely to view its capital in a more charitable and philanthropic light than is the business enterprise. The joint-stock company is likely to show a greater awareness of opportunity cost than is the university's teaching hospital. Any system of remuneration able to influence the one will not necessarily have an identical impact upon the other.

Modes of ownership and the associated patterns of motivation can be disparate and varied, but one fact does stand out: the majority of hospitals (and this irrespective of the specific national context) are not commercial undertakings orientated primarily toward the pursuit of profit. Many industries are known to be return-seeking, mercenary and maximising. Not so the hospital industry, where the typical supplier cannot, it would appear, reasonably be modelled as if guided by gain. The difference in orientation is striking – particularly so since the minority of hospitals that do pursue profits have convincingly demonstrated that money can indeed be made from misery.

One reason for the difference might be the possibility, in the words of Kenneth Arrow, 'that the association of profit-making with the supply of medical services arouses suspicion and antagonism on the part of patients and referring physicians'[1], who therefore prefer to obtain their services from a non-profit outlet instead. The profit motive, it is argued, simply does not inspire confidence on the part of the consumer; while the practitioner, aware that he will not retain the patient's trust if he is seen to make referrals to hospitals that overtreat and overcharge, has in any case an ethical commitment of his own such as causes him to rank institutions that primarily want to heal above institutions that primarily want to earn. Social values are frequently hostile to the exchanging of cash for health. The moral revulsion is, arguably, especially strong in the case of the hospital service, where the consumer's ignorance coexists with a high level of vulnerability in the light of the severity of the complaint that led to the admission. Pleading that the revulsion is exaggerated, one could point out that private nursing homes and private laboratories are widely accepted; that equipment manufacturers and pharmaceutical companies are profit-seeking corporations – and that hospital professionals (unless they are on performance-related pay or happen also to share ownership in their respective organisations) have no personal incentive to economise on Hippocratic responsibility in order to expand an institutional surplus in which they have no individual interest. Logical or foolish, the fact is that arguments such as these may fall upon deaf ears. Where profits and hospitals are generally regarded as incompatibles, there the profit-seeking sector is not likely to flourish.

Another reason might be the tendency of the not-for-profit sector to be so heavily subsidised that commercial entrants are simply not able to compete. Thus socialised institutions tend to be subsidised from public finance and charitable foundations to be given tax exemptions similar to the tax concessions enjoyed by wealthy donors with respect to the altruistic gifts that provide the start-up capital, but the commercial hospitals are normally accorded relief no more generous than an assessment from the Revenue. Equity and efficiency alike would seem to suggest a level playing-field – that the favourable tax treatment, where it cannot be terminated for the non-profit supplier, should as an expensive second-best be extended to the profit-seeking hospital as well. In this way the fight would be made less unfair and the more entrepreneurial would be less impeded by discriminatory artificialities from offering the consumer a better service at a lower price. At any rate, the existence of the differential position with respect to subsidies and taxes might be a significant barrier to competitive entry and thus an explanation for the paucity of profit-seeking enterprise in the hospital sector.

A third reason why profit-orientated hospitals have been slow to develop might be overall consumer satisfaction with the established system. Should non-profit institutions be efficient (and be perceived to be efficient), should supply in addition be tolerably well matched to need, then profit-seekers would have neither the opportunity to undersell through lower average cost nor the chance to tap a significant pool of neglected customers. The efficiency of the not-for-profit sector would be particularly great in the case of a national health service genuinely successful on a large scale in planning manpower and coordinating institutions, spreading its overheads in the process. A national health service has the additional attraction to the consumer, public payment being married to public provision, that the marginal cost of utilisation is low or nil. The cost of the private sector service would in contrast be a very real burden. The national finance entitlement (in the absence of a voucher system) is non-transferable from the State sector to the private; the State sector is seldom prepared to countenance an opting-out from the taxes that cover its costs; and the consumer keen to go private must therefore reconcile himself to the fact that in rejecting the non-profit in favour of the for-profit sector he will in effect be paying twice. No one likes to pay twice when he need pay only once. Thus it is that consumers' preferences given the institutional constraints help to explain the relative lack of success of the profit-orientated hospital in a nation able to tempt with a more competitive product.

A fourth and last reason for the disproportionate success of the non-profit institution has to do with the self-interest of the professionals themselves. Where doctors hold property rights, still they might not see the need to put profit before conscience: should the team be large, each profit-maximiser might decide to ignore all but medical considerations, hoping in that way to take a free ride on the profit-maximisation of his fellows and being in his turn frustrated by their ill-founded determination to take a free ride on his. Where doctors do not hold property rights, the incentive is great to keep down the prices charged by the hospitals in order to keep up the fees demanded by the consultants themselves: there are limits to the bills that the uninsured will be able to pay, there are limits to the totals that the insurers will be prepared to fund, and such a zero-sum perception of the division of a limited reward will no doubt stimulate self-interested doctors to favour hospitals that do not inflate their charges with profits. Self-interested professionals, where consulted, are more likely to advise the hospitals to install expensive equipment that will boost the specialist's productivity, but less likely to propose a lengthening of in-patient stays at the expense of independent surgeons deprived by reduced throughput of potential fees. Self-interested professionals, in short, may be a reason in their own right for the fact that the representative hospital has evolved not-for-profit.

Whatever the reason, the fact that the representative hospital (most of all so in the acute sector) does not take profit as its maximand would seem to suggest that it is to organisational psychology rather than to maximising economics that the theorist must turn for a model of the goals of the firm. The model will focus not on commercial incentives but on institutional politics. Its predictions will be as precise as change which is constant and as clear as conflict which is continuous. Meetings are held, compromises struck, lunches eaten, whispered secrets exchanged. The most that can be said is that the bundle of objectives which emerges may without reservation be regarded as the bundle of objectives which emerges. The alternative being no model at all, such precision and such clarity are bound to exercise a certain attraction.

Thus some present at the meetings, the model will argue, will press for an economical deployment of inputs and a minimal average cost per unit of output. The reason might be the devoted bureaucrat's pride in good husbandry; or the teleologist's commitment to maximal social service squeezed out of a given resource endowment; or the grasping doctor's dedication to high pay facilitated by low cost. From whichever the constituency, the demand will be for efficiency in operation. Others within the organisation will, however, call first and foremost for an increase in the size and rate of growth of the hospital (as measured by patients admitted, say, or by numbers of staff employed). Development may be seen as serving the interests of the customer or, for that matter, as an investment in the standing and security of the staff member. For whatever the reason, the goal that will emerge will be the expansion of the hospital.

Then there will be those members of the team who will argue in favour of high quality care as identified (perhaps, in terms of effectiveness, erroneously) by low patient–staff ratios and state-of-the-art equipment. Such alpha-plus facilities boost job satisfaction and attract distinguished physicians; while big names in combination with the capital prerequisites for technical virtuosity confer upon a hospital a reputation for medical excellence which (allowance made for the waste associated with over-skilling and over-mechanisation) is often entirely merited. Such a reputation (quite apart from the consumer satisfaction and the social purpose for which it may stand proxy) is itself a commercial asset. An administrator knows that he can use prestige as an argument in a fund-raising campaign. He will also, if applying for an internal promotion or a better job elsewhere, have personally to rely on impressionistic evidence such as the image of the institution in the absence of the more quantitative information that would be conveyed, say, by data on profits.

Constrained by the hospital's budget, it is clear, a number of goals will figure prominently in debates as to organisational purpose and a number of constituencies will expect to enjoy an input. Most influential among these will be the hospital consultants. Not that the doctors can be regarded as a united coalition: perhaps hostile as a group to a management that wants to spend scarce resources on paintings for the executive offices, that antagonism will be as nothing when compared to the dog-eat-dog competitiveness of the open-heart section locked in conflict with the psychiatrists and the psychologists for a non-incremental share in the annual budget. United or divided, this much remains true, that it will be the doctors who decide on the admissions, the nature of treatment, the length of stay that are the essence of the hospital's activities. Pauly and Reddish, referring specifically to the non-profit institution, have not unexpectedly written as follows: 'The critical assumption of our model is that the physician staff members enjoy *de facto* control of hospital operations and see to it that hospitalization services are produced in such a way as to maximize their net incomes.'[2]

Administrators too have power, of course. They can put pressure on doctors to grant staff privileges to additional competitors. They can, for that matter, demand that doctors boost in-patient attendances at times when occupancy rates would otherwise be low. Yet administrators have few sanctions to back up their guidelines (whereas doctors can always threaten to transfer to another hospital if denied capital or if instructed to limit diagnostic procedures). Their position, when all is said and done, can hardly be regarded as strong. In Fuchs's memorable phrase: 'From the point of view of the hospital administrator, running a hospital is like trying to drive a car when the passengers have control of the wheel and the accelerator. The most the administrator can do is occasionally jam on the brakes.'[3] The administrator's lot is not a happy one. At least he can take some comfort from the fact that, in the non-profit institution, he is exempt from the pressure to show a competitive return on capital. Since he cannot pay out a surplus as dividends, since he must aim only at a budgetary balance, since there is little chance that his organisation will be 'sold' by its 'owners', his struggles over shares will tend to be internal to the hospital and free from the interference of prying gain-seekers pushing for profit. Nominally accountable to the trustees, such an administrator will enjoy an operational autonomy which will make him the envy of the commercial manager compelled to fight simultaneously not on one front but on two.

The doctors and the administrators are two of the groupings that expect to enjoy an input in the decision-making process. So do a plurality of other constituencies within the broad church that is the organisation. The owners and the trustees of a private hospital, the politicians (local or national) in the case of a publicly-owned one, the bureaucrats who are given the monopolist's licence to issue guidelines and directives, the catchment population with the patient's-eye perspective on priorities, the security guards and the kitchen staff (and their trades unions) – there is no reason to think that the utility-functions of the heterogeneous members of these disparate groupings will be identical but considerable reason to think that many if not most will be determined to be consulted on policy. The outcome of the internal relations will be the precise mix or combination of motives that then serves as the maximand of the organisation. In advance of the internal negotiations there is no theory that can render that maximand predictable.

A posteriori there are few if any unambiguous truths about motives and their consequences that can ever be teased out by empiricism. In Pauly's words:

> The heart of the theoretical problem is that the objective function is usually unobservable. Utility always is unobservable, and direct test of whether profit or physician income is at its maximum is usually impossible.[4]

A priori the goals and their outcomes are never much easier to deduce and anticipate in a real-world organisation of blood and bone characterised not so much by the microeconomic calculus as by what Herbert Simon calls 'the patterns of who-talks-to-whom-how-often-about-what'[5]. Cyert and March are particularly open in owning up to unknowledge when they admit that they are not sure precisely how to model the behaviour of the firm: 'It makes only slightly more sense to say that the goal of a business organization is to maximize profit than to say that its goal is to maximize the salary of Sam Smith, Assistant to the Janitor.'[6] Unknowledge means what unknowledge says; and unknowledge does not therefore mean that the price and the quantity that will be set by Sam Smith and his discussion partners will ultimately be any different from the price and the quantity that would have been set by Old Moneybags and his profit-maximisers. Perhaps they will be different and perhaps they will be the same. Whether *a posteriori* or *a priori*, all that unknowledge can say with any certainty is that it hasn't a clue. The typical organisation is, when all is said and done, very much a black box – and the hospital is in that sense very much a typical organisation.

Irrespective of what happens in the blackness of the organisational box, this much at least can be stated with confidence, that the not-for-profit hospital, like its profit-seeking counterpart, will be constrained in its activities by its resources. Budgets matter; and the payment of hospitals must therefore be regarded as an important topic in health policy. Here, as it was in the case of the doctors, the principal modes of remuneration are three in number.

The *first*, the fee-for-service homologue, is to reward the hospital on the basis of the work performed. The dismal scenario would be the case where the hospital takes full advantage of the blank cheque by supplying services – in exchange for fees – that are either medically unnecessary in themselves or else of a standard of quality too high to be warranted. Reimbursement controls operated by the insurers can provide some check on this abuse. Even so, the idea that spurious treatment might be supplied in order to finance thick carpets (*de facto* dividends in kind) or high wages (*de facto* dividends in cash) is not an attractive one. Looking on the brighter side, however, the cheerful scenario would be the multiple choice environment of the competitive market, where rivalry leads to product differentiation in search of revenue and survival itself (even of the non-profit undertaking that desires only to break even) presupposes cost-consciousness, economy and efficiency. Just as the former scenario can involve marginal tests and expensive scans, of course, so the latter can cause some patients to be discharged too soon for the treatment to be effective and others to face the discomfort and even the danger of travel by taxi rather than by ambulance. Combined with monitoring of performance through standard medical success indicators (survival of the patient, recurrence of the complaint, relief from pain, full recovery of function, early return to work), it is clear nonetheless that the payment of the self-governing hospital on the basis of the business it attracts can provide a strong incentive to the institution both to please patients and to trim waste.

The *second* mode of remuneration, analogous to the capitation fee paid to the general practitioner, is the annual subscription paid by the client (normally an insuring agency) directly to the hospital. The hospital undertakes in return for the lump sum to meet the in-patient requirements of the insured parties for the period of the contract. It knows that if it fails satisfactorily to do so the unhappy patient and his family doctor will propose to the insuring agency that the bloc arrangement in the next decision-making round be concluded with a different supplier. Here again the hospital competes by means of its service and of its price. Here again that rivalry ideally serves, in the non-profit as in the for-profit sector, as the patient's *de facto* guarantee.

The *third* option, similar to the doctor's salary, is the annual allocation. The budget is fixed (say, by the politicians who control the funding of a public hospital); the transfer is capped (save perhaps for agreed supplementation to purchase capital equipment); and the hospital is then left to its own devices to determine the use that it makes of the resources. Here too there is a dismal scenario, that it increases the share of its income that it devotes to thick carpets and high wages while cutting back on the cost-conscious conduct that would have made scarce resources go further in the service of patients. Here too there is a cheerful scenario, that it reduces length of stay and promotes home convalescence in a bid to reduce waiting times and promote surgical admissions. Here too there is a penumbra of doubt as to the precise strategy that the institution will ultimately adopt. On the one hand there is the studied laziness which will appeal strongly to social actors with an interest in the quiet life: thus assessment and preparation might be scheduled exclusively post-admission, in order to keep down the percentage of cases in the surgical phase that is so expensive in terms of time and money. On the other hand there is the drilled commitment to the best practice for the greatest number that is the psychic income of a not-insignificant part of the hospital community: such professionalism and pride might cause the hospital to make more efficient use of its fixed budget (a practical option where additional resources cannot otherwise be obtained) in order to expand its throughput (a service to patients so much in keeping with the medical objectives that are the hospital's charter). The sceptic will reason that the fixed budget is far less likely to be associated with drilled commitment of this kind than it is with the studied laziness that is in one sense the more natural reaction to a mode of remuneration in which extra productivity attracts no extra payment. A more scientific approach would, however, be to adopt an agnostic posture: the maximand of the hospital will be that mix of objectives that emerges from the internal negotiations in which all the hospital-constituencies will seek to play some part. In advance of the internal negotiations there is no theory that can render that maximand predictable.

10.2 ENTRY

A nation wants hospitals but it does not want only hospitals. A nation is prepared to pay for the services of hospitals but it does not want to pay over-the-odds because the hospitals that supply the services happen to be non-optimal in size. Too few hospitals will mean the high average cost that results from the diseconomies of large scale at near-capacity utilisation. Too many hospitals will mean the high average cost that is brought about by unexploited economies and underemployed potential. No one will want to ignore the danger that some persons will be offered no in-patient treatment at all in the case of the *too few*. Nor, for that matter, will anyone want to ignore the wastes and perils associated with supplier-induced demand in the case of the *too many*. Yet no one will want to assert that the question of optimal numbers is anything other than closely linked to the question of optimal size: if the cost-curve of the hospital truly manifests the familiar U-shape, then it is clearly in the interests of good husbandry that the point of minimum average cost be properly identified. Only when that point has been isolated can a society wishing to combine expansion or contraction of output with low average cost and eonomies of scale have any confidence that it is not making the mistake of varying the size of the institutions (number being kept constant) when it would have been more rational to vary the number of the institutions (size remaining fixed at the lowest-cost point).

The minimum must be isolated; but the task of identification is by no means a simple one. A cost-curve is a far easier instrument to employ when it is constructed from the logical abstractions of the economics textbook than when must be reconstructed *as if* behind a thick veil of the purest confusion *ab initio* from the raw data of experience. Yet reconstructed it must be if the minimum is indeed to be isolated; and that in turn means the making of crucial decisions with respect to the two key variables of cost and quantity.

(a) Cost

With respect to cost, one obvious definitional problem will involve the time-period. In the short-run, the bulk of the inputs will be fixed overheads (hospital buildings, operating theatres, staff on contract) and very few indeed will be genuinely variable (notably the less expensive inputs such as drugs, dressings, laundry and meals). In the short-run the relevant cost for decision-making purposes will, ignoring the bygones that are forever bygone, be the marginal cost and the relevant average will be not the average total but the average variable. In the long-run, however, even constants become choices, extra blood merges with extra blood banks, and the proper focus then becomes the sum total of all the resources. One implication is that a patient might be admitted at low additional cost in the short-run (at a time, say, when the hospital has excess capacity) but denied treatment on grounds of cost in the long-run (a period, being specific, when the hospital has the freedom to dispose of surplus scale and to rethink its costings in the light of active decisions rather than in the darkness of passive residuals). The time-period is of obvious importance to any specification of cost, but it must also be stressed how difficult it is in the real world to operationalise the scholarly abstraction: 'Time.... is itself absolutely continuous'[7], a great nineteenth-century economist once confided, 'nature knows no absolute partition of time into long periods and short'[8], and the hospital will have in the circumstances to recognise just how arbitrary will be any cut-off point that is selected.

Further complications arise in connection with the estimation of capital. Some statisticians use historic cost while others prefer replacement value. Some researchers incorporate opportunity-cost while others deny that irreversibilities are capable of enjoying next-bests. No scholar is ever entirely sure at what rate to depreciate a technology-intensive investment project that is vulnerable at any moment to sudden death from premature obsolescence. Given these complications, the compromise struck can be as extreme as the decision to count the machines but not to value them. It can also be as self-defeating as the choice simply not to calculate the cost of capital at all.

Capital causes complications, but so too does labour. Thus manpower inflexibilities might be at the root of under-utilisable plant (as where staff unions refuse rotation schemes permitting round-the-clock surgery). Traditional demarcations, similarly, might be the reason for delayed substitutions (as where a rigidity that could be eliminated at a stroke survives well into the long-run because of the conservative's distaste for non-gradual adaptations). Clinical freedom is always a problem (as where doctors cling to inculcated professionalism even in the face of new thinking on best practice). So is outside tendering for hotel and catering concessions (nutrition and hygiene being regarded by some observers as ancillary to medicine but by others as inseparable from care). Conventions as well as capital, in short, introduce lags and fixities so severe as to call into question the relevance of a *continuous* curve.

A further problem in the area of cost has to do with comparability. Studies normally generalise on the basis of pooled data rather than with reference to a single institution tracked historically over time. Aggregation being the key, it is clearly of importance either to group hospitals by broad similarity of casemix or to standardise for variations in such a way as to net out heterogeneities. The unifying factor in both instances might be the percentage of patients in the specified diagnostic categories or it might be the percentage of expenditure that arises in each. What it cannot be is a simple enumeration of the services offered: such a statistic relates to institutional potential but, revealing nothing about relative significance and utilisation, conveys no information that can confidently be employed in the context of cost.

Proper allowance should also be made for the unique circumstances that will always characterise specific institutions. Thus one hospital will have inherited old and decrepit buildings (a history-bound exogeneity necessitating an abnormal expense of repair); another might have to pay significantly above the average (in the absence of a standard national scale) in order to attract scarce skills to an unpopular location; a third will be a teaching hospital (and in that capacity a supplier of medical education and medical research in addition to the medical treatment that it dispenses to its patients); a fourth might cater for a community that is abnormally polluted or disproportionately elderly (a community, in other words, in which complaints recorded in each category are in practice above-average in severity); a fifth will enjoy a non-representative institutional subculture (longer stays, for example, or a higher propensity to operate). Inconvenient though these differences undoubtedly are, it is clear that meaningful generalisations cannot properly be made on the basis of pooled data until the statistics have been adjusted in such a way as to make them reasonably comparable.

Especial difficulties arise in the course of adjusting for the quality of care. Intuitively, one feels that there is likely to be a difference in the standard of treatment as between the different hospitals. Empirically, however, one recognises that there is simply no unambiguous indicator that proxies the suspected dispersion.

To shadow the quality of inputs by the nature of outcomes is an obvious procedure. Yet it is a procedure which is by no means a satisfactory measure of relative performance. Follow-up evidence is not always available with respect either to medical success (survival, say, for at least five years subsequent to the intervention) or to medical failure (not just the death in surgery or the cross-infection picked up in the ward but the less visible pathology such as the early readmission, all-too-often recorded erroneously as a separate admission rewarded with a new cure). Patient's health does not in any case depend solely on formal care (let alone on formal *hospital* care): age-adjusted and sex-adjusted though they ideally will be, the calculations will to that extent continue to embody an element that is illogical in theory and haphazard in practice. Perverse incentives present a further difficulty. Institutions aware that standards are being monitored through recoveries will be rationally motivated to turn away the seriously ill lest the admission of the incurable bring with it the stigma of failure. Assuming that Florence Nightingale was right in her contention that the hospital ought not to do the sick any harm, no premature death brought on by the conscious pursuit of statistical quality will ever be a number with which the student of the hospital can feel entirely comfortable.

To shadow the quality of inputs by the nature of outcomes is evidently not an ideal procedure. Not to weight the value of the eggs by the tastiness of the omelette is, however, to force the statistician to find a proxy for standards that concentrates exclusively on what care *is*, not at all on what what care *does*. By far the most popular proxy in this respect is the quantitative index of relative expenditure. No one can prove that two nurses per bed are better than one in the ward. No one can deny that non-profit hospitals with no alternative outlet for their trading surplus will plough back even in underutilised equipment. No one can maintain that insuring agencies make no contribution to unnecessary upgrading by removing from the client the need to shop around. No one can argue that there is not an inherent absurdity in an estimation which on Monday thanks high cost for quality but on Tuesday uses it to demonstrate deplorable inefficiencies such as organisational slack. No one, in other words, can be entirely happy with the notion that *more* will inevitably be better and *less* invariably mean worse. Perhaps not; but no one, equally, will find it easy to think up an alternative proxy that mobilises significantly more consensus in the nebulous area of quality of care.

Many studies of hospitals' costs are aggregative to the level of the institution. Others, less comprehensive and less global, prefer to concentrate on the costs of a single department or of a single service. The hospital being a multi-product firm, different treatment centres experiencing different cost-functions, there is a certain attraction in a procedure that sets out to examine individual activities rather than the bundles and packages to which they add up. The microscopic approach is attractive (perhaps as a complement to the more ambitious study of the whole), but the requisite information, sadly, is not always accessible. Some can be manufactured from data referring *in toto* to the joint costs of the shared inputs: thus a *pro rata* attribution can be made of the collective overheads (the laundry, the pharmacy, the post-operative recovery room, the kitchen, the administration, the intensive care unit) that, while not perfect, is still not arbitrary. Yet much information will nonetheless not be available at a microscopic level; and that is why the more aggregative studies are likely also to be the more precise.

Information is a problem in the calculation of cost. Not least is the problem a serious one when the investigator is seeking responsibly to make an allowance for wider social cost despite the fact that no such statistic will normally be included in the hospitals' own accounts. Thus the accounts might show that the large hospital is better placed than is the small one to spread the fixed costs of capital-intensive services and to provide a wide range of specialised treatments – but might not show the magnitude and incidence of the associated spillovers which it must therefore be the task of the outsider to establish. One of these will be the longer travelling times and higher travelling costs that are imposed by the larger catchment area on staff, patients and visitors. Then there are the private psychic costs, complementing the private pecuniary costs, that take the form of frustration felt when public transport does not run regularly, anxiety experienced at the thought that death or medical complications might result before the casualty can reach the more distant clinic. Since the rich have more purchasing power and own more private transport than do the poor, the social costs tabulated will clearly have implications not just for efficiency but for equity as well.

Within the large hospital, further human costs can arise. Sometimes these will take the form of poor human relations in a coldly bureaucratic structure (low *morale* leading in turn both to lower involvement of staff and greater alienation of patients). Sometimes they will consist in a radical divorce of the treatment-centre from the local community (a green-field empire often finding it difficult to conduct local fund-raising events or to enlist local volunteers). Sometimes, of course, the human costs will take the form, the sign reversed, of collective *benefits* such as reduce total burdens rather than augment them. One example would be the closure of uneconomically small hospitals (including doctor-owned proprietaries) and the concentration of the functions on a single site: such size might then mean a professional staff so large and so heterogeneous that it can no longer arrive at the mutually acceptable compromises that previously had reinforced its restrictive practices. Here the spillover that the accounts will not record will be a diminution in traditionalised regimentation and a greater role for innovativeness and adaptability. This viscosity too must the investigator of the hospitals' costs strive in his unknowledge most assiduously to quantify in order that his statistic might become as robust as any such statistic can ever be when situated so centrally in a definitional minefield from which no two measures of cost will ever emerge identical.

(b) Quantity

As with cost, so with quantity, where different studies include different information for the simple reason that there is no general consensus on how best to estimate the product that the institutions supply. The medical objectivist will argue that improvement in mortality or morbidity alone can be called the value-added of the hospital's intervention: the insight is plausible but, the relationship between status outcomes and hospital treatments being so loose, no easy task to operationalise. The medical subjectivist, dissatisfied with cold enumeration, will call instead for consumer's valuation and revealed preference: sample surveys being expensive and inconclusive, market prices being distorted by ignorance, insurance and professional restriction, the signals that are recorded are unlikely to satisfy all students. There being no convincing indicator either of medical improvement or of economic welfare, the statistician is obliged to do the best that he can with the data that is accessible. What this typically means is that he must select a proxy estimator for the hospital's output. That proxy is in practice very often the hospital's input. A wound dressed is a dressing applied. A phobia obviated is a pill dispensed. The reasoning that the outputs can be tracked by means of the inputs used up to produce the outputs is in the circumstances clear enough. The patient whose stitches fester into gangrene will not, of course, share the statistician's complacency with respect to the treatment, and nor will the dissident sedated by psychotropia despite the fact that his lunacy is no more than a simple difference of ideology. Inputs are not outputs. In more cases than not, however, the statistician will be prepared to settle for the proxy he can see rather than waiting for the ideal to which his access is barred.

This is not to say that the statistician is unaware of the difficulties associated with the use of the proxy – or of the curious economics that it bequeaths to the cost/quantity relationship that he is seeking to reconstruct. The standard procedure in the microeconomics textbook is to depict the Marshallian

U with the aid of a vertical axis that shows the cost of production and a horizontal axis that indicates the quantity of output. The standard procedure of the statistician with the proxy is to replace the numbers of outputs that he does not know with the numbers of inputs that he does. His logic may be sound but still his economics will be curious: his dependent variable will be the pecuniary value of the inputs, his independent variable will be the physical quantity of the inputs, and his methodological framework will be open to attack from those critics who will insist that the axes are too close to be convincing. The statistician will not deny that to correlate input with input is no more satisfying than to treat the eggs employed with a view to producing an omelette as identical to the tastiness of the omelette that the ingredients were brought in to bring about. What the statistician will say, however, is that a second-best methodology is better than no methodology at all. The problem, the statistician will say, is that there is simply no obvious alternative to the hardly satisfying approach of employing the means as the indicator of the end that is not in sight.

Means are numerous and heterogeneous; but normally the investigator can spare himself the labour of aggregation. The reason is that there is a single input which, absolutely central to the treatment provided by the hospital, may be regarded in and of itself as a good index of the hospital's productive activity. That input is beds. Beds being the input and the input being the output, therefore beds are the output. Only a bed-factory can say as much.

Beds are important, but they are also ambiguous. That is why the investigator must devote some thought to the precise form in which he wants to present his statistic. The simplest option is the crude bedstock or number of beds available in a hospital for the purpose of treating patients. Such an aggregate is of undeniable relevance to the broader concept of volume of activity, but it is also in several ways a misleading proxy for the quantity of care. On the one hand it introduces a downward bias by omitting the contribution of treatments without beds: the (non-constant, non-standard) contribution of out-patient departments is a case in point. On the other hand it overstates the quantity of attention supplied by virtue of the fact that makes no correction for beds without treatments: physical potential is a poor indicator of operational capacity where a non-negligible proportion of the bed-plant, undeniably installed, cannot be devoted to the delivery of patient care because of the lack either of a budget to cover current cost or of complementary inputs such as balanced teams of professional manpower. A better indicator of actual output (as opposed to potential output) will in the circumstances be not the naked beds *per se* but rather the occupancy levels of those beds.

The average daily census has the attractive feature as a measure of quantity that it picks up no beds save those being utilised by patients. In that way it translates metals and mattresses into the more cordial language of patient-days and/or patient-nights. Yet the average daily census does have the disadvantage that it makes no distinction between occupancy associated with long stays and occupancy associated with rapid throughput; whereas the nature of the stay is in truth significantly cross-correlated with the behaviour of hospital costs. In order to clarify the position the investigator might decide to combine his statistic on occupied beds with additional data on the caseflow per bed per year. Such an amplification would at the very least permit a distinction to be made between a high average cost due to long in-patient stays (a possible sign of administrative inefficiencies, manpower bottlenecks, avoidable failures in communication and control) and a high average cost due to fast in-patient turn-around (a benefit to the case on the waiting list even if a burden to the constituency that must finance the expensive surgery more frequently performed). Beds, one concludes, are more like a range of choices than a single statistic. That property, moreover, they have in common with virtually all the other estimators that might conceptually enter into an empirical investigation of the cost/quantity relationships that obtain in the modern hospital. Given the disparity in the variables, a disparity in the results is only to be expected.

That said, the real-world evidence that has been collected on the hospitals' cost/quantity relationships does seem to lend support to the theoretical anticipation of the familiar U-shape: the average cost per bedded case does seem initially to fall (as specialised facilities are used more effectively) and eventually to rise (the most likely cause being the managerial diseconomy).

The real-world evidence does not speak with a single voice on the precise location of the cost-minimum but it does suggest that maximum scale economies are best reaped by relatively large institutions: whether as low an in-patient census as 190 in the study conducted by Carr and P.J. Feldstein[9] or as high a bed-stock as 438 in the work of Mann and Yett[10], what is clear is the extent of consensus among American authors that considerations of cost-minimisation given production indivisibilities point to institutions larger than the bulk of voluntary hospitals in the United States. The voluntary hospital is the principal mode of hospital care in the United States (as estimated by numbers of hospitals, numbers of beds, total assets): the public sector is second, the for-profit sector is third. The inference is that there are too many small hospitals in the United States, and that average cost might fall were there to be a smaller number of larger ones. On the other hand, if the results of Lave and Lave are to be believed, it is unlikely to fall very far: 'Our results indicate that if economies of scale exist in the hospital industry, they are not very strong.'[11] The U is shallow, Lave and Lave conclude, but it does exist.

The scale of diseconomies in Ontario would appear, in the research of R.G. Evans, generally to confirm both the presence and the flatness that had been detected by Lave and Lave further south. Thus Evans reported (his results sensibly accompanied by a warning not to expect universality from specific findings forever grounded in time and place) that the province enjoyed a U but that the troughs and the peaks in Ontario tended only to be weakly differentiated:

> The final equation suggests a U-shaped cost curve with minimum at 258 beds. The marginal response of costs per day to bed size in terms of dollars per 100 beds increase is small, being 7¢ for a 300 bed hospital, 43¢ for a 500 bed, and $1.34 for a 1000 bed hospital. Only at the extreme end of the spectrum, where observations are few and differential case severity is most likely to be a problem, do we find a strong scale economy.[12]

Evans' finding, that there are long-run economies and diseconomies but few that are exceptional, is relatively neutral as between the advocates of cottage hospitals on the one hand, supermarket-scale institutions on the other. Economically speaking, Evans found, there is a minimum size; but still its advantages ought not to be exaggerated in view of the general flatness of the surrounding terrain.

A not dissimilar result was reached in the course of the methodologically very important study that was carried out in England and Wales, just over a decade after the establishment of the National Health Service, by M.S. Feldstein.[13] Feldstein's data related to 177 acute, non-teaching hospitals, all of them reasonably large in terms of expenditure. The smallest mustered 72 beds and the largest 1064. The mean was 302.9. The statistics referred exclusively to a single point in time, a single accounting year: the cross-section of a group is far easier to calculate than is the time-series of an institution, even if the historical methodology that incorporates the recorded past trends and the expected future developments in a single hospital's cost/quantity relationships is probably the more satisfying. Feldstein's conclusion was a guarded defence of economies of size, but also a dual one. Depending on the adjustments made, he was able to identify the minimum point on the average cost curve as occurring at the level either of 310 beds or of 905 beds. Both figures are high. The latter is very high indeed.

The figure of 310 was derived from the data after an allowance had been made for the differences in the numbers of cases treated in each of the specialist areas (obstetrics, ENT, paediatrics and so on). Feldstein found that 'approximately one third of the observed interhospital variation in cost per case is due to casemix differences'[14]. Some, he said, were unambiguously correlated with hospital size (as where large institutions take on a disproportionate share of the more expensive work); but casemix and size, he insisted, remain for all that conceptually separate and not to be confused. The allowance made, the calculation then yielded its result: 'The average cost function, when adjusted for casemix, is a shallow U-shaped curve with a minimum at the current average size (310 beds). Costs rise beyond this size but level off after 600 beds at about 10 per cent above the minimum cost.'[15] Average costs rise following the long intermediate range from 250 to 350 beds in which the curve is almost horizontal. The cause of the rise (which, at no more than 10%, is clearly not very great) apparently has much to do with the fact that larger hospitals treat fewer cases per bed per year than do smaller ones: 'The failure to achieve economies of scale is primarily due to the lower case-bed ratio in larger hospitals, even after adjusting for casemix differences. This probably reflects a lower level of 'managerial' or labour efficiency and, in particular, a slower hospital pace.'[16] Communications and control so often grow weak as organisations grow large, and the hospital is no exception. The cost that rises from 310 beds is the proof: 'If it were not for this lower intensity with which the hospital plant is used, these larger hospitals would have lower costs per case.'[17] On the other hand, the increase in average cost is exceedingly small as hospital size effectively doubles from 310 to 600 beds (and beyond 600 beds the diseconomies finally disappear altogether). All in all, therefore, the flat U-shape as identified in Feldstein's pioneering investigation does not provide a strong argument for any obvious size in particular: 310 may be the minimum but all around it is flatness, and thus 'on balance size has little effect on cost'.[18]

The figure of 905 was derived from the data after correcting for the slower flow that is a standard characteristic of the larger institution: 'When costs are adjusted for case-flow rates, cost per case decreases throughout the observed range of hospital size to a value of £49.30 at 905 beds, some 12 per cent below average cost.'[19] Scale in such a case is quite clearly capable of producing a worthwhile reduction in the average cost of hospital care: 'If the case-flow of larger hospitals could be improved so that it was not lower than the rate in other hospitals – primarily by decreasing average lengths of stay – operating cost per case in larger hospitals could be reduced to better than 12 per cent below current average cost.'[20] Faster case-flow, in Feldstein's study, is the key to lower cost per case, and shorter length of stay the key to faster case-flow. The impediment to the achievement of lower cost per case is evidently not the occupancy-rate of the institution (not, in other words, an ineffectively low level of utilisation of the fixed factors of bed capital and ward nursing) but rather the long period of time spent by patients in beds awaiting doctors. Logically, therefore, the average cost per case could be cut if expanding budgets were to be skewed in favour of the bottleneck-input: 'Output would increase if a greater proportion of total expenditure were devoted to medical staff and less to nursing and housekeeping activities.'[21] Were, more specifically, the resources to be skewed not towards medical staff in general but towards medical staff in *large* hospitals in particular, there the fall in average cost per case in consequence of additional cases per bed-year would be especially marked. Big then would ultimately be more beautiful than small. To the tune of 12 per cent.

Feldstein does not deny that falling cost per case is likely to mean rising cost per institution: accelerated throughput clearly means a greater proportion of in-patient census in the expensive surgical phase and therewith a smaller proportion at the cheaper pre-operative and convalescent stages. Nor does he entertain any illusions that shorter stays and more admissions will make any significant dent in waiting lists: 'The evidence does not indicate that there is a level of supply at which the demand for beds would be satisfied.[22] If anything, the evidence would seem to suggest the opposite, that the anxious will always clamour for the marginal, that shorter waits attract in discouraged abstainers, that consumers' needs are not exogenous but supply-conditioned, and that, in sum, 'bed-day demand increases proportionately with availability'[23]. Thus it is, the treatments becoming more bunched and the built remaining defiantly the filled, that the total cost per institution is likely to rise even as the average cost per case may be expected to fall. Feldstein's results, like all inductions no more than the frozen portrait of a single time and a single place, must not be assumed to be all-encompassing and general. That said, the story they tell is clear enough: the larger hospital was found by Feldstein to be the hospital potentially the best situated to reap the technical economies of lower cost per case.

Technical efficiency is without a doubt a laudable objective for a society determined to make the most of its scarce resources. No one would deny that the lowest point on a U-shaped relationship is bound to enjoy a *ceteris paribus* superiority to a higher average cost associated with a less economical level of output. Yet no one would even so maintain that there is no more to prudent management than the simple pursuit of the physical minimum. What is necessary for the engineer must not, in short, be confused with what is sufficient for the economist. Berki is only one among many to have issued a warning against a reliance on the partial and the incomplete:

> It is clear that no productive organization need necessarily be on its economically efficient production function: it may use a technically efficient production function with the 'wrong set' of inputs or it may use a technically inefficient one (manual record keeping in a 1000 bed hospital) or unnecessarily costly inputs may be used (registered nurses making up beds).[24]

Where there is more than one technical relationship between the various inputs, more than one physical means of delivering a named output, there it makes little sense to identify the lowest point on a single curve without also isolating the most economical combination, the lowest attainable cost.

To specify the production function that is economically the most efficient presupposes that the prices of the inputs can all be carefully evaluated in the light of the respective marginal productivities: administered scales, traditional differentials, national agreements and aggregated statistics serve as a reminder that the calculation will not be an easy one. The information collected, gainful substitution of the cheaper for the more expensive factor must be possible to effect: institutions being resistant to adaptation, workers opposing unemployment even when they acknowledge the advantage of automation, it must not be supposed that inflexible reality will enjoy the same freedom of manoeuvre that is the great attraction of textbook theory. Even if the most economical combination could correctly be isolated, still it must be conceded that the lowest cost will sometimes not be an attainable option. Social patterns and the conservatism of convention will see to that.

The economical hospital will cost inputs and effect substitutions. It will also price the outputs and compare the alternatives. There is much logic in its attempt to juxtapose the extra cost of a given treatment both with the extra revenue that that treatment brings in and with the extra return that some other treatment might be expected to occasion. As a measure of economic welfare, of course, the procedure can never be entirely satisfactory. Third-party payment and price discrimination obscure the felt significance of subjective sacrifice. Price reimbursable is very often the average revenue per diagnostic group and not the marginal revenue per differentiated uniqueness. Most problematic of all, perhaps, is the fact that the marginalist calculus is unlikely to be adopted by any save the profit-maximising institution: the typical hospital being not-for-profit, the incentive will simply not be present to proceed along a preferred cost–quantity curve until that unique point is reached at which the extra revenue will be precisely the same as the extra cost. This is not to say that the not-for-profit hospital will not be motivated to be efficient, only that its internally-negotiated goals and norms are unlikely to correspond to those that the textbook would associate with economic efficiency. In that sense there is a notion of organisational efficiency that, coexisting with the technical and with the economic, considerably complicates the task of predicting and recommending.

Considerations of economic efficiency may lead to the selection of a lower curve, considerations of organisational efficiency to the choice of a different point. That they can do. What they cannot do is to transcend the U-shape in the cost/quantity relationship that would appear to be a technical fact of life. Thus it is that the U-shape becomes an important argument in the debate concerning the proper number of entrants that can reasonably be permitted into an industry where average cost per producing unit is prone to rise whenever output per firm is either too small or else too large. No society wants its hospitals to waste scarce resources. Whether State or market provides the better barrier to preventable costliness is, however, a more controversial matter.

Most modern industries have a U. The hospital's U tends if anything to be a remarkably flat U as compared with the cost relations of a range of other sectors. Observations such as these, however persuasive in their own right, would appear to have done little to weaken the commitment to entry controls of those members of the community who regard State restriction as the *sine qua non* for hospitals' efficiency. Their enthusiasm for restriction is shared both by that constituency which sees stringent licensing as the bulwark against substandard quality and that grouping which fears that free entry will unjustifiably inflate health budgets. The protection of standards by means of entry controls is an argument identical in its substance to the discussion of legislation, liberalisation and lawsuit, recommendation, regimentation and regulation which constituted the bulk of Chapter 9.2 on the access of the doctors to their profession. The containment of costs by means of entry controls is a defence of limitation as an antidote to supplier-led escalation that is bound to appeal strongly to all readers who take the view that the wise planner is always superior to the uncoordinated market in the unusual area of health.

Standards and costs set to one side, the verdict must be that the case for State-administered barriers in order to concentrate production at the lowest point on the producer's U can hardly be regarded as proven. Excess capacity and overfull employment can still raise average cost even where each new entrant has duly secured a certificate of need. Novelty and innovation are luxuries rather than necessities once the State has taken upon itself to exclude the competitive challenge of cost-cutting new rivals. Technical efficiency ought not in any case to be confounded with economic efficiency: only a person of very limited imagination could assign any normative significance to a single point on a single U when the pursuit of optimality can in truth never mean the attainment of an *optimum optimorum* beyond which all history becomes no more than the unthinking perpetuation of the past's *status quo*. Ideally omniscient and beneficent, the real-world State might not in practice live up to the high expectations entertained by the advocates of control.

The alternative to State limitation is market freedom. In such a system it is the spontaneity of the suppliers and not the guidance of the regulators that determines the number of producers and influences the level of costs. Competition compels hospitals to be active in the pursuit of efficiency. It also provides a reason for gains made to be passed on to the consumer in the form of prices reduced. Local monopoly must remain a cause for concern in a genuine emergency: while no one should underestimate the power of the producer when time is of the essence, still the national and international character of the hospital industry is bound to undermine the imperfection in that overwhelming majority of cases when treatments are elective or postponable. Duplicated capitalisation and under-utilised beds must remain a spectre of surplus that can never be laid: unwelcome as the consequent rise in average cost must *ceteris paribus* be, the community as a whole might nonetheless be prepared to pay the price of monopolistic competition if in return for the higher charge it were to be offered a choice of quality and a menu of differentiation. Nor is it obvious that over-expanded capacity and unnecessarily high prices will always and everywhere accompany the market freedom of entry and exit: competitive shake-out and client-led closure can be the source of good quality at reasonable cost, even as the over-bedded society can all-too-easily degenerate into supplier-induced demand and economically wasteful practices. The experience of beds in hotels may indeed be the model that beds in hospitals might usefully be encouraged to emulate. Perhaps it may; but still the pragmatist in the market for health will demand convincing proof that the circumstances are sufficiently the same before he recommends the same medicine in the one case that he would without hesitation have prescribed for the other. Only the most blinkered of doctors will recommend cervical cytology for every patient, male or female. Only the most doctrinaire of ideologues, similarly, will reach automatically for supply and demand when what is first required is a careful examination and a balanced report.

Part IV

Conclusion

11 The Value of Life

Morally speaking, there is something deeply repellent about the counting of the cost where the benefit in question is a human life. Morally speaking, there is something absolutely unacceptable about the compressing of a human life into the monetary units of the economic market. A life is an infinite treasure that cannot, must not command a market value. A life, transcending all price, is not a thing to be bought and sold in a car-boot sale.

Morally speaking, the value knows no bounds. Practically speaking, it does. Practically speaking, scarce resources constrain ethical absolutes and make difficult choices inescapable in the troubled area of preserving life, of 'preventing death',[1] with which this concluding chapter is concerned. Practically speaking, as Fuchs insists,

> choices *must* be made and every choice necessarily reflects a set of values. These values underlie all implicit and explicit weighing of costs and benefits. Because resources are scare relative to wants, we do not have the option of evaluating or not evaluating. The only option is whether to evaluate explicitly, systematically, and openly, as economics forces us to do, or whether to evaluate implicitly, haphazardly, and secretly, as has been done so often in the past.[2]

Choices *must* be made, and it is clearly important that they be made in such a way as to appeal to the broad swell of the social consensus. Sometimes that consensus will want to devolve responsibility to the level of the individual and sometimes it will wish to concentrate power in the hands of the professionals. Sometimes, more collectively, it will make the decision that sensitive decisions are more effectively made when made the charge of an accountable leadership. The patient, the practitioner and the public are at any rate the three key decision-making constituencies that can potentially be approached by a troubled consensus compelled by scarcity to put an economic value on a human life.

The three constituencies, the subject of Chapters 2 and 3, will be examined in turn in the three sections of the present chapter. The conclusion reached is that extra life-years purchased through an expensive drug or a bone-marrow transplant will undoubtedly enjoy a high social valuation—but so too will upgraded education such as assists the less-advantaged to escape from the vicious circle of poverty; or industrial investment such as creates new jobs; or economic growth such as expands the tax base; or additional consumption such as elevates the human life above the level of the bare existence. Choices *must* be made, and no one but a calendar-year fetishist would suggest that they be made in such a way as to satisfy but a single maximand. Hippocrates will turn in his grave and those about to die will not salute us. The grounds for discontent are real enough. No less real, however, is the need to compromise on the second-best in the face of the inevitable.

11.1 THE PATIENT

Pebbles on the beach are not known to derive pleasure or pain from the myriad of influences, actual and potential, to which their pebbleness leaves them exposed. Unscreened from the hot sun, swept out to sea by the waves, trod upon by careless holiday-makers and their thoughtless children, pebbles never ask to be consulted in advance or complain afterwards about their treatment. Pebbles are poor philosophers and dull conversationalists and are seldom invited a second time except to apologise. Pebbles do, on the other hand, clearly have the redeeming feature that, unlike persons, they do not believe themselves to be in possession of a unique individuality and a discrete subjectivity which in some sense make each somehow difference from all. Pebbles are easy to deal with and persons are not. It is in the circumstances no surprise that doctors find their trips to the beach so restful.

Persons like to think of themselves as unique and discrete, and one inference from that self-perception might be that the life-and-death decision is ideally entrusted to the individual decision-maker. Only the individual can know the precise satisfaction which he derives from marginal life-years of varying quality or compare a felt benefit with the felt cost to which it gives rise. Only the individual can flesh meaning into medicine by assigning perceived values to fear and anxiety, tolerance and acceptance, pain and risk. Only the individual, in short, can say with any confidence what best accords with her own view of the good life or where he personally would want to draw the line. Thus it is, as Gavin Mooney points out, that the morbidity tables and the objective probabilities can never provide more than a part of the guidance in the case of any given intervention:

> While the doctor may be in a position to tell me what the risks are he is in no position to tell me how I ought to weight risk of death against risk of blindness. If I am little concerned with losing my eyesight but have a great fear of death then I may well decide that I will not have the

> operation. What we have here therefore is a combination of a measurement of objective risk supplied by the State's representative and the consumer's sovereignty applying when the weights to be attached to diferent risks are being determined.[3]

For the full story to emerge, the patient as well as the disease must evidently be taken into account.

If the consumer in indeed to be consulted, then some means must be found of measuring the direction and intensity of the individual's valuations. It is seldom easy to quantify the unquantifiable. That said, the following approximations to the value attached to life by the life-holder himself are likely to generate some fleeting indication at least of the contents of the invisible mind that is forever closed to guests.

(a) Payment for Care

Marginal payment tendered in exchange for incremental service supplied is the intellectual hard core of market-orientated economics. It is also the essence of that democratic and decentralised methodology which derives finite valuation first and foremost from revealed preference. Actions speak louder than words in the greengrocer's shop and the money placed where the mouth is determines the price in the butcher's. The value of the apples and the oranges, the pork and the lamb, is generally taken by the methodological individualist to be the supply-and-demand equilibrium that is sequentially negotiated by the interested buyers and the calculative sellers. The value of life, the methodological individualist would no doubt maintain, ought ideally to be derived in the same manner, through the detached observation of the economic sacrifice that is made by the life-holder himself when he digs deep into his own pocket to settle the bill for care.

Certainly, the payments in question are far from unknown. Cancer patients abandoned as incurable by their doctors are observed to travel abroad at their own expense in pursuit of treatment. Heart patients denied a wonder drug by their insurers are seen to sell their home to raise the cash. In instances such as these the individual consumers may be regarded as providing interesting insights into the subjective meaning which they and they alone attach to the value of life. So, incidentally, does the case of the ailing pensioner who, keen to leave his heirs an undepleted bequest, spends money on a lethal injection in order to liquidate a substandard existence, self-perceived. The rule is the familiar one of 'you pays your money, you takes your choice'. The consumer of the wonder drug and the purchaser of the lethal injection will clearly not be motivated to make the same choices. Still, however, they will have this in common, that the preferences they reveal will be most fundamentally their own.

The methodology underlying the inference from payment is a familiar one and the evidence on the trade-offs is empirically accessible. Yet there are sound reasons nonetheless for treating the generalisations made with a considerable degree of caution.

Individuals, for one thing, are more differentiated than are the pebbles on the beach. The consumer of the wonder drug and the purchaser of the lethal injection will not indicate the same relationship between expected satisfaction and extra sacrifice: statements about the value of life are in that sense the prisoner of the sample that is selected. Interpersonal comparison of heterogeneous subjectivities, difficult at the best of times, is complicated still further by the non-constant utility that is likely to be associated even with the standardised payment of an identical sum. The logic of the variance is the deduction that the marginal utility of money is likely to move inversely to the individual's spendable resources. The variance accepted, the idea that a representative rich person will experience less distress per unit of expenditure than will a typical poor one must inevitably make the aggregated revelations observed by no means easy to interpret. The life cycle compounds the ambiguity introduced by income and wealth: should older persons (perhaps because 'you can't take it with you') be more willing to spend than are younger ones, the data on payment for care ought ideally to be age-adjusted in order to pick up the lower utility of money in the later years of life.

Insurance status raises further problems. Willingness to pay, if it is to supply reliable information about the value of life, must involve genuine choices backed up by next-bests foregone. Where care is reimbursable through cover, however, there the consumer is able to command the service without incurring any personal obligation to surrender a *quid pro quo*. No one would suggest that the consumer would rush to acquire a double by-pass merely because it is cheap; or that the third party would automatically validate any and every wish, however marginal. Yet there will understandably be a residual suspicion that the payment authorised by Ego but made by Alter will exceed to some non-trivial extent the payment that would be authorised by Ego if also financed by Ego.

Payment proportioned to psyche is the *sine qua non* for revealed preference to be taken as the basis for attitudinal generalisation. That being the case, there is a strong temptation for investigators to confine their studies to data generated out-of-pocket – to the payment for care, in other words, of the totally-uninsured (including those who have exhausted their cover) and of the partially-uninsured (notably those subject to high deductible thresholds and a major co-payment involvement). Such observations are the economist's *desiderata*: the money being the actor's own, the actions observed are more likely to move in step with the actors' thoughts than they would if it were Alter and not Ego who had to pay.

The information collected may be authentic. Given the atypical nature of the sample, however, it is most unlikely to be representative. The uninsured tend to be below-average either in their aversion to risk or in their level of affluence. Where the uninsured are optimistic chancers convinced that 'it can't happen to me', they will entertain gambles with their lives that the more prudent mainstream will consensually regard as excessive. Where the uninsured are impoverished and unemployed, they will reveal preferences for what they can afford that the wider community will treat rather as the make-dos of the also-rans than as the *optima* appropriate to the integrated. Better information could, of course, be generated were the normal to be forced into the marketplace through the effective suppression of health insurance for any and all. Such an expedient would put teeth into willingness to pay by stimulating representative shoppers to register choices with respect to life-saving care that are logically on a par with those that they are prepared to record for beer and bread. No doubt it would; but still it is unlikely ever to be mooted. No one with any respect for the feelings of his fellow citizens will ever be keen to propose the winding-up of all insuring agencies, private and public, merely to encourage generalisable intelligence through the emergence of authentic markets trading specifically in premature death prevented. Responsibility for payment is unlikely ever to be made fully individual. The presence of insurance is bound therefore considerably to complicate the interpretation of real-world evidence on the purchase of care intended by the consumer to be life-saving in nature.

Even if the responsibility were to be individualised, moreover, still there would remain an important obstacle to extrapolation from payment for care. The problem, eloquently captured by the Hobson's choice of 'your money or your life', is that there is only one value that will logically be articulated by the known loser with the life-threatening complaint when he contemplates the maximum sum he is just prepared to spend to secure the revocation of the *de facto* death sentence that is represented by his illness. That one value will be the equivalent of all that he can pay. Aware that it is he who has drawn the blank in the lottery of life in the form of the bullet with his name on it, what the rational life-lover is likely to decide is that his willingness to pay is little short of infinite, however much his ability to pay might be limited by his practical circumstances. Such a person will pay all that he can to continue his life and (precisely because he would not be around to spend the proceeds) will refuse any bribe that would be offered to him to sell his place in the queue for treatment: 'In ordinary circumstances', Professor Mishan writes, 'no sum of money is large enough to compensate a man for the loss of his life. ... If, in ordinary circumstances, we face a person with the choice of continuing his life in the usual way or of ending it at noon the next day, a sum large enough to persuade him to choose the latter course of action may not exist.'[4]

In extraordinary circumstances it might: thus an old person (one, perhaps, with a waning attachment to life) might refuse care in order to maximise the legacy passed on to heirs and an altruistic parent might volunteer for a suicide mission in a period of famine in exchange for an agreed payment adequate to ensure the survival of his family. In ordinary circumstances it will not. The losers might seek to buy out the rights of the winners but they are unlikely despite their efforts to attract many takers. A cat may have nine lives but a person has only one. Having only one life, a person cannot normally reap any gains from trade by means of swapping that life for money. Having only one life, most persons will probably deny that any welfare-surplus can be generated in consequence of such a transfer of assets in the time-honoured manner of Pareto. The infinite value which most persons will probably assign to their lives is clearly an important obstacle to the extrapolation of the value of life from the individual's willingness to pay for life-and-death care. Where infinite means infinite and all means all, a life-maximising society will have no choice but automatically to convert the whole of the national product into a giant clinic – and that no balanced community is likely ever to wish to do.

No society deficient in an infinite supply of productive resources will be able in practice to assign an infinite value to the morally priceless commodity that is a human life. Yet no society committed to the market approach to consultation and consensus will wish to impose a cap on life-saving expenditure that is somehow at variance with the preferences that are revealed by its citizens when they manifest their willingness to pay in real-world situations. On the one hand scarcity, on the other hand participation – the Rawlsian veil once drawn aside to identify the wounded, the value of life once defined to be the willingness of the hard cases to pay for care, it is clear that no society constrained by resources but also committed to individualism will be able simultaneously to satisfy its twin objectives.

Nor should it be forgotten that the lexicographic ranking of life above all else is at one and the same time a choice to rank certain individuals above equal citizens with different needs. A society in which some know themselves to be well while others know themselves to be ill is *de facto* a pluralistic polity, a divided community in which the healthy will demand education and indulgence while the desperate will devote all that they have to care. To scale up on the basis of the ill is to deprive the healthy of pleasure. To scale up on the basis of the well is to deprive the desperate of life. To select the constituency to be consulted is evidently to rank one value of life above another in a society where not all individuals will reveal the same preferences because not all will have the same requirements. Just as individualism can be at odds with scarcity, so, it must be stressed, can one individual's demands be at variance with the wants of another. Thence the not insignificant objection to the practice of inferring value of life from payment for care, that it is unworkable and unsuitable in precisely those democratic conditions in which the search for a non-arbitrary, non-authoritarian standard of evaluation is most likely to be conducted.

Willingness to pay for care is unlikely to generate a finite or a consensual valuation of human life: the Rawlsian veil once drawn aside, the politician wondering how much of society's scarce resources to devote to ambulances and underpasses, medical research and street lighting, will in the circumstances derive little guidance from the induction. Willingness to pay for the *probability* of care is, however, a different matter: where the probability is known but not the identity of the victim, there the decision made as if situated behind an impenetrable veil of radical ignorance is more likely to embody a bounded and a shared valuation that the politician can employ in formulating a national policy towards early detection, liver and bowel transplants, the disposal of plutonium waste, the transportation of explosives, the earthquake-proofing of collapsible structures. Where the life to be saved is, in other words, a *statistical* life, where the life to be saved is neither one's own life nor that of a named individual whose photograph has appeared in the newspaper, there the citizen is in a position to make as detached and as rational a decision as can ever be made in so emotionally-charged an area of human activity.

Once the expected replaces the actual and the factual gives way to the uncertain, so, of course, is the qualitative specification of the value of life itself made subject to a subtle transformation. The question that generated the information that a human life has an infinite value was a question addressed to an identified life-holder recognising himself to be in need of life-saving care. The question that produces the finite value is the more relaxed query as to the extra cost that a calculative life-preserver would be just willing to authorise in order to escape an extra risk of avoidable mortality. The former question generated the answer that the criminal under irrevocable sentence of death would pay all that he could to be sprung from his cell. The latter question produces a different answer precisely because of the revised definition of the underlying problem that is well illustrated by Blomquist's usage:

> Value of life is the marginal value of a change in risk of death. It can be interpreted as an individual's value of a small change in his own probability of survival or alternatively as an individual's value of saving the life of an unidentifiable person in a large group to which the individual belongs.[5]

The new question refers to the common valuation of an unnamed probability's future death prevented. The original question referred to Mr. X's valuation of Mr. X's life preserved once Mr. X had learned with absolute certainty that disease Y had made his body its home. The questions are not the same. Nor are the answers that those questions are likely to elicit.

Policy-makers will rank the finite values that are thrown up by anxious unknowledge above the infinite values that are the free gift of a frightened certainty. Not every observer will endorse the choice. Not every observer will be prepared to accept that the leadership's preference for the expected (the *ex ante*) over the actual (the *ex post*) is founded on intellectual considerations more robust than administrative convenience alone. Thus John Broome, arguing against the notion that the value of the risk of dying may be regarded as a good substitute for the value of life itself, has taken the view that it is little short of murder to treat a statistical life as if in some way inferior to the personalised life of Mr. X suffering from disease Y: 'It does not seem correct to distinguish in value between the death of a known person and of an unknown person.'[6] Broome's conclusion, that the value of the anonymous life must be upgraded until it equals the value of the named life, has the beneficial property as seen from the perspective of utilitarian philosophy that it leads directly to an increase in the numbers of survivals. So literal an interpretation of the injunction to love one's neighbour as oneself might be expected, indeed, not merely to increase but actually to maximise the census of lives saved. No one dwelling in the ignorance of the *ex ante* can ever be entirely confident that it will not be his or her own life that will one day constitute the marginal *ex post*. No one, accordingly, should be too quick to find fault with Broome's contention that no economic value short of infinity can ever be assigned to a human life. Because Mr. X's willingness to pay for care is infinite, perhaps his community's valuation of life must also be infinite and can never be less.

All humanitarians will wish most sincerely to be able to follow Broome in the direction of the infinite commitment. Realists among the moralists will, however, point out that Broome's idealistic first-best is unable to provide practical guidance in the second-best world of scarcity. Besides that, as Buchanan and Faith observe, Broome's concentration on the objective consequences to the virtual exclusion of the subjective calculus in effect distorts the nature of the preferences that real-world individuals are actually observed to reveal:

> To say that 'costs' are infinite for the person who loses his life in the draw of a lottery in which he rationally chose to participate is to say nothing at all about the *value* that such an individual placed on life in the moment at which the choice was made. These ex post 'costs' can, in no way, influence the choice behavior that created the consequences.[7]

Buchanan and Faith are adamant that Broome's infinites are rooted far more in the accountant's historicals than ever they are in the selection of options that must remain the essence of the democrat's quest: 'The central flaw in his whole argument lies in a misunderstanding of *cost*. When does any attempt to *value* life arise for an individual or for a collectivity? Only when a *choice* is confronted does a valuation process become necessary. And only when choice is confronted is opportunity cost meaningful.'[8] Even if the *ex post* were able to supply usable criteria, Buchanan and Faith would maintain, still it must be rejected on methodological grounds for the simple reason that real-world men and women are wont to make their decisions in advance of knowing the outcomes—and that no responsible government will employ standards that deviate significantly from those of the citizens who elect it into power.

The arguments aside, the *ex ante* perspective is in the event the more frequently adopted of the two possible vantage points. Thus it is that the relevant willingness to pay is more frequently the willingness to pay for *probability* than it is the willingness to pay for *care*: 'Briefly, the fundamental premises of the willingness-to-pay approach are (a) that social decisions should, so far as possible, reflect the interests, preferences and attitudes to risk of those who are likely to be affected by the decisions and (b) that in the case of safety, these interests, preferences and attitudes are most effectively summarised in terms of the amounts that individuals would be willing to pay or would require in compensation for (typically small) changes in the probability of death or injury during a forthcoming period. Consequently, the willingness-to-pay approach tends to be concerned principally with individual marginal rates of substitution of wealth for risk of death or for risk of injury.'[9]

Concerned as it is with the individual and the subjective in the context of expectation and risk, the *ex ante* perspective is exposed, however, to the serious difficulty that the contents of people's minds are non-observable and non-empirical. It is by no means easy to estimate other people's willingness to pay if they are not in practice being called upon either to show the willingness or to make the payment. The estimation is not a simple one, but nor is the attempt necessarily doomed to failure. Simply, the search will have to be for the shadow rather than for the substance that is likely to remain frustratingly elusive.

In the *ex post* case the proxy for willingness will be the payment for care. In the *ex ante* case the equivalent proxy may be derived from one or more of the following four sources of introspective evidence: attitudes reported in questionnaires and surveys, choices made involving safety and security, differential remuneration regarded as compensatory for differential danger, life insurance purchased as a cushion for dependent survivors. Each of the four sources of introspective evidence will be examined in turn. None will be seen to be ideal. Each nonetheless will retain a certain attraction to the methodological individualist who stubbornly insists that the patient alone can ever have the right to assign an economic value to a human life.

(b) Questionnaires and Surveys

Always assuming that people are self-aware rather than intuitive, always assuming that they are articulate and not tongue-tied, the most obvious means of capturing the economic value that they themselves attach to the risk of dying would clearly be to ask them outright for a number. The number would refer to their willingness to pay for a small change in probability and it would almost certainly fall short of infinity. People might be prepared to sacrifice all that they own and more when conscious that they have already fallen victim to a life-threatening illness; but they might for all that be somewhat less generous to themselves when imagining no more than the purchase of a probability. Questionnaires and surveys are employed to pick up the finite numbers that real-world individuals cite when asked how much they would be just willing to pay in order to conclude just such a purchase.

The object of the exercise is not to observe preferences revealed through expenditures made but rather to collect information by means of direct inquiry. Sometimes the question asked will be open, explicit and transparent: here the participants will be invited without any further prompting to state precisely how much money they would be just willing to spare in exchange for a named improvement in the likelihood of survival. At other times the question asked will be fleshed out with detail in an attempt to stimulate the respondent's thought processes: thus they might be required to specify the maximum supplement they would be prepared to pay to upgrade an airline ticket to a carrier with a better safety-record, or the additional fuel bill they would regard as acceptable in order to secure a given reduction in risk of death from an accident at a nuclear power plant, or the increment in local taxation they would countenance in connection with a campaign to improve street lighting and police services. However the question is phrased, the object of the exercise is clear enough: it is to generate, proceeding bottom-up, a reasonable indication of the true marginal rate of substitution of personal wealth for risk of death in a given community at a given point in time. The quantification made, policy-makers then have a democratic benchmark to which they can refer when faced with the life-and-death choices that will inevitably be as common as they are difficult in any society that looks to its State to implement policies affecting safety and care.

One such benchmark is $28,000, this being the implicit value of a human life (entirely dependent, of course, on the specific questions that were asked) in the study conducted in Boston by J.P. Acton.[10] Acton canvassed the opinions of 100 Bostonians. He informed them that for the purposes of his investigation they should take the probability of a heart attack as 1/100 (.01) and the probability of a heart attack proving fatal as 2/5 (.40). He then asked them how much they would be willing to pay for a programme (an air-ambulance service, for example) which would reduce from 2/5 to 1/5 (.20) the likelihood that the heart attack would be followed by death: the average sum quoted was $56. As the initial chance of death was (.01) (.40) and the chance of death contingent on the policy change was (.01) (.20), Acton was able to establish the ratio of the extra cost (the proposed expenditure of $56) to the extra benefit (the expected fall in the risk of death of .004-.002 = .002). He then solved for the average value of a human life on the basis that $56/.002 = $28,000.

Questionnaires can pick up such magnitudes, but they can pick up much subsidiary information as well. Thus Jones-Lee and his associates (who sampled over 1000 Britons, nationally dispersed) asked no less than 37 questions and came up with some valuable supplementary data. They found, for example, that respondents were not indifferent (financial burden assumed constant) as between death in a car accident, death from heart disease and death from cancer: asked to say which form of death they most wanted to see reduced by 100, the respective tallies were 11, 13 and 76 per cent. Perhaps this result (a clear warning that differentiated modes of decease are not easy to aggregate) picks up the disutility of dying alongside the disutility of the death itself. Most people will probably regard a slow death from stomach cancer (a painful process involving morbidity as well as mortality) as somehow inferior to a sudden death in a car crash (a disease-free end which is economical of both discomfort and anxiety).[11]

Jones-Lee and his associates were also able to establish by means of finely-tuned questioning the extent to which, at least for some people, death *per se* is not the worst possible outcome. With respect to the loss of a leg, for instance, 6.2 per cent of the respondents said the status was as bad as death, 2.4 per cent slightly worse than death, 1.2 per cent much worse than death, 0.3 per cent very much worse than death, while for the permanently bedridden status the results were 33.4, 11.9, 11.2 and 6.9 per cent respectively.[12] The discovery, that 10.1 per cent of the respondents believed the loss of a leg to be at least as bad as death, that 63.4 per cent held the same belief when asked to contemplate the prospect of being permanently bedridden, is a salutary reminder that most human beings are unprepared to conflate the discrete notions of being alive on the one hand, continuing to exist on the other. That reminder serves in turn to underline the importance of psychometric investigations into relative valuations of different health-states.

One such investigation is the study carried by Kind, Rosser and Williams into the quality (and not just the quantity) of the life-years that might through intervention be rescued from the jaws of death. The authors point out that there exists a continuous range of intermediate states that lie between perfect health on the one hand, total extinction on the other. They also take the view that thosc states are not merely to be regarded as earning instrumentalities, irrespective of the level of satisfaction of the unique individuals actually entrusted with the living of the lives. Kind, Rosser and Williams explain that it is their objective to construct 'what might be called "warmblooded" or joy-of-living valuations, in the value-of-life jargon.'[13] They pursue their investigation with the aid of a questionnaire incorporating eight permanent states of disability: these range from no disability at all at one pole to complete unconsciousness at the other, with a series of compromise conditions in between (being bedridden, being housebound, being unable to perform more than light housework only). Each state of disability is susceptible of identification with four discrete degrees of subjective distress: none, mild, moderate and severe.

Seventy subjects were interviewed, the sample being chosen in such a way as to include some patients, some doctors, some nurses and some healthy volunteers. Each subject was asked to provide information both ordinal (whether state A was preferred to state B) and cardinal (*by how much* the happiness associated with A differed from that derived from B).

The results contained some surprises: doctors, for example, ranked an above-average number of states as worse than death and also showed an above-average sensitivity to suffering. More important than the results are, however, the aspirations. The investigators correctly recognised that measured life-years have little meaning until they have been quality-adjusted to allow for perceived utility. They also demonstrated a technique by means of which the multiple characteristics of the product known as living can in practice be estimated and weighted.

Questionnaires and surveys offer ordinary individuals the opportunity to reveal their preferences. Attractive to the democrat as such consultation must inevitably be, yet it would be a mistake nonetheless to erect too robust a structure of economic and social policy on the problematic foundations which are often the best that the process is able to provide.

One obvious difficulty is that the respondents might simply not grasp what exactly it is that they are being asked to quantify. Not all persons have so great a fluency in the language of the *might-be* that they are able intelligently to state how much they would be just willing to pay now in exchange for a reduction of .002 per cent in the statistical probability of premature death: as Jones-Lee admits, there must always be 'cause for concern about the capacity of most subjects for *imagining* their response to this type of question in the first place.'[14] Thought experiments involving small changes in statistical lives are never easy to conduct; and the charge is therefore real that the answer supplied to the hypothetical question will have much of the character of a number plucked out of the air by a person too confused and too embarrassed to be calculative. Aware of the possibility, the sensible investigator will naturally want to include internal cross-checks in the questions asked in order to confirm that risk-rankings are indeed transitive. Such cross-checks might in the event prove counter-productive. Should they establish that the representative respondent is genuinely prone to plucking numbers out of the air, the demonstration of irrationality is bound to undermine confidence in the value of the results.

A second difficulty involves the active role of the questions that are asked. It is well-known that, most people being anxious to please, a question beginning 'would you agree...' is more likely than not to evoke an affirmative response. It is widely accepted that, most people being creatures of compromise, a scale with an odd number of steps will offer an unhealthy temptation to the undecided automatically to converge on the middle. In cases such as these, clearly, the investigator might *willy nilly* be influencing his replies merely by virtue of the way in which he words his questions. Not that it is always apparent precisely when bias is likely to be engendered. Intuitively one would have expected that rational individuals would react in the same manner to the probable saving of – human lives, irrespective of the precise formulation of the questions asked. Empirically, however, the experimental results established by Tversky and Kahneman would appear to suggest that there is considerably more to the psychology of choice than the mathematical mean alone: 'The prospect of certainly saving 200 lives is more attractive than a risky prospect of equal expected value, that is, a one-in-three chance of saving 600 lives. ... The certain death of 400 people is less acceptable than the two-in-three chance that 600 will die.'[15] Thence the 'common pattern' that dominates the 'majority choice': 'Choices involving gains are often risk averse and changes involving losses are often risk taking.'[16] Presumably there is perceptual imperfection in any mode of decision-making that reacts more strongly to a certain loss than it does to a probable gain of an equivalent magnitude. Perhaps they are imperfect; but still the perceptions must be respected as the individual's own. Thus it is that the investigator must think long and hard about the method of attack that he or she adopts: 'In a question dealing with the response to an epidemic, for example, most respondents found "a sure loss of 75 lives" more aversive than "80% chance to lose 100 lives" but preferred "10% chance to lose 75 lives" over "8% chance to lose 100 lives", contrary to expected utility theory'.[17] Questions, in short, have consequences; and the investigator would therefore do well to keep in mind the possible bias deriving from the active role.

The final difficulty has to do with the selection of the sample. It being impractical to canvass the opinions of the citizenry as a whole, a cross-section must be identified which speaks with the voice of the median, the representative and the typical. Once upon a time the estimation of the consensus presented no real problem: scholars had the great good fortune of being able to sample at Random (a village in Derbyshire distinguished by the fact that its much-interviewed inhabitants thought precisely as did the silent majority of the nation's population). Later came the Fall: Random having been razed to clear a path for a motorway, scholars were forced for themselves to single out the subset that possessed the relevant characteristics of the wider whole.

The shadow referendum is a difficult one to conduct. The distance-factors being numerous, the results will not be conclusive even if allowance is made for the least-hidden heterogeneities of age, sex, occupation, income, wealth-ownership in the form of a car or a house. Respondents are always self-selected to the extent that there is no compulsion to respond (the less-than-100% response rate carrying with it the possibility that those who are concerned enough about risk to reply will happen also to have an above-average valuation of both the quantity and the quality of life). A sample size of 70, 100 or even 1000 participants can hardly be regarded as large enough to be unambiguously free from bias (whereas a meaningful trawl might, of course, have to be so ambitious as to impose a prohibitive cost). Different pools and different risks will produce different values: the not-inconsiderable range in the replies recorded points in itself not to generalisable inferences so much to a history-bound account of *who* was once asked, and about *which* threat to life. Such variability, such mutability, inevitably reduces the usefulness of the attitudinal data to the policy-maker who wants to be in touch with the mainstream. Disillusioned with words but committed to consultation, the leadership might decide in the circumstances to turn directly to deeds for the guidance it requires on the popular valuation of a human life.

(c) Safety and Security

Questionnaires and surveys invite grouped individuals to verbalise numbers while fielding hypothetical plus-perfects. Studies of real-world experience do not ask but merely observe. Making the tacit assumption that aggregated outcomes normally constitute a fair simulacrum of individuals' intentions, such studies deduce preferences from actions and take the actual as an index of the desired. Should human behaviour be fundamentally unmotivated, the observational method will produce results that are no more than isolated occurrences and freak one-offs. Should human behaviour be fundamentally purposive, however, there may be much in an approach that infers subjectivity from phenomena and states of mind from choices made. Not least with respect to the value of life, where real-world experience in the general area of safety and security may serve as a sensitive indicator of popular attitudes to the inescapable trade-off between resources and risk.

Thus the piece-worker is observed to dispense with protective goggles and inconvenient safety-catches in order to boost his per-hour output. The pedestrian saves time – but endangers life – by crossing against the lights. The party-goer chooses an unlicensed taxi in preference to a more expensive alternative that is more frequently inspected. The tenant accepts the polluted environment of the main road and the nuclear reactor in exchange for a rent that is moderate. The holiday-maker searches out the deserted beach despite the fact that it is the congested beach that boasts the lifeguard. The amenity-lover goes by road and sometimes speeds despite the fact that the train is both less dangerous and less costly. The drinker drinks and the smoker smokes despite the fact that the former knows of the threat to his liver and the latter is aware of the danger to her lungs. In these and other ways the members of the community may be said to be revealing their preferences through the medium of their actions. Quantified, those preferences provide insights of a sort into the value that individuals themselves attach to their life.

The evidence, needless to say, lends little support to the supposition that individuals on balance are of the opinion that an infinite sum may reasonably be paid for a small increase in the probability of survival. What the evidence does do is to confirm that individuals on balance are frequently prepared at the margin to swap some probable survival for some present advantage. The evidence also gives an indication of the equilibrium price at which those sales and those purchases are by implication being effected. Being actual rather than imagined, the evidence has the additional advantage that it provides a measure of the *which* and the *by how much* that is based entirely on what people do and not at all on what people say. Such evidence will have a strong appeal to all observers convinced that actions speak louder than words.

The voluntary installation of a collapsible steering column is a useful illustration of the general proposition that the risk of death is at least in part a self-selected endogeneity. A further illustration is the voluntary recourse to the car seat-belt. Here the driver who wears the belt incurs no less than three sets of costs – the paid-out cost of buying and fitting the belt; the time-cost of earnings foregone while putting on and unbuckling the belt; and the discomfort-cost of motoring when restrained by the belt. On the other hand, the driver knows that the sacrifice is rewarded by an identifiable benefit in the form of a heightened probability of enjoying continued life as a direct result of employing the belt. Benefits as well as costs are clearly involved in the voluntary recourse to the car seat-belt. Blomquist, writing at a time when the car seat-belt was not compulsory in the United States, set himself the task of quantifying the economic value of human life that was implicitly being revealed by the 23 per cent of American drivers who voluntarily invested in the risk-reducing device. The value calculated would obviously have been a different one had Blomquist concentrated his attention not on the 23 per cent who did but on the 77 per cent who did not. A democracy debating whether to ban all flights over urban areas lest one crash provoke a horrific catastrophe will be seriously exposed to unpopular error where it takes as representative a calculation that relates specifically to a minority. That said, even a minority can express an opinion; and it is explicitly the opinion of the 23 per cent that Blomquist sought to reconstruct.

Thus Blomquist first added up the marginal cost per driver belted: he was able to rely on a time-and-motion study for the vital information that the average American who buckled and unbuckled required 3.3 hours per annum for the activities, and he made an arbitrary imputation of his own to cover the inconvenience entailed. He then incorporated the appropriate benefit, which he took to be the reduction in risk of mortality as is documented in objective statistics. Finally, basing his computation on the ratio of extra cost to extra benefit, he worked out that the implicit value of a human life, as revealed by the protective practices of the belted themselves, was approximately $370,000.[18] Of particular interest was Blomquist's conclusion, derived from his real-world data, that this estimate was no less than double the value that would have been suggested by the human capital approach. What this means, if Blomquist is correct, is that the willingness to pay yields better predictions of popular attitudes that does the more objective measure that conflates the value of living life with the value of productive life. Most readers, one suspects, will probably warm to such a result.

Calculations pyramided on crash-helmets bought or not bought, fatty foods eaten or not eaten, cod liver oil swallowed or not swallowed, fitness-centres attended or not attended, all offer promising insights into subjective valuations. If those perceptions are truly to serve as sensitive indicators permitting meaningful generalisations, however, then it is clearly of some importance that the group selected for study should be a reasonably representative sample of the wider society's overall orientation. The task of identifying so ideal a sample is, alas, by no means an easy one. Life at Random was so much simpler. But we start from here.

Some members of the community will be positive towards risk. Attracted rather than repelled by the threat to life and limb, such persons will actually prefer the excitement of dangerous living to a lower probability of premature death. Ranking cliff-hanging life-years above tea-drinking life-years, such persons are observed deliberately to seek out hazardous activities such as motorcycle racing, bare-knuckle boxing and hockey played without helmets. Often they provide some indication of the pleasure they derive from the flirtation with death by means of the fee they pay to enter the game (the subscription required, say, to join a free-fall parachuting society). Thrilled by hang-gliding and injecting, seduced by abseiling and sequential infidelity, risk-lovers will clearly be a world away from the attitudes of the radical averters with whom they are obliged to share their social space. Negative towards danger, such committed averters will treat caffeinated coffee as a forbidden narcotic and will judge it irresponsibly careless to cross the road other than with the support of a well-trained warden. Such persons prudently shop twice daily in order to ensure that their food is fresh; they dwell in ground-floor units in order to facilitate evacuation in the event of fire; and they sink scarce resources in fully-equipped fall-out shelters lest a terrorist's device render them the victims of a nuclear winter.

Somewhere in between the cliff-hangers and the tea-drinkers are the skiiers and the footballers, the airline passengers and the chain-smokers. Desirous on the one hand of enjoying life but on the other of holding on to it, such moderates constitute the compromising middle group to which Blomquist's 23% will presumably belong. The problem for the policy-maker is to decide whether to accept the valuations of the seat-belt wearers as characteristic of the median citizen or whether, alternatively, to formulate policy in the chosen image of the fearless mountaineer or of the persistent hand-washer. Given the heterogeneity of orientations that obtain in the pluralistic society, it can hardly be an easy task for the mixed economy to identify the ideal position on the spectrum that separates the citizens who wrestle with sharks from the citizens who spend sensibly on good galoshes.

Nor is it obvious that the highest frequency will necessarily correspond to the greatest intensity: where the vast majority derives only limited pleasure from cliff-hanging whereas a tiny minority drinks in the profoundest of satisfaction with its tea, the democrat who treats the majority's view as the representative one will be acting in a time-honoured tradition that is also, cardinally speaking, seriously suspect. To infer the economic value of a human life bottom-up from individuals' perceptions no doubt reflects the loftiest of aspirations. The search for the representative being fraught with such difficulties, however, there would seem to be a persuasive argument, here as elsewhere, for cutting back on the generalisable in order to concentrate on the anthropological. Blomquist's 23 per cent may or may not have the attitudes of the median citizen. What it does have is the attitudes of the median belter – and that value of life is in itself by no means without interest.

Always assuming, of course, that the subjects in the study are reasonably aware of the actual probabilities that attach to the safety devices and the security measures that they are observed to employ. In the case of the questionnaire or the survey the respondent is authoritatively informed as to the magnitude of the risk: he is then required only to put a pecuniary value on his reaction to the reduction. In the case of the revealed preference for the filter-tip over its high tar cousin, however, the consumer is most fundamentally on his own. Frequently in the dark as to the statistical probabilities, not certain where to turn for reliable evidence, aware that pooled frequencies are not named individuals, disheartened in any event by the negative utility always associated with the contemplation of one's own death, the consumer who scrupulously cuts the fat off his meat in order to reduce the probability of a fatal heart attack may well be revealing preferences that are more indicative of directions than they are of magnitudes. Choices so imprecisely formulated make calculations built upon the observations at once artificial and ambiguous. The citizen's-eye view of the value of life, it is intended, should be estimated through the comparison of the extra cost with the extra benefit – of the price, say, of a residential smoke alarm with the improved life expectancy that the purchase procures. Yet it is clearly impossible to grind out a finite value where the citizen, aware of the marginal burden, is ignorant of the marginal gain that the investment is likely to secure.

When in doubt the observer can, of course, fall back on the objective probabilities that the rational actor ought to have employed. Thus the observer might shunt in the data from the mortality tables even when the actor who incurs the marginal cost is not believed to have made use of such statistics and frequencies. Factual information undeniably generates a value as well as a sign, a magnitude as well as a direction. Should the real-world individual not have acted upon the same solid statistic, however, the value of life that is manufactured with its aid will have no real-world relevance. It will be a normative value of life, a value of life that would predictably have been enunciated by rational men and women if in possession of all the relevant information. It will no doubt be a very fine value of life – but it will not for all that be the value of life that is implied by the revealed preferences of real-world men and women when they are seen to spend on safety and security.

An alternative procedure would be for the observer, eschewing altogether the factual evidence, to rely exclusively on the misperceived odds and the unrealistic expectations that real-world actors themselves make the subjective basis for their recorded choices. Perhaps they will overvalue the well-publicised but infrequent occurrence such as the militant's bomb. Perhaps they will undervalue the small but regular risk like the chip-pan fire that, statistically speaking, will represent the greater threat. Instinctively, the observer will have the scientist's reservations about any calculation that makes deliberate use of overvaluations and undervaluations such as these. Respect for persons is uncompromising, however; and it must not be forgotten how frequently it is that such misapprehensions constitute the very bedrock of the liberal democracy. As Gavin Mooney puts it: 'Although it may be accepted that where public funds are involved we ought not to use a fool's valuation in deciding upon their allocation, if... society is comprised solely of fools, then the valuation of these fools is the correct one to use.'[19] All in all, there is a strong case to be made in favour of using *perceived* probability rather than *actuarial* probability when performing any calculation of the value of life as seen from the perspective of the authentic life-holders themselves. A strong case – except for one thing: statistics on the probable survival that real-world actors think they are purchasing are inconveniently thin on the ground.

One reason for the deficiency in the data is the simple fact that most people do not think things through with the precision that is the *sine qua non* for the computation to be made. Even if a perceived 10 per cent is conspicuously unequal to an actuarial 20 per cent, it at least allows the observer to calculate the implicit value of a human life. Where the basis of the choice is the guesstimate or the gut reaction, the number-cruncher's lot will be a far less happy one.

Besides which, the very apperception of the 'a little bit less', the 'a whole lot more', presupposes that the observer has somehow made contact with the hidden mind which alone can sense the trade-offs. Yet such a contact is in truth by no means an easy one to establish. Questionnaires and surveys come encumbered with shortcomings so marked as to drive the observer from words to deeds: it would be in the circumstances an admission of defeat for the observer to retreat from deeds to words again. Inference of the subjective probability from the result obtained will only be possible if both the economic cost of safety and security and the economic value of a human life are themselves already known: how the value can be produced in advance of the computation being performed is, however, as shrouded in mystery as the reason why anyone should want to gain a purchase on the probability after gaining a purchase on the value of life for the calculation of which the probability is explicitly being sought. Thence the conclusion, that the data is often deficient precisely because the observer has no dependable means of making contact with the invisible mind which alone can tell its 10 per cent from its 'a little bit more' – or admit that it 'hasn't a clue'.

A final reason for the deficiency in the data has to do with the conspicuous conjunction of joint products. Individuals switch off the mains electricity before they open the fuse box because they harbour a fear of death through electrocution: in that sense they are clearly sacrificing time and effort in order thereby to avoid the diswelfare of premature mortality. Yet they also incur the burden because of quite separate anxieties relating not to the *length* but rather to the *enjoyment* of life: while not actually welcoming extinction, neither are they keen on pain and suffering, sustained injury and permanent disability. Their willingness to pay in such a situation ought properly to be recorded as the extrapolation of two utilities rather than as the payment made for only one. To the extent that an adjustment is not made for spoiled existence, the crucial element of quality of life will have been missed out and the remaining element, the quantity of life, misleadingly estimated upward by default. Different investigators, of course, will make different adjustments. Rightly so; since no division of a single payment can ever be other than by means of the guesstimate or the gut reaction that in the limit will equal the arbitrary.

(d) Differential Remuneration

There exist few markets in certain death. There exist few exchanges that regularly transfer the life-holder's established property rights to a homicidal capitalist offering a market price. There exist few solicitors who know how to do the conveyancing and few judges who would be prepared to enforce the contract. But risk of death is different. Pecuniary compensation for the increased probability of premature death is a common characteristic of the market for labour, where a danger-differential is the accepted inducement that encourages the nervous to overcome their aversion. That marginal payment may be regarded as a revelation of preference with respect to cash definite versus death possible. Should it reasonably be so regarded, the implicit bribe can then be employed in the reconstruction of the individual's-eye perspective on the value of life.

Danger money is the creature of the marginal hazard, not of the total position. Thus it would be unhelpful to use the construct to predict that workers in high-risk occupations will normally receive more pay than will workers in low-risk employments. Window cleaners do not normally earn more than senior civil servants. *Ceteris paribus* perhaps they would; but still the fact remains that differences in educated skill and demanding responsibility are seen more than to cancel out the differential exposure to occupational accident. If danger money is truly to yield meaningful predictions, it is clearly preferable that the use of the concept be reserved for cases where like is unambiguously being juxtaposed to like. It would, for example, be entirely appropriate to use the concept to predict that coalminers blasting with explosives underground will command a better remuneration than will coalminers pushing buttons on the surface. Such a comparison is very likely to give a democratic insight into the representative miner's subjective trade-off between extra risk on the one hand, extra money on the other.

Where the representative miner is not also the representative citizen, it would obviously be an error to generalise for the wider population on the basis of the value of life that is implied by the outlier and the exception. A risk-averting collectivity contemplating the costs and benefits of an anti-smoking campaign would obviously do well to ignore the atypical valuations of the deep-sea driver, the bomb-disposal expert, the circus snake-charmer, the drug dealer's courier, the pilot of the crop-sprayer and the incinerator of toxic waste when it searches for the median even in the bosom of the sample. Where the representative miner happens also to be the representative citizen, however, there it may make good sense to generalise for the whole on the basis of a part that is not the extreme but rather the norm.

Good representatives must be selected; and Lionel Needleman has suggested that construction workers might be a suitable choice. Needleman does not say how he knows that the pool in question is neither atypically adventurous nor atypically timid in its attitude to risk. What he does say is that the group he identifies enjoys average industrial earnings and appears, in terms of its objective characteristics, to be 'reasonably typical of male manual workers in general'.[20] The bias in favour of the younger, the manual and the male is an admitted shortcoming (not least because the middle aged, the professional and the female would probably prove more cautious in their approach to life-threatening tasks). Needleman nonetheless maintains that the sample he selects is an adequately indicative one.

The occupational group selected, Needleman proceeds to collect information on the premium payments that British workers manage to secure as the concomitant of their volunteering for abnormal duties. Thus he records the following result, which relates to the subjective measure of working at heights: 'The hourly rate on one of [the] sites was two pence at heights between 30 and 75 feet, four pence at between 75 and 100 feet, six pence at between 100 and 150 feet, and thereafter six pence for each additional 50 feet.'[21] Particularly at risk were the roofing workers, the scaffolders and the steel erectors. Not surprisingly, these were also the grades of construction worker that cornered the lion's share of the danger money.

Needleman had access to objective data on incremental risk: he knew, for example, that the average labourer who volunteered to become a scaffolder was exposing himself to an extra 0.52/1000 chance of premature death. He also had statistics on differential remuneration: thus he was aware that the average labourer who became a scaffolder would be able to command 10–15 per cent more money than that same person would have earned on the ground. Equipped with that information, Needleman compared the extra cost with the extra benefit in such a way as to derive the following implicit valuations for selected human lives: £7,845 for a roofing worker, £16,565 for a steel erector and £45,980 for a scaffolder.[22] Different studies using different samples have, of course, derived different results – the results reported by Marin and Psacharopoulos being very different indeed: 'If the sample is split into groups, the value of life implied for manual workers is ... in the £600,000–£700,000 range, while the value of life implied for non-manual workers is over three times as high. This is expected given that safety is a superior good.'[23] Different samples imply different values. And Random is gone forever.

If compensating differentials are to be consulted in the search for the value of life, than it is naturally of some importance that pay should be free to fluctuate: observed variations in earnings can hardly be regarded as in proportion to subjective attitudes to fatalities where the payments in question are insensitive when they ought to be flexible. Yet the simple fact is that the real world is characterised by institutional rigidities and collective conventions such as render observed differentials signally resistant to individualised settlements. Collective bargaining, so favourable to standardisation over groups, can be an impediment to risk-shading. Imperfect knowledge of alternative employments, significant barriers to mobility (occupational and geographical), the high transaction costs of change, all dictate that disequilibrium relativities can survive even for long periods of time. The force of the objection should not, of course, be exaggerated – the very existence of danger money being living proof that the heightened risk of death at work remains a marketable commodity even in a corporatised economy. Still, however, a doubt must be voiced as to the extent to which the differentials will pick up the precise magnitudes rather than simply the general directions to which the differences will point.

Not that the resultant pay structure will even then be easy to interpret. The earnings-differential might indeed be the proportioned counterpart to the statistical fatality and to nothing else. Equally, however, the extra pay might incorporate a recognition of accompanying disamenities such as the oil-platform's damp and dirty conditions or the non-fatal fall from heights of the roofer who slips. Clearly, the task must be first to recognise the disamenities and then to correct for them: only in that way can death-related differentials be derived such as provide the purified indicator of the value of life. Perhaps too the sample should be divided by insurance status. A steel erector who must pay out-of-pocket for medical care will arguably be less willing to take chances than will a scaffolder who has comprehensive cover. Health insurance may not prevent death but it does pay for injuries to be treated. In that way it reduces the differential that must be paid for disamentity – but only for the worker who is insured.

Just as the differentials should be free to fluctuate, so it is important that the variance should be informed. There is little to be explained with reference to danger money where the contract is concluded in ignorance of the probabilities involved: the revealed preferences of the consumer of life will hardly be approximated by the mortality-differential where the individual is unaware of the threat. Yet objective probability is one thing, subjective estimation is another; and the truth is that individuals' calculations will often be based on frequencies quite different from those that are induced by the scientist from the evidence. In the words of Marin and Psacharopoulos: 'Workers' demand for extra compensation is not necessarily based on the actual risks of each job but on what they think the risks are. Many of the occupational causes of death are not obvious.'[24] Not obvious, not noticed and not known. Thus does the statistical death give way to the fool's valuation in a complicated world where few decisions are ever taken on the basis of perfect information.

In the real world, the frequency of newsworthy fatalities tends to be biased upward, the malignancy of the boringly mundane simultaneously to be under-estimated. Cardiovascular disease among low-grade civil servants does not make the front pages. The violent death of a police officer is covered even at the cost of the evening's soaps.

Separation in time is a further cause of perceptual misapprehension. Consider the statistic that occasional porters performing light tasks only tend to experience a mortality rate far in excess of that recorded for coalminers working underground. Such a *datum*, unimpeachable in itself, will conceal as much as it reveals where the whole truth turns out to be that the terminal illness was actually contracted at the seam, even if the premature death was separated from the occupational hazard by the intermediate transfer to safer surface employment. Risk-comparison is especially vulnerable to inter-temporal latencies where the typical worker holds a succession of jobs (in which case the carcinogenic effect of asbestos fibres lodged early in the lung might never come to light) or where the risk is a newly-established one (where the pay-differential, in other words, cannot risk-rate the compensation for the obvious reason that the long-run impact cannot be known in advance).

Space too can be the reason for error. Thus a scaffolder is in a poor position to compare his danger-money with that of a whaler: ill-informed about the conditions in the other industry, he simply knows too little about the deaths and the bonuses to be able to calculate the opportunity costs or to conduct meaningful arbitrage. He will be far better placed to speak with authority about his own particular industry. A scaffolder will have seen so large a number of falls from heights that he will be in a good position to rule-of-thumb the extra fatalities and the appropriate differentials. Perceptual error, always a problem, will clearly be less of a problem in a closed society such as that of Needleman's construction workers than it will be in a heterogeneous pool where accidents at work are less visible. Needleman's workers were consistently myopic about outside risks: it is striking that the scaffolder, the steel erector and the roofer tended to demand extra money for an extra threat that was the statistical equivalent of one-third that of riding a motorcycle, one-half that of smoking 20 cigarettes a day. Weak on outside probabilities, the important thing is that Needleman's workers knew quite a bit about themselves. They were, in other words, adequately informed about themselves to make an intelligent estimation of the danger-differential that could then be employed to produce the workers' implicit valuation of their own human lives.

(e) Life Insurance

Dublin and Lotka, in 1930, formulated an economic approach to the money value of a man which in effect defined his value as his value to his dependants:

> Every individual who insures himself for the protection of the members of his family has in mind providing them, in the event of his death, with a sum of money that shall, as nearly as possible, take the place of his contribution to them while living. Human life in this sense may be equated to a sum of money.[25]

Human life in this approach is to be estimated soley in terms of expected net future earnings foregone (allowance made for the individual's own anticipated future consumption). Sentimental attachment and the grief of those left behind do not enter into the calculus: for all their felt immediacy, Dublin and Lotka warned, still the emotions are deficient in those 'practical, tangible quantities capable of numerical estimate in dollars and cents'[26] that are the *sine qua non* for precision and objectivity. Suffering, Dublin and Lotka said, has no financial counterpart capable of measuring up to the unexpired stream of expected payments, discounted so as to produce a single present value and quantified with reference to age-specific mortality rates. Besides that, Dublin and Lotka indicated, there is little in the economists' tool box that would enable them to deal effectively with bygones that are forever irreparable. Economists ought in the circumstances to confine themselves to the calculations they are professionally equipped to perform.

The idea that the individual's purchase of life insurance is some measure of the individual's valuation of human life is undeniably a tidy one. Especially attractive is the combination of the subjective decision voluntarily to insure with the objective evidence embodied in the earnings data. Yet there is a problem. Life insurance is a mode of compensating the survivors. Its aim is to ensure that those who rely upon another's earnings enjoy protection against economic loss in the event of the premature death of the breadwinner. Its aim is not to provide a payment for the deceased person himself in recognition of the satisfactions denied him when his life is so early snuffed out. Life insurance is thus more nearly the premium-payer's valuation of his life as a capital sum to be handed on to his heirs than it is a measure of the costs and benefits that attach specifically to himself. Life insurance expressly puts a value on death. Whether life insurance simultaneously puts a value on life is more debatable.

The insurance method has the further disadvantage that it is ethically suspect – obviously so, since any differential valuation of human life that parallels the economic differentials of the income distribution would seem to convey the perhaps unpalatable information that the death of a high earner is in some sense a greater loss than would have been the case had the deceased been less well-paid. Such a valuation is morally objectionable save in a community of which the members are nothing but slaves, marketable commodities to be bought and sold. It is economically objectionable as well to the extent that pay is an imperfect proxy for productivity and the cross-section of today an incomplete indicator of the time-series that is to come.

Life insurance, moreover, provides no guidance as to the value of life of the totally uninsured. An infant child is a case in point. That life must have some value but the child, lacking cover, will nonetheless have failed to assign a price to it. Nor it is clear what the appropriate price ought to be: uninsured children, like uninsured adults, differ so widely in their talents, their drive, their luck, that no national average can ever replace the unique and personal estimation that is unavailable where the uninsured put no price upon their life.

The assurance method, finally, does not take into account the possibility that the very existence of the protection itself might alter the parameters of the trade-off. Where the individual becomes less anxious about his own demise and therefore less safety-conscious, the disutility of his own death diminishes in his own mind. His own life, subjectively speaking, is of less value to him than it would have been had he not enjoyed the guarantee that dependant stake-holders with a financial interest in his earning capacity would be given pecuniary compensation in respect of the unexpected liquidation of the core asset. The amount replaced is the value of his life to them. It need not be the value of his life to himself; and in the case where he becomes reckless in consequence of the protection for his heirs it palpably is not. The life assurance valuation in such circumstances gives misleading signals to the policy-maker intent on dispensing with questionnaires and surveys but determined nonetheless to obtain subjective guidance on the value of life.

Life insurance makes its pay-outs to individuals by definition different from those who have borne the costs. In that sense the selfish premium-payer would be better off disabled. Accident insurance against what Dublin and Lotka call the 'acquired incapacity to fulfil the ordinary tasks of life'[27], the 'depreciation of the economic value of the individual'[28], gives rise to a claim in favour of the premium-payer himself; life insurance only compensates beneficiaries spared both the contributions and the mishap. Also, in the event of the 'incapacity' and the 'depreciation' the payment made by the insurer is often topped-up by a court order such as compels the tort-feasor to redress the grievance of the victim. The award is *ex post* (whereas the questionnaire is *ex ante*); and considerable disparities are often alleged to obtain as between the different judges (whereas the good survey will poll a representative sample). Interestingly, Kind, Rosser and Williams found nonetheless that there existed a close correlation between the valuations articulated by the 70 calm, detached subjects whom they interviewed and some 202 court awards made for compensation: 'It appears that, compared with the psychometric evidence, legal awards tend to assign more moderate relative valuations to the most severe states, but otherwise there seem no identifiable source of systematic bias between the two.'[29] The subjectively-aware might therefore wish, economising on the questioning, to rely altogether on the sensitivity of the judge.

Accident sometimes means damages for the party directly affected. Death, however, is different: then the judge, setting the distress of the deceased decisively to one side, concentrates his attention soley on the injuries suffered by the living. In proceeding in this manner, the court will make an assessment of the economic value of a human life which will reflect the same considerations as those which underlie the pay-out promised by the life insurance. First and foremost, in other words, the court will measure subjective disamenity in terms of objective variables such as the value to surviving dependants of earning capacity extinguished through negligence.

The measure is not an ideal one. Relating to a named individual, it has none of the detached impartiality that is the great attraction of the statistical probability. Acknowledging private cost while ignoring social, it demands no damages for the nation in respect of the premature destruction of education and potential. Excluding the dead to target the living, it introduces an additional bias in the downward direction by virtue of the qualitative dimension that is deliberately excised when the judge makes no allowance for the utility foregone by the deceased. Clearly, the award is unlikely to give adequate guidance to the social policy-maker so long as the value of life that is proclaimed by the court neglects something of the importance of the pleasure of living that would have been experienced by the casualty. This is not to say that the judges ought to be in the business of posting cheques to plots in graveyards, only that questionnaires and surveys, safety and security or differential remumeration might provide a more comprehensive account of the crucial subjectivities that are the essence of the patient's-eye perspective on the market for life.

11.2 THE PRACTITIONER

The first approach, in line with the principle of exchange, was to quantify the value of life on the basis of the marginal payment the representative individual would be just willing to make in order either to prevent the loss of his life or to ensure that the probable sacrifice be properly compensated. The second approach, falling back on authority, is to delegate to the representative professional the difficult task of deciding which life to save – and at what cost.

Delegation is attractive. It is attractive to the ignorant and the uncertain who, lost in the thick fog of behavioural unknowledge, are only too prepared to make the trained their guide. It is attractive to the nervous and the anxious who, comfortable with the notion of capital punishment, wish it nonetheless to be the judge and not themselves who briefs the hangman. It is attractive to the constitutionalists and the proceduralists whose concern is with preannounced rules and impersonal standards: so long as the same criteria are rigorously applied to all, such advocates of impartiality through convention will consistently maintain, at least each denial of care will reflect the same just process and no patient refused a life-saving drug will have grounds to die with the bitter cry of *ad hominem* on his lips. It is attractive, last but not least, to the doctors and the experts themselves: convinced that their traditions and precedents are rational rather than casual, insistent that the tried-and-tested is an indispensable bulwark against fashionable enthusiasms without a track record, such educated conservatives will say that their craft has so greatly benefited from learning-by-doing that the outsider is today entirely right to say that the doctor knows best. Doctors and experts, clearly, will find delegation attractive. They will hardly be alone in so doing.

Delegation is attractive. It is also familiar. Doctors, of all citizens the most experienced in the making of life-and-death decisions, have long been charged with the responsibility for choosing marginal means and for establishing ultimate ends. Doctors have long had to weigh alternatives and contemplate options in an economic world where one person's life-support machine costs another person his clot-busting thrombolytic. Doctors are familiar with the decisions and the patients are familiar with the doctors. There is in the circumstances a certain reassurance to be gained from the delegation of life-and-death decisions to well-trained medical professionals whose demonstrated expertise has retained confidence time-out-of-mind.

Doctors are unlikely, of course, to be in a position to articulate the precise valuation which they put upon a human life or to verbalise decision-making criteria which frequently they never learned but merely absorbed. The conditioned reflex, the knee-jerk reaction and the automatic response are valuable short cuts in a medical emergency; but they do mean that the underlying values and standards, implicit rather than explicit, must often be gleaned from actions and not from words. Doctors presumably will greet the substitution of empiricism and induction for questionnaires and surveys with a great sense of relief. No sincere Hippocratic with an ethic of service will want to stand up and declare that he is regularly choosing to let some lives lie where they fall. Observation of practice will be far less stigmatising to the committed teleologist aware for all his dedicated perfectionism that finitude of resources has condemned him to an eternal second-best.

Thus it might happen that doctors in a given medical system are seen to refuse treatment for a life that would have cost a known amount to save but at the same time are observed to spend an identical sum to save a different life. These results convey information that is both ordinal and cardinal. Replicated often enough to convince the *de facto* detective that they must count as representative rather than as idiosyncratic, the *de facto* bloodhound will then be able to use them as the basis for the inference that the doctors did what they did because they believed the second life to be of greater value than the first, the first life to be of lesser value than the second. The criteria are left to be sketched in afterwards. Like the philosopher, the theory only arrives *post festum*.

As with individual patients, so with individual treatments. Long-term haemodialysis for chronic renal failure provides a useful illustration. Buxton and West found that the cost to the National Health Service was £3500 per year of life extended through hospital dialysis (£2600 where the dialysis took place in the home). They based their calculation on the sum of £23m that was the discounted cost in England and Wales of institutional dialysis provided to 1000 patients for a sequence of 20 years. Buxton and

West, the calculation made, then went beyond mere estimation alone by suggesting that the values reconstructed might realistically be regarded as revealed preferences: the amounts the decision-makers are observed willing to spend, they said, 'may be considered to represent one estimate of the price society is prepared to pay to maintain life.'[30] If the decision-makers were prepared to pay all of £3500 for an additional life-year made possible through haemodialysis, then, the inference would seem to be, those decision-makers must have believed the annualised value of the incrementalised existence at least to be the equal of the £3500. And thus does the implicit become the explicit, the doctor's gut reaction solidify into the accountant's bottom line.

Practitioners' valuation is not unfamiliar. Nor, however, is it unproblematic; and one obvious difficulty is the danger that the inculcated attitudes of medical professionals might have survived intact despite a radical transformation of circumstances and conditions. Incrementalism and guesstimation, careers and committees, might have bent traditions from the ideal formulations that cool consideration would have suggested. Administrative convenience might have squeezed quantitative evidence into the confining straitjacket of average cost from which the marginal cost will find it difficult to escape. An insistence on medical convention when economic assessment identifies a more cost-effective technique might have opened up a gulf between two conceptions of optimality that resolute replication will make it impossible to transcend. Cases such as these demonstrate just how problematic it is to seek rational guidance from professional practice: where the standards employed are the unplanned outcomes of past processes, the preferences revealed by the practitioner may in truth be far more indicative of the over-socialised traditionalist's determination to conform that they are of any intellectual justification underlying the values that are implied.

Rules, however out of touch, at least promise what authorities can seldom deliver, that like will be treated as like and not *ad hoc*. Yet no constitutional settlement is ever free from some ambiguity necessitating some interpretation and allowing some independence. Good or bad, one consequence of such discretion and such initiative is that different doctors come to do different things. In the zone of autonomy, it is clear, different doctors will imply different magnitudes for the economic value of a human life.

Particularly susceptible to variance will be borderline cases where what is at stake is not so much the straightforward probability of technical success as philosophical fundamentals and ethically-charged issues. Doctors are unlikely to agree on the minimal bundle that is a human being (is an unconscious patient properly alive even if suspended in a coma virtually certain to be irreversible?); or on the exact specification of the state known as death (does it set in when the heart ceases to beat, when the brain becomes oblivious to external stimuli, when breathing becomes impossible without an artificial respirator?); or on the extent to which the unseen lives of waiting-list patients ought to constitute an argument in the practitioner's equation (should a hopeless incurable be repeatedly resuscitated when to switch off the support would be to free up the bed for a fellow creature of no less moral worth?); or on the moment when a mix of potentials becomes an unborn child that it would be murder to destroy (does a foetus have rights and what should happen when mother and child are at odds over those entitlements?). Different doctors will provide different answers to questions such as these. Through their actions they will in effect be putting different prices on one and the same asset. The observer concerned to reconstruct professionals' standards from a simple inspection of professionals' practice will naturally wish to equip himself with a representative sample. It is in the nature of the zone of autonomy, however, that one-offs will be common but representatives not always easy to locate. Clinical freedom can have its costs as well as its benefits. Not least to the patient: denied life-years by one doctor that would have been supplied by another, the client is bound to wonder *which* doctor it is, exactly, who happens in the event to know best what the circumstances decree.

Sometimes corporatised (and lacking flexibility), sometimes individualised (and prone to inconsistency), what is clear is the lack of hands-on accountability that must always characterise an inward-looking system dependant most of all upon the medical profession for the crucial decisions. Arm's-length accountability will generally be seen as socially legitimate so long as the public interest is consensually believed to be at one with the private. Quite different will be the level of tolerance, however, where the public is convinced that the professionals are making choices that are at variance with the values, the externalities and the institutions that exercise the wider collectivity. There, the public might conclude, the value of life that is being implied by the closed corporation is simply not the value of life that is held by the nation and the society of which the doctors are but a part.

One source of conflict will involve the unequal distribution of economic power. Thus the doctor might, rationing by price, be prepared to sell life-saving treatment to any patient with the income, the wealth and the insurance entitlements sufficient to cover the fee; but still the wider community might, concerned about the poor, deem it inequitable that patients unable to pay should be implied valueless and turned out to die. The wider community might in addition see to it that income maintenance continues the good work begun by medical intervention. The doctor clearly does the amputee or the paraplegic no lasting service if, unable to work, that patient sees the life saved through surgery rapidly fall forfeit to starvation. It is not normally the concern of the doctor to take a view on the ethics of medical rescue succeeded by economic assassination. It is more frequently the concern of the doctor's community, however, to situate the physical survival in its broader economic context.

Impartiality can prove a further source of tension. Disinterested professionalism prevents the doctor from treating like as unlike. Not so his fellow citizens, who might not be prepared to accept that scarce resources should be diverted from young productives to comfort elderly incurables or that the life of an unemployable alcoholic should be put on a par with that of the most brilliant engineer. There is a popular perception that the State and not the market is the friend of the weak. Where that State discriminates by age and function, however, where public policy favours the value-adder while treating the non-employed as parasitical, there, it is clear, the interests of the weak will not be well-served by a polity that takes the majority's position. In the case of the elderly incurables and the unemployable alcoholics, it would appear, the doctor and not the consensus will be the deviant's true friend.

Yet the doctor cannot in all circumstances reliably be counted upon to defend the patient's preferences. Sometimes it happens that the willingness to pay is frustrated from the start by an unwillingness to *be* paid that prevents effective demand ever from translating itself into quantity supplied. This mismatch between the purchaser and the provider is a further reason for thinking that the doctor's-eye view of the value of life will not in practice be an unproblematic one. A person who dies of skin cancer because ethical practitioners have refused to perform scientific experiments on animals may well feel as bitter and resentful as another person who dies of a rare sclerosis because economical majorities prohibit minority treatments with high average costs. The individual who wishes to live will not think kindly of authoritarian technocrats who deny him care for a low-quality existence that he himself stubbornly ranks above no existence at all. The individual who wishes to die will not feel himself better served by a Hippocratic opposed to assisted suicide than he will by a law banning all suicides in the economically-active age-groups. Clearly, the inculcated reactions of the medical practitioners will on some occasions go against the manifested desires of the paying patients, even as they will on other occasions act to protect those desires from the tyranny of the democratic mass. Where the agent does not see eye-to-eye with the principal, the doctor's perspective on the value of life is unlikely to command the complete confidence of the patients and the public who will demand the final say.

11.3 THE PUBLIC

The advocate of economic exchange will take as his ideal the market for life in which unique individuals alone decide how much of the commodity they wish to consume and at what marginal cost. The supporter of professional authority, on the other hand, will argue strongly in favour of decision-making by professionals and experts with knowledge and experience on their side. The two perspectives are a world apart in the attitudes which they embody. As separate as section one and section two of the present chapter, they are linked nonetheless, in a democratic society, by the underlying conviction that neither the former position nor the latter can legitimately be adopted as the basis for public policy where that position is not also buttressed by the power of public opinion. The public is in that sense the ultimate authorising agency, even where that which it authorises turns out to be as microscopic as the unique individual's distinctive choice, as paternalistic as one doctor's conventional response.

Yet it would be a mistake to assume that public opinion will always and everywhere see democratic intervention as being confined to the legitimation of the patient or of the practitioner, of the consumer or of the supplier. The range of social choices, like the range of social attitudes, is in truth somewhat broader than two alternatives and nothing more. The range, like those attitudes, has both economic and non-economic dimensions such as are considered respectively in the first two parts of this section. The final part of the section draws together the various approaches to the economic value of a human life and asks what, if anything, the theories have to contribute to the quality of debate.

(a) The Wealth of Nations

The social consensus, taking issue with the splendid individualism both of the sovereign consumers and of the Hippocratic professionals, might cleave to the notion that the value of a life is inseparable from the life-holder's anticipated contribution to the nation's gross product. So judgemental a consensus would not accept that a person's a person for a'that. Nor would it agree with the notion that there can exist some absolute right to health which does not carry with it a concomitant duty to add value and foster growth. Instead, the economystic mind would maintain, the value of a life prolonged is both to be estimated and to be justified in the hard currency of expected productivity (predicted earnings serving as the proxy) in the balance of the individual's expected working-life (the actuarial standing in for the actual). If the value of a life is to be taken as the value of that life to the appropriate life-holder in the case of the crash-helmets, to the nominated heirs in the case of the life insurance, then it is self-evidently the value of that life to the collectivity as a whole that the economic man will have in mind when he studies the patient's tax returns and promotion prospects – probable absorption of scarce food and clothing duly deducted – prior to authorising access to the society's scarce medical resources. A collectivist ethos need not be a compassionate one.

A selective standard would not be a selective standard if it stubbornly refused to select. The criterion that access should be performance-related cannot reasonably be criticised for any such failure to discriminate: the hurdle is as precise as the discounted present value of the future earnings stream, the orientation as intuitive as the team manager's preference for the footballers most likely to advance the cause of the whole. Taking human capital as a measure of human worthiness, the work-centred approach is content to regard 'the economic impact of untimely death', in Schelling's telling phrase, 'more as a loss of livelihood than as a loss of life'.[31] The policy inference is clear enough: a self-interested nation, stronger on materialism than it is on sympathy, would do well to skew scarce resources towards young graduates on high salaries (particularly those with dependants that might become a public responsibility) and away from the incurable and the senile, the mentally severely subnormal and the physically severely handicapped. The value-adder is unlikely openly to advocate capital punishment for passenger-citizens who, supplying no manpower and generating no tax, nonetheless impose a burden upon the capacity that is created by the active. The distinction between the *de jure* and the *de facto* is blurred at the margin, however, where the inference that is drawn from the standard is such as to deny to the pensioner the treatment that would have saved his life.

The logic is harsh, given that priorities can kill. Human capital is important but so too is human dignity. The portfolio of considerations must inevitably undermine the belief that the value of life can reasonably be estimated with unidimensional reference to growth alone. Things are important but so too are people. Thus it is that the humanitarian will take to task the economystic for developing an obsession with a part when what really interests the nation is the whole. Teachers are paid disproportionately in the form of psychic income – few people will say that their low money earnings are also proof of low marginal value. Housewives are unwaged and outlast their husbands in retirement – few people will accept that a female life costs more and is worth less than a male one. Grandparents and great-grandparents are descendant generations' final utilities – few people will deny that happiness can be afforded by their survival and sorrow bred by a subsequent bereavement. Any human life, even a non-producing life, can be a source of satisfaction to the life-holder himself – few people will regard it as sound economics to build in the instrumentality of investment while deliberately ignoring the end that is consumption. Today's incontinent infant is tomorrow's incontinent geriatric – few people will look askance at good care targeted at young productives merely because the costly by-product of the current benefits will later be an ageing population and a higher ratio of the retired to the working. Few people will want to argue that productivity and priorities can never mix. Few people nevertheless will want to argue that the truth is the part when in truth it is the whole. Where the consensus ranges so widely, it it clear, there the selective standard adopted is unlikely to enjoy overall social legitimation so long as it relates to human capital alone.

(b) The Gift Relationship

An alternative to the achieved status of the performance test is the ascribed status of belonging and *Gemeinschaft*. In the former case it is the will of the community that the patient should be required to justify his access to life-saving intervention in the quite specific terms of his expected contribution to collective affluence. In the latter case, however, it is the choice of the consensus that the selective standard should be less judgemental and more accepting, less concerned with *to do* and more concerned with *to be*. The model is the love and identification of the family, the emotive tribalism of the non-calculative community. The model is not the *quid pro quo* of the economic market that auctions its entitlements for labour or for cash.

Membership and solidarity being of the essence, the caring polity is unlikely to treat the deaths even of bedridden unemployables as indicators of social success. One result is that a number of lives will acquire value which in a community less averse to fear and suffering might well have had none. Committed humanitarians will, for example, be more generous towards the long-stay hospitalisation of the terminally ill than will economic men and women who see a life as no more than a means.

Not that sympathy and pooling will always work to the benefit of the patient who wants to live. Sometimes they will not: witness the disparity between survival and socialisation that is occasioned whenever a redistributing polity denies to the rich the opportunity to pay privately for medical intervention until such care can be brought within the choice-set of the disadvantaged as well. Such a rejection of demand and supply on the grounds of equity will be the caring community's counterpart to the identical refusal on the grounds of economy that will be the growthman's unequivocal response to the threat that the rich retired might purchase a right to live that properly belongs to the impoverished up-and-coming. Whether because of the gift relationship or because of the wealth of nations, it is clear, the social consensus will sometimes want to reject the individual's own value of life in favour of a value that is more in line with the community's priorities. It is not likely to be of much comfort to the rejected marketeer that his fate was sealed not by random chance but by the vast majority of his fellow citizens.

The rejected marketeer, contemplating his future with all the enthusiasm of the voted-down, will no doubt ask something along the lines of 'Whose life is it, anyway?' The rejected marketeer must expect to be horrified with the reply he receives from the sleeping life-holders who, tactfully abstaining from totting up the scrap value of his ribs, nonetheless insist that they have bought heavily into his pancreas and commandeered a capital in his joints. Everyone likes the democratic process but no one likes the rejection that can so easily be its outcome. The inference must be that no democracy can reasonably expect all the citizens at the town meeting to return home equally happy. Or at all.

(c) Market and Life

Public policy is able to influence the life span – of that there is no doubt. At the curative stage the State is able to reduce mortality rates by means of expanding access to resuscitation units and emergency theatres, clean blood for transfusion and healthy organs for transplant. At the preventive stage, meanwhile, the State can vaccinate, educate and screen; it can ban all cigarette smoking and strictly enforce a snail's pace on the motorways; it can require that all braking mechanisms be tested at six-monthly intervals for roadworthiness and that all household wiring become subject to spot checks for frays and overloads. The State can make health insurance comprehensive, compulsory, subsidised and regulated; it can insist upon protracted trials for new drugs and prescription-only for existing ones; it can demand the rigorous licensing of professionals and institutions in an attempt to exclude the fakes and keep out the butchers. The State can commit itself to road safety, pedestrian subways, traffic lights, good policing, gun control and the destruction of dangerous pets. It can veto all military response, irrespective of provocation, lest someone get hurt. In these and other ways the State is able to influence the life-span – of that there is no doubt.

The ability of public policy to influence the risk profile is not in question. Yet the technical capacity of collective intervention to save statistical lives, always permissive and never imperative, must not be taken to imply that the State has some obligation (as if marginal survival were the same as total) to do everything in its power to prolong expectancies. It does not; for the simple truth is that cost impels moderation while consensus points to balance. Helicopter blood banks and lifeboat rescue teams, however beneficial in themselves, might not seem worth the sacrifice to the citizenry that must support the expense. Building regulations and air safety standards, irrespective of the incremental existence that they may well deliver, might have nonetheless to be rejected by a community that resents the higher prices and the restricted availabilities, the avoidable absorption of capital and the wasteful unemployment of labour. Laws restricting the fatty and prohibiting the fried, even if endorsed by the impeccable authority of credentialed opinion, might still not be popular in an imaginative democracy that enjoys its cholesterogens at least as much as it values its skiing. What the State *can do* for health is not, in short, the same as what the State *ought to do* for health. Stranded somewhere between individualism and direction, the most that the sensitive State can hope to do is to match the public policy that it supplies as closely as possible to the public policy that its citizens most wish to demand.

The undertaking is an ambitious one. The questionnaire is often at variance with the seat-belt which contradicts the wage-differential which is inconsistent with the court award which is incompatible with the human capital which is overridden by the doctor who knows best which is overridden by the second opinion that knows different which is overridden by the public interest that is measured by the questionnaire. The thinking democrat who in the circumstances opts for *laissez-faire* out of frustration and doubt should not, one suspects, be accused too rashly of unwarranted defeatism: there can be no meaningful match of policy supplied to policy demanded where different citizens employ different measures to capture the essence of the common and the shared.

Nor is there any reason to think that the consensual and the agreed will necessarily resemble buried treasure to be found even in a real world of plurality and mix. Integrated totalities have a single hump in their value distribution: free market for health or managed market for health, the median member will conveniently voice the median view when properly consulted. Heterogeneous collectivities are, however, somewhat more of a problem for a leadership that sincerely wants to follow: where the social constituencies are multiple and the intellectual positions are diverse, there it might prove impossible to make useful generalisations for the simple reason that each representative will be true only unto its own individual idiosyncrasies. Such circumstances throw up few certainties and discourage the search for the unique ideal that is forever the optimal. One man's meat will then be another man's poison; and that is why the welfare-maximum in a real world of plurality and mix must never be allowed to become the single-valued endstate that is the victor's trophy in the zero-sum conflict. Rather, the image of the good life must always relate to the just process of discussion and negotiation, debate and argumentation, which alone can reconcile antitheses and resolve contradictions. One man's *explicandum* is another man's *conundrum.* It isn't exact and it isn't precise; but that's the way it is in a market for health that must also be a market for ideas.

Notes and References

2. Principal and Agent

1. K.J. Arrow, 'The Welfare Economics of Medical Care' (1963), in M.H. Cooper and A.J. Culyer, (eds.), *Health Economics* (Harmondsworth: Penguin Books, 1973), p. 16.
2. O.E. Williamson, *Markets and Hierarchies* (New York: The Free Press, 1975), p. 14.
3. A. McGuire, J. Henderson and G.H. Mooney, *The Economics of Health Care* (London: Routledge & Kegan Paul, 1988), p. 156.
4. P. Smith, 'Information Systems and the White Paper Proposals', in A.J. Culyer, A. Maynard and J.Posnett, (eds.), *Competition in Health Care: Reforming the NHS* (London: Macmillan, 1990), p. 118.
5. W.M. Strull, B. Lo and G. Charles, 'Do Patients Want to Participate in Medical Decision Making?', *Journal of the American Medical Association*, Vol. 252, 1984, p. 2990.
6. M.H. Cooper, 'Economics of Need: The Experience of the British Health Service', in M. Perlman, (ed.), *The Economics of Health and Medical Care* (London: Macmillan, 1974), pp. 93–4.
7. T.F. Andersen and G.H. Mooney, 'Medical Practice Variations: Where Are We?', in T.F. Andersen and G.H. Mooney, (eds.), *The Challenges of Medical Practice Variations* (London: Macmillan, 1990), p. 7.
8. A.L. Sorkin, *Health Economics* (Lexington, Mass.: Lexington Books, 1975), p. 5.
9. Cited in M.L. Johnson, 'Patients: Receivers or Participants?', in K. Barnard and K. Lee, (eds.), *Conflicts in the National Health Service* (London: Croom Helm, 1977), p. 74.
10. I. Illich, *Limits to Medicine* (Harmondsworth: Penguin Books, 1977), p. 239.
11. *Ibid.*, p. 223.
12. G.L.S Shackle, 'The Bounds of Unknowledge', in J. Wiseman, (ed.), *Beyond Positive Economics?* (London: Macmillan, 1983), p. 37.
13. *Ibid.*, p. 32
14. R.G. Evans, 'Supplier-Induced Demand: Some Empirical Evidence and Implications', in Perlman, *op.cit.*, pp. 163–4.
15. A. Maynard, M. Marinker and D.P. Gray, 'The doctor, the patient, and their contract', *British Medical Journal*, Vol. 292, 31 May 1986, p. 1439.
16. A. Williams, 'Need'—An Economic Exegesis', in A.J. Culyer and K.G. Wright, (eds.), *Economic Aspects of Health Services* (Oxford: Martin Robertson, 1978), pp. 32–3.
17. V.R. Fuchs, 'The Supply of Surgeons and the Demand for Operations' (1978), in his *The Health Economy* (Cambridge, Mass.: Harvard University Press, 1986), p. 147.
18. *Ibid.*
19. J.D. Bunker and B.W. Brown, Jr., 'The Physician-Patient as an Informed Consumer of Surgical Services', *New England Journal of Medicine*, Vol. 290, 1974, p. 1053.
20. C.E. Phelps, 'Induced Demand—Can We Ever Know Its Extent?', *Journal of Health Economics*, Vol. 5, 1986, pp. 360–1.
21. M. Calnan, 'Towards a Conceptual Framework of Lay Evaluation of Health Care', *Social Science and Medicine*, Vol. 27, 1988, p. 931.
22. R.D. Auster and R.L. Oaxaca, 'Identification of Supplier Induced Demand in the Health Care Sector', *Journal of Human Resources*, Vol. 16, 1981, p. 329.
23. *Ibid.*, p. 341.
24. M.V. Pauly and M.A. Satterthwaite, 'The Pricing of Primary Care Physicians' Services', *Bell Journal of Economics*, Vol. 12, 1981.
25. J.D. Bunker, 'Surgical Manpower: A Comparison of Operations and Surgeons in the United States and in England and Wales', *New England Journal of Medicine*, Vol. 282, 1970, p. 143.

26. *Ibid.*, p. 139.
27. E. Vayda, 'A Comparison of Surgical Rates in Canada and in England and Wales', *New England Journal of Medicine*, Vol. 289, 1973, p. 1228.
28. Bunker, *loc.cit.*, p. 140.
29. A. Smith, *The Theory of Moral Sentiments* (1759) (New York: Augustus M. Kelley, 1966), p. 122.
30. *Ibid.*, p. 166.
31. F. Hirsch, *Social Limits to Growth* (London: Routledge & Kegan Paul, 1977), p. 139.
32. A.C. Enthoven, *Reflections on the Management of the National Health Service* (London: Nuffield Provincial Hospitals Trust, 1985), p.16.
33. J.R. Hampton, 'The End of Clinical Freedom', *British Medical Journal*, Vol. 287, 29 October 1983, p. 1237.
34. *Ibid.*, p. 1238.

3. The Public Interest

1. K.E. Boulding, 'The Concept of Need for Health Services', *Millbank Memorial Fund Quarterly*, Vol. 44, 1966, p. 31.
2. Cited in G.E.R. Lloyd, (ed.), *Hippocratic Writings* (Harmondsworth: Penguin Books, 1978), p. 67.
3. Cited in A. Giddens, (ed.), *Emile Durkheim: Selected Writings* (Cambridge: Cambridge University Press, 1972), p. 101.
4. *Ibid.*
5. B. Abel-Smith, 'Whose welfare state?', in N.I. Mackenzie, (ed.), *Conviction* (London: MacGibbon & Kee, 1959), p. 67.
6. Ministry of Health, *A National Health Service*, Cmnd. 6502, 1944, p. 26.
7. J.P. Newhouse, 'Commentary', in M. Olson (ed.), *A New Approach to the Economics of Health Care* (Washington, D.C.: American Enterprise Institute, 1981), p. 206.
8. Cited in *Hippocratic Writings*, *op.cit.*.
9. J.S. Mill, *On Liberty* (1859), G. Himmelfarb (ed.) (Harmondsworth: Penguin Books, 1974), pp. 68–9.
10. G.H. Mooney, *Economics, Medicine and Health Care* (Hemel Hempstead: Harvester Wheatsheaf, 1986), pp. 27–8.
11. A.J. Culyer, *Need and the National Health Service* (London: Martin Robertson, 1976), p. 89.
12. M.V. Pauly, *Medical Care at Public Expense* (New York: Praeger, 1971), p. 21.
13. M. Friedman, *Capitalism and Freedom* (Chicago: University of Chicago Press, 1962), p. 15
14. Hirsch, *Social Limits to Growth*, *op.cit.*, p. 91.
15. R.M. Titmuss, *Essays on 'The Welfare State'*, 2nd ed., (London: George Allen and Unwin Ltd., 1963), p. 39.
16. R.M. Titmuss, *The Gift Relationship* (Harmondsworth: Penguin Books, 1973), pp. 254–5.
17. A. Bevan, *In Place of Fear* (London: MacGibbon & Kee, 1961), p. 100.
18. W. Niskanen, *Bureaucracy and Representative Government* (Chicago: Aldine, 1971), p. 41.
19. A. Downs, *Inside Bureaucracy* (Boston: Little, Brown and Company, 1967), p. 97.
20. J.M. Buchanan, *The Limits of Liberty* (Chicago: University of Chicago Press, 1975), p. 157.
21. G. Tullock, *The Vote Motive* (London: Institute of Economic Affairs, 1976), p. 25.
22. D. Owen, *In Sickness and in Health* (London: Quartet Books, 1976), pp. 89,91.

4. Health and Insurance

1. The illustration, from Alfred Marshall, is cited in E.A. Benians, 'Reminiscences', in A.C. Pigou, (ed.), *Memorials of Alfred Marshall* (1925) (New York: Augustus M. Kelley, 1966), p. 79
2. A.C. Enthoven, *Health Plan* (Reading, Mass.: Addison-Wesley, 1980), p. 8.
3. V.R. Fuchs, 'The Contribution of Health Services to the American Economy' (1966), in Cooper and Culyer, *Health Economics, op.cit.*, p. 163.
4. M.V. Pauly, 'The Economics of Moral Hazard: Comment', *American Economic Review*, Vol.58, 1968, p. 534.
5. Hirsch, *Social Limits to Growth, op.cit.*, p. 5.
6. M. Olson, *The Logic of Collective Action* (Cambridge, Mass.: Harvard University Press, 1965), p. 166.
7. *Ibid.*, p. 91.
8. R.H. Tawney, *Equality* (1931) (London: George Allen & Unwin, Ltd., 1964), p. 43.
9. R.M. Titmuss (with others), *The Health Services of Tanganyika* (London: Pitman Medical Publishing Co., Ltd., 1964), p. 124.
10. J. Rawls, *A Theory of Justice* (Oxford: Clarendon Press, 1972), p. 302.
11. Titmuss, *The Gift Relationship, op.cit.*, p. 274.
12. H.J. Aaron, *Serious and Unstable Condition* (Washington, D.C.: The Brookings Institution, 1991), p. 51.
13. B.A. Weisbrod, 'The Health Care Quadrilemma', *Journal of Economic Literature*, Vol. 29, 1991, p. 534.

5. The Private Sector

1. Aaron, *Serious and Unstable Condition, op.cit.*, p. 150
2. P.J. Feldstein, *Health Care Economics*, 3rd.ed. (New York: Wiley, 1988), p. 326. Emphasis Added.
3. Enthoven, *Health Plan, op. cit.*, pp. 120–1.
4. See on this H.S. Luft, *Health Maintenance Organizations* (New York: Wiley, 1986).
5. R.H. Tawney, *The Attack and Other Papers* (London: George Allen & Unwin, 1953), p. 169.

6. The State Sector

1. Cited in R. Klein, *The Politics of the National Health Service* (London: Longmans, 1983), p. 38.
2. H. Phelps Brown, *Egalitarianism and the Generation of Inequality* (Oxford: Clarendon Press, 1988), p. 331.
3. Cited in *ibid.*, p. 340.
4. D. Collard, *Altruism and Economy* (Oxford: Martin Robertson, 1978), p. 138.
5. J.K. Galbraith, *Journey to Poland and Yugoslavia* (Cambridge, Mass.: Harvard University Press, 1958), p. 28.
6. J.M. Buchanan, *Technological Determinism Despite the Reality of Scarcity* (Little Rock: University of Arkansas for Medical Sciences, 1990), p. 23.

7. The Individual

1. Joy Townsend, 'Economic and Health Consequences of Reduced Smoking', in A. Williams, (ed.), *Health and Economics* (London: Macmillan, 1987), pp. 140–1.

2. *Ibid.*, pp. 144–5.
3. T.H. Marshall, 'The Right to Welfare' (1965), in his *The Right to Welfare and Other Essays* (London: Heinemann Educational Books, 1981), p. 91.
4. T. McKeown, *The Role of Medicine*, 2nd ed. (Oxford: Blackwell, 1979), p. 90.
5. *Ibid.*, p. 124.
6. *Ibid.*, p. 9.
7. *Ibid.*, p. 118.
8. *Ibid.*, p. 147.
9. *Ibid.*, p. 170.
10. V.R. Fuchs, *Who Shall Live?* (New York: Basic Books, 1974), p. 6.
11. *Ibid.*, p. 28.
12. *Ibid.*, p. 16.
13. D.G. Green, *Which Doctor?* (London: Institute of Economic Affairs, 1985), p. 46.
14. *Ibid.*, p. 45.
15. M. Friedman (with R.D. Friedman), *Free to Choose* (Harmondsworth: Penguin Books, 1980), p. 245.
16. W.M. Wardell, cited in S. Peltzman, *Regulation of Pharmaceutical Innovation* (Washington, D.C.: American Enterprise Institute, 1974), p. 89.
17. Friedman, *Free to Choose*, p. 247.
18. Fuchs, *Who Shall Live?*, p. 29.
19. R. Dubos, *The Mirage of Health* (New York: Harper, 1959), p. 110.

9. The Doctor

1. B. Abel-Smith, *Value for Money in Health Care* (London: Heinemann Educational Books, 1976), p. 62.
2. H.E. Frech III, 'The Long-Lost Free Market in Health Care: Government and Professional Regulation of Medicine', in Olson, *A New Approach to the Economics of Health Care*, *op.cit.*, p. 56.
3. Friedman, *Capitalism and Freedom*, *op.cit.*, p. 146.
4. *Ibid.*
5. J.P. Newhouse, *The Economics of Medical Care* (Reading, Mass.: Addison-Wesley, 1978) p. 35.

10. The Hospital

1. Arrow, 'The Welfare Economics of Medical Care', in Cooper and Culyer, *Health Economics*, *op.cit.*, p. 23.
2. M.V. Pauly and M. Reddish, 'The Not-For-Profit Hospital as a Physicians' Cooperative', *American Economic Review*, Vol. 63, 1973, p. 88.
3. Fuchs, *Who Shall Live?*, *op.cit.*, p. 58.
4. M.V. Pauly, 'Nonprofit Firms in Medical Markets', *American Economic Review* (Papers and Proceedings), Vol. 77, 1987, p. 258.
5. H.A. Simon, *Administrative Behavior*, 2nd ed. (Glencoe: The Free Press, 1965). p. xx.
6. R.M. Cyert and J.G. March, *A Behavioral Theory of the Firm* (New York: Prentice-Hall, 1963), p. 30.
7. A. Marshall, *Principles of Economics*, 8th. ed. (1920) (London: Macmillan, 1949), p. vii.
8. *Ibid.*
9. W.J. Carr and P.J. Feldstein, 'The Relationship of Cost to Hospital Size', *Inquiry*, Vol. 4, 1967, p. 60.
10. J.K. Mann and D.E. Yett, 'The Analysis of Hospital Costs: A Review Article' (1968), in Cooper and Culyer, *op.cit.*, p. 288.

11. J.R. Lave and L.B. Lave, 'Hospital Cost Functions', *American Economic Review*, Vol. 60, 1970, p. 394.
12. R.G. Evans, '"Behavioural" Cost Functions for Hospitals', *Canadian Journal of Economics*, Vol. 4, 1971, p. 209.
13. M.S. Feldstein, *Economic Analysis for Health Service Expenditure* (Amsterdam: North-Holland, 1967).
14. *Ibid.*, p. 51.
15. *Ibid.*, p. 86.
16. *Ibid.*
17. *Ibid.*, p. 57.
18. *Ibid.*
19. *Ibid.*, p. 86.
20. *Ibid.*
21. *Ibid.*, p. 123.
22. *Ibid.*, p. 194.
23. *Ibid.*, p. 198.
24. S.E. Berki, *Hospital Economics* (Lexington: Lexington Books, 1972), p. 85.

11. The Value of Life

1. See T.C. Schelling, 'The Value of Preventing Death' (1968), in Cooper and Culyer, *Health Economics*, *op.cit.*, p. 293.
2. V.R. Fuchs, *How We Live* (Cambridge, Mass.: Harvard University Press, 1983), p. 48.
3. G.H. Mooney, *The Valuation of Human Life* (London: Macmillan, 1977), p. 23.
4. E.J. Mishan, 'Evaluation of Life and Limb: A Theoretical Approach', *Journal of Political Economy*, Vol. 79, 1971, p. 693.
5. G. Blomquist, 'Estimating the Value of Life and Safety: Recent Developments', in M.W. Jones-Lee, (ed.) *The Value of Life and Safety* (Amsterdam: North-Holland, 1982), p. 37n.
6. J. Broome, 'Trying to Value a Life', *Journal of Public Economics*, Vol.9, 1978, p. 94.
7. J.M. Buchanan and R.L. Faith, 'Trying Again To Value A Life', *Journal of Public Economics*, Vol. 10, 1979, p. 246.
8. *Ibid.*, p. 245.
9. M.W. Jones-Lee, M. Hammerton and P.R. Philips, 'The Value of Safety: Results of a National Sample Survey', *Economic Journal*, Vol. 95, 1985, p. 49.
10. J.P. Acton, *Evaluating Public Programs to Save Lives: The Case of Heart Attacks* (Research Report R-950-RC) (Santa Monica: Rand Corporation, 1973), p. ix.
11. Jones-Lee, Hammerton and Philips, 'The Value of Safety', *loc.cit.*, p. 58.
12. *Ibid.*, p. 54.
13. P. Kind, R. Rosser and A. Williams, 'Valuation of Quality of Life: Some Psychometric Evidence', in Jones-Lee, *The Value of Life and Safety*, p.159.
14. M.W. Jones-Lee, *The Value of Life* (London: Martin Robertson, 1976), p. 133.
15. A. Tversky and D. Kahneman, 'The Framing of Decisions and the Psychology of Choice', *Science*, Vol. 211, 30 January 1981, p. 453.
16. *Ibid.*
17. *Ibid.*, p. 455.
18. G. Blomquist, 'Value of Life Saving: Implications of Consumption Activity', *Journal of Political Economy*, Vol. 87, 1979, p. 556.
19. Mooney, *The Valuation of Human Life*, pp. 126–7.
20. L. Needleman, 'The Valuation of Changes in the Risk of Death by those at Risk', *Manchester School*, Vol. 48, 1980, p. 233.
21. *Ibid.*, pp. 235–6. The data refers to 1970.
22. *Ibid.*, p. 240.
23. A. Marin and G. Psacharopoulos, 'The Reward for Risk in the Labor Market: Evidence

from the United Kingdom and a Reconciliation with Other Studies', *Journal of Political Economy*, Vol. 90, 1982, p. 848. The data refers to 1975.
24. *Ibid.*, p. 831.
25. L.I. Dublin and A.J. Lotka, *The Money Value of a Man* (New York: Ronald Press, 1930), p. v.
26. *Ibid.*, p. 3.
27. *Ibid.*, p. 68.
28. *Ibid.*, p. 102.
29. Kind, Rosser and Williams, 'Valuation of Quality of Life', *loc.cit.*, p. 165.
30. M.J. Buxton and R.R. West, 'Cost Benefit Analysis of Long-Term Haemodialysis for Chronic Renal Failure', *British Medical Journal*, 1975, Vol. II, p. 376.
31. Schelling, *loc.cit.*, p. 295

Index